CHARLES JOHANSSON

Mastering the Art of
FREEZE DRYING

100 INNOVATIVE RECIPES

A COMPREHENSIVE GUIDE TO FOOD
PRESERVATION, RECIPES, AND
TECHNIQUES FOR EVERY HOME COOK

© Copyright 2025 - All rights reserved.

ISBN 979-8-9996932-0-4
Library of Congress Control Number: 2025919351

The content contained within this book may not be reproduced, duplicated or transmitted without direct written permission from the author or the publisher.

Under no circumstances will any blame or legal responsibility be held against the publisher, or author, for any damages, reparation, or monetary loss due to the information contained within this book, either directly or indirectly.

Legal Notice:

This book is copyright protected. It is only for personal use. You cannot amend, distribute, sell, use, quote or paraphrase any part, or the content within this book, without the consent of the author or publisher.

Disclaimer Notice:

Please note the information contained within this document is for educational and entertainment purposes only. All effort has been executed to present accurate, up to date, reliable, complete information. No warranties of any kind are declared or implied. Readers acknowledge that the author is not engaged in the rendering of legal, financial, medical or professional advice. The content within this book has been derived from various sources. Please consult a licensed professional before attempting any techniques outlined in this book.

By reading this document, the reader agrees that under no circumstances is the author responsible for any losses, direct or indirect, that are incurred as a result of the use of the information contained within this document, including, but not limited to, errors, omissions, or inaccuracies.

CONTENTS

INTRODUCTION xi

CHAPTER 1: INTRODUCTION TO FREEZE DRYING 1

   The Many Benefits of Freeze Drying 1
- *Long Shelf Life* 2
- *Lightweight and Portable* 2
- *Nutrient Preservation* 2
- *Ease of Preparation* 2
- *Customizable* 2
- *Versatile* 2
- *No Refrigeration Needed* 3
- *Taste Preservation* 3
- *Eco-Friendly* 3
- *Convenience* 3
- *Time-Saving* 3
- *Emergency Food Supply* 3
- *Reducing Waste* 4
- *Cost-Effective* 4

   Freeze Drying as a Safety Net 4
   Community Freeze Drying Projects 4
   Freeze Drying vs. Other Preservation Methods 5
- *Canning* 5
- *Dehydrating* 5
- *Freezing* 5
- *Smoking and Salting* 6

   Why Freeze Drying Is Gaining Popularity 6
   Key Terminology 7

CHAPTER 2: HOW FREEZE DRYING WORKS 10

   How Does Freeze Drying Work? 10
   The Phases of Freeze Drying 11
   Common Myths vs. Facts 12
   Safety Considerations 14
   Freeze Drying Without an Appliance 15
- *Using Your Freezer (Preferably a Deep Freezer)* 16

Freeze Drying With Dry Ice 16

CHAPTER 3: CHOOSING THE RIGHT FREEZE DRYER 18

Difference Between Home and Commercial Freeze Dryers 19
Features 19
Structure 19
Capacity 20
Time 20
Cost 20
Overall Comparison 20

Overview of Popular Brands 21
Harvest Right 21
Vevor 21
Cuddon 22
Blue Alpine 22
Excalibur 22
GEA 22
Telstar 22

New, Used, Refurbished, or Repaired? 22
New Freeze Dryers 23
Used Freeze Dryers 23
Refurbished Freeze Dryers 24
Repaired Freeze Dryers 25

How Do I Know Which Appliance Is Right for Me? 26

CHAPTER 4: SELECTING AND PREPARING INGREDIENTS 28

Best Foods for Freeze Drying 28
Foods to Avoid 29
Pre-Treating Herbs and Fresh Spices 30
Pre-Treating Meat 31
Pre-Treating Vegetables and Fruits 32
How to Blanch 33

Sourcing the Ingredients 33
Homegrown and Homemade 33
Store-Bought 34
Bulk Buying 35

CHAPTER 5: THE FREEZE DRYING PROCESS STEP-BY-STEP 36

Preparing the Freeze Dryer 36
Setting Up 37
Test Run 37

- Loading Trays Properly 38
  - *Silicon and Parchment Liners* 38
  - *Bulk Density* 39
  - *Load All Trays* 39
- Drying Time 39
- Techniques of the Masters 40
- When Is the Freeze Drying Process Done? 41
  - *Use Your Senses* 41
  - *Be Scientific* 41
- Drying Times 42
- Moisture Content 43
- Pampering the Machine 43

CHAPTER 6: PACKAGING AND STORAGE FOR A LONG SHELF LIFE 45

- Packaging Options 45
  - *Mylar Bags* 46
  - *Mason Jars* 46
  - *Vacuum or Nitrogen?* 47
- Commercial Packaging Machines 47
- Ideal Storage Conditions 48
- Oxygen Absorbers 48
- Labeling Done Right 49
- Why Rotate? 50
- Has It Gone Bad? 50
- Rehydrating 51
- Shelf Life Comparison 52

CHAPTER 7: TROUBLESHOOTING AND GOOD ADVICE 54

- Common Issues 55
- Good Advice for Top Freeze Drying 58
  - *Regular Maintenance on a Real Schedule* 58
  - *Quality In, Quality Out* 59
  - *Getting Chilly* 59
  - *Defrosting for Pre-Treatment* 59
  - *Hot Stuff* 60
  - *A Good Start* 61
  - *Clean Your Food* 61
  - *Spreading Germs* 61

CHAPTER 8: GETTING CREATIVE 63

- Freeze-Dried Candy 63

  Gifts 64
  Herbal Remedies and Teas 65
  Starting a Freeze-Dried Food Business 66
   Is Your Own Freeze Drying Business Worth It? 67
   The Business Plan 68

CHAPTER 9: WHAT NEXT? 69
  Emergency Food Supply 69
   Be Prepared 70
   Planning the Food Supply 70
  Community Resources and Online Groups 71
  Experimenting With Freeze Drying 72
   Freeze-Dried Flowers 72
   Manuscripts and Artifacts 73
  Frequently Asked Questions (FAQs) 74

CONCLUSION 77

RECIPES 79

HERBS, SPICES, AND SEASONINGS 81
  Herbs and Spices 81
   Ready-to-Use Oven-Roasted Garlic 81
   Smoky Paprika 82
  Seasonings 83
   Tzatziki Seasoning Blend 83
   Classic Burger Spice 84
   Onion Soup Seasoning 85

SAUCES, DRESSINGS, PUREES, AND SIDES 86
  Sauces 86
   Naturally Sweet Applesauce 86
   Marinara Homestyle Sauce 87
   Sugar-Free BBQ Sauce 88
   Creamy Parmesan and Tomato Sauce 90
  Dressings 91
   Tangy Herb Dressing 91
  Purees 92
   Baby's Favorite Food 92
   Year-Round Pumpkin Puree 93
  Sides 94
   Classic Butter Herb Stuffing 94

SOUPS AND BROTHS 96

Soups 96
- Beefy Bean Taco Soup 96
- Cheesy Basil Potato Soup 97
- Creamy Potato Ham Soup 98
- Chicken Enchilada Bowl 100
- Chicken and Spinach Soup 101
- Golden Turmeric Turkey Noodle Soup 103
- Cheddar Lover's Broccoli Soup 104
- Lemon and Herb Chickpea Soup 106
- Rosemary and Sage Butternut Soup 107
- Vegan Veggie Soup 109

Broths 110
- Nourishing Veggie Broth 110

STEWS AND CASSEROLES 112

Stews 112
- Rosemary Beef Stew 112
- Smoky Bean and Quinoa Stew 114
- Country-Style Chicken Stew 115

Casseroles 116
- Sausage and Hash Brown Casserole 116
- Mozzarella and Sausage Pizza Casserole 118
- Ultimate Cheeseburger Mac Casserole 120
- Creamy Spinach and Cheese Casserole 122
- Creamy Chicken and Bacon Casserole 124
- Cheddar-Topped Green Bean Bake 125
- Squash and Ricotta Casserole 127
- Marshmallow-Topped Sweet Potato Delight 128
- Cheesy Eggplant Casserole 130
- Creamy Zucchini and Chicken Casserole 132

MEAT DISHES 134

Chicken 134
- Lemon–Garlic Chicken 134
- Chicken and White Bean Chili 136
- Smoky Bacon Chicken Chili 138
- Cheesy Chicken Pepper Fajitas 141
- Chicken Pot Pie 142

Turkey 144
- Turkey Meatballs 144

  Liquid-Smoke-Brined Turkey 146
 Beef 148
  Shredded Beef 148
  Timeless Cottage Pie 150
  No-Fuss Comfort Pot Roast 152
  Hearty Texas Beef Chili 154
  Beef Stroganoff 156
 Pork 157
  Tangy Pork Tacos 157
  Smoky BBQ Pulled Pork 159
  Rustic Root Beer Beans 161
  Nutritious Homestyle Chili 162
 Mixed Meats 164
  Steak and Chicken Cheese Melt 164

PASTA AND RICE DISHES 166
 Pasta Dishes 166
  Cheesy Oven-Baked Jumbo Shells 166
  Rich Carbonara Pasta 168
  Creamy Macaroni and Cheese 170
  Easy Three-Ingredient Egg Noodles 173
  Simple Buttery Parmesan Fettuccine Alfredo 174
  Cheesy Broccoli Pasta 176
  Delicious Cheesy Veggie Lasagna 177
 Rice Dishes 179
  Fiesta Rice 179

SALADS 181
 Colorful Bean Chili Salad 181
 Chicken and Mayo Salad 182
 Summer Pasta Salad 184
 Celery and Chicken Tossed Salad 186

LIGHTWEIGHT CAMPING AND HIKING MEALS 187
 Chili for the Trail 187
 Couscous and Brothy Mushroom Soup 188
 Portable Low-Fat Lasagna 190

FRUITS, VEGETABLES, AND VEGGIE DISHES 192
 Fruits 192
  Freeze-Dried Fruit 192
 Vegetables 194

  Freeze-Dried Vegetables 194
 Veggie Dishes 196
  Ginger Veggie and Tofu Stir Fry 196
  Crunchy Seasoned Peas 198
  Seasoned Veggie Chips 199
  Tangy Salt and Vinegar Zucchini Chips 200
  Creamy Garlic Mashed Potatoes 201
  Veggie Crispies 202
  Sweet Potato Crunchy Chips 203

DESSERTS AND SWEET TREATS 204
 Desserts, Puddings, and Sweet Treats 204
  Chill and Shake Soft Serve Ice-Cream 204
  Granny Smith's Secret Apple Pie 205
  Smooth and Creamy Cocoa Pudding 206
  Cinnamon Pumpkin Roll Treat 208
  Freeze-Dried Berry or Fruit Cheesecake 210
  Chocolate Bark 212
 Frostings and Sweet Ingredients 213
  Raspberry-Kissed Buttercream Frosting 213
  Homemade No-Cook Sweetened Condensed Milk 214

CANDY, SNACKS, AND HEALTH BARS 216
 Candy 216
  Butterscotch Treats 216
  Fluffy Pillow Marshmallows 217
  Chewy Jelly Gummies 219
 Snacks 220
  Classic Blueberry–Vanilla Muffins 220
  Creamy Citrus and Vanilla Cookies 222
  Mini Yogurt Treats 223
  Crunchy Power Snack 224
 Health Bars 225
  Blueberry Power Bars 225
  Fruity Crunch Bars 226
  Spiced Pumpkin Oat Bars 227
 Super Quick Freeze-Dried Yummies 229
  Veggie Party Dip 229
  Savory Summer Popsicles 230
  Fruit Leather 230
  Trail Mix 230
  French Toast Voilà! 230

    Next-Level Yogurt Snack 230
    Sweet and Red Bites 230
    Oatmeal Refuelers 231
    Peckish for a Pickle 231

BEVERAGES 232
    Floral and Fruit Fusion Water 232
    Peach Pineapple Refresher 233
    On-the-Go Lemonade Blend 234
    Berry Bliss Lemonade 235
    Festive Berry Bliss Punch 236
    Immunity Boosting Emergen-C 237
    Nature's Green Boost Smoothie 238
    Nutmeg-Kissed Creamy Eggnog 238
    Sweet Strawberry Milk Blend 240
    Icy Strawberry Coconut Milk Delight 241

PETS AND HOME 242
  Dog Food 242
    Tail-Wagging Turkey and Veggie Mix 242
  Cat Food 244
    Kitty's Purrfectly Tender Chicken Delight 244
  Pet Treats 245
    Meat and Sweet Potato Bites 245
    Peanut Butter Sweet Banana Treat 245
    Liver Slivers 246
  Home Essentials 246
    Natural Heartwarming Simmer Pot 246

ABOUT THE AUTHOR 247

REFERENCES 249
  Image References 260

INTRODUCTION

Have you heard the buzz about freeze drying and wondered what it's all about? Perhaps you're concerned about food security, want something ready in the pantry for emergencies, or just want to try something new. In this book, you'll find everything you need to become a master of any freeze-dried food use you can imagine, and we'll guide you every step of the way.

Freeze drying is taking the cooking world by storm. Campers take freeze-dried foods with them to the great outdoors, mothers use freeze-dried foods to feed their families nutritious meals without spending hours in the kitchen, and hosts wow their guests with freeze-dried cuisine containing out-of-season fruits. Preparing for emergencies and unexpected guests becomes less stressful when there's a selection of freeze-dried foods in the pantry. Whether you're attracted to the convenience of freeze-dried foods or the endless possibilities, in these pages you'll find the information you need to use freeze drying in the most efficient way.

From choosing an appliance, to recipes, to starting your own freeze drying business, this book has you covered. Are you ready to explore the world of home freeze drying and to take advantage of a simpler-than-it-looks method that offers food security, convenience when outdoors, long-term savings, long shelf lives, and versatility? Jump right in!

We'll kick off our introduction to freeze drying in Chapter 1 with a look at the many benefits of freeze drying. Because we live in uncertain times where we have to plan for political upheavals and natural disasters, we'll discuss freeze drying as a safety net. The initial cost of a freeze drying appliance may be too much for one person on a strict budget, but we'll overcome this obstacle with advice on community freeze drying projects. Then, we'll compare freeze drying with other preservation techniques to explore the advantages of freeze drying for preservation. We'll end the chapter with the key terminology you'll encounter in freeze drying cookbooks and communities.

Chapter 2 is all about how freeze drying works. Don't worry; this isn't a science textbook, and there won't be a test on the last page! We'll look into the phases of freeze drying using simple, clear language to take the sting out of the technical details. This will be followed by a section where we dig out the truth from the common myths surrounding freeze drying. The chapter ends with some safety considerations to help you freeze dry food without harmful bacteria spoiling the food—and the fun!

It can be overwhelming to choose the right freeze dryer, especially if you're new to freeze drying. Chapter 3 to the rescue! We'll examine the difference between commercial and home freeze dryers and put some popular brands under the microscope. This is followed by a discussion of the pros and cons of used and new machines. The last section of this chapter will help you make sense of the information given and choose the appliance that's perfect for you.

The first step to becoming a master freeze dryer is to know your ingredients. In Chapter 4, we'll discuss the best foods for freeze drying and which foods aren't suitable for this method of preservation. You'll also find practical tips on the pre-treatment of ingredients, and we'll compare homegrown, store-bought, and bulk-buy food sources.

Chapter 5 will walk you through the freeze drying process step by step. You'll learn how to prepare the food and the machine, how to load the trays for the best results, how the settings and timings work, and how to know when the drying process is done. The final section of this chapter will show you how to clean your appliance safely without damaging your machine.

One of the best things about freeze-dried food is the long shelf life. In Chapter 6, we'll find out how to store freeze-dried food. We'll explore the best ways to package, label, and rotate the food, and we'll compare the shelf lives of various freeze-dried foods. A well-organized pantry containing perfectly preserved foods and treats will make you proud.

Although freeze drying is easy once you get the hang of it, sometimes things go wrong. Chapter 7 will help you troubleshoot common issues. We'll address potential problems such as uneven heating, food not drying properly, temperature and pressure fluctuations, high power consumption, and more. Issues that arise during freeze drying are usually easy to fix and won't cost an arm and a leg.

If you're looking for new challenges with your trusty freeze dryer or simply more uses for freeze-dried foods, Chapter 8 will give you plenty of ideas. Get creative with freeze-dried candy, freeze-dried gift baskets, and freeze-dried herbs and teas, and find out how to start your own freeze-dried food business.

Before we conclude this book with a brief recap, join us in Chapter 9 to discover how you can incorporate freeze-dried food into an emergency food supply. We'll discuss community resources and online groups, and learn how you can start your own club for freeze drying enthusiasts. The chapter ends with some FAQs to round off everything you need to know to be a master of the art of freeze drying.

And of course, once you know your way around a freeze dryer, you'll want to try out recipes that use freeze-dried ingredients and freeze dry prepared meals. The "Recipes" section at the end of the book contains a wide variety of recipes that will have your mouth watering for the delightful, full-bodied flavors that only freeze drying can bring to the table. With both meat and veggie dishes, pastas, salads, desserts, sides, and even drinks, there's truly something for everyone—you'll even find freeze-dried pet treats for your furry friends, as well as lightweight camping and hiking meals.

Onward to the next page, where we'll find out what freeze drying is and why it's gaining popularity.

CHAPTER 1
INTRODUCTION TO FREEZE DRYING

Freeze drying (or lyophilization if you're technically inclined) is a process that removes the water from food. The water in the food gets frozen, then a vacuum causes the ice to become vapor. The remaining product has the same shape, nutrients, and taste as before the freeze drying. Let's find out more about the benefits of the freeze drying process, as well as why it's trending worldwide, and explore some terminology.

The Many Benefits of Freeze Drying

Freeze drying is becoming trendy because more and more people are falling in love with its many benefits. Below are the benefits you can enjoy if you freeze dry food.

Long Shelf Life

Water content is one of the main factors that determines a food's shelf life because the microorganisms that cause food spoilage (bacteria, mold, and yeast) need moisture to grow. Since freeze drying removes so much water that the final product contains only around 2% moisture, the shelf life will be much longer than that of the fresh version of the food. Some freeze-dried foods can last for more than 30 years (*Shelf Life*, n.d.).

Lightweight and Portable

Campers and hikers know the frustration of having to pack enough food but not so much that it will weigh them down or take up too much space. Freeze-dried food is very lightweight since the water weight is eliminated, resulting in a product that is up to 90% lighter (D'Argy, 2023a). This ensures that lovers of the outdoors can enjoy the fresh air accompanied by a filling, tasty meal or snack that is light and small when packaged.

Nutrient Preservation

Freeze drying only removes the water content, which means that the nutrients—such as proteins, minerals, and vitamins—are left in the food. The freeze drying process leaves the cell walls of the food intact so that the nutrients don't leak out, which can happen with canning or cooking. As an added bonus, the nutrient profile isn't spoiled by having to add artificial preservatives.

Ease of Preparation

What could be easier than merely adding some water into a Mason jar or pouch? That's really the only requirement to rehydrate a freeze-dried meal. No slaving in front of a hot stove for seemingly endless hours, no watching the clock to prevent burns, and no scrubbing of pots and pans afterward.

Customizable

You can make freeze-dried food suit your tastes and needs. Ingredients can be freeze dried whether they are sliced, diced, shredded, cubed, or grated. Full meals, such as pies and lasagna, can be freeze dried. Freeze-dried foods can be mixed in any combination you desire. You can even freeze dry candy and ice cream!

Versatile

Freeze-dried food is ideal for every occasion. Whether you're packing snacks for a day visit to a park or picking ingredients for an haute cuisine dish to impress your dinner guests, you can't go wrong with freeze-dried foods.

No Refrigeration Needed

Freeze-dried foods can last for years, even decades, if they are properly packaged and stored correctly in a dry, cool area. No need for the fridge or freezer!

Taste Preservation

The taste, texture, and aroma of foods are preserved, which means that freeze-dried foods taste the closest to fresh. The flavor of most fruits and vegetables is not only preserved but also concentrated during the freeze drying process, which explains why these foods are sought-after snacks.

Eco-Friendly

Help save the environment by reducing the food waste caused by buying food with short shelf lives, producing less packaging waste, eliminating the use of harmful preservatives, and saving energy by not having to refrigerate.

Convenience

Have you ever had moments of sheer panic when you have unexpected guests and no idea what to feed them? Or times when you simply didn't feel like cooking but craved some homemade comfort food? Having a pantry stocked with a variety of freeze-dried full meals is the convenient, practical solution. What could be more convenient than merely adding hot water to transform a packet of freeze-dried food into a delicious dish?

Time-Saving

Modern life can be a crazy dash from one activity to the next, with precious little time to unwind. Give yourself more free time by simply adding hot water to a freeze-dried meal. If you have a little stockpile in your pantry, you'll also save time (and gas money) thanks to less frequent trips to the grocery store.

Emergency Food Supply

Natural disasters are often unforeseen and can leave you without electricity or access to stores for days. Their long shelf life and lack of need for refrigeration make freeze-dried foods the ideal emergency food supply for any "just in case" scenario. Unlike other food stockpiles, freeze-dried meals only need added water and don't need to be cooked or defrosted before eating.

Reducing Waste

If you feel guilty about throwing away leftovers, your fridge can easily end up cluttered with a variety of containers storing odds and ends such as half a sandwich, a few spoonfuls of soup, a half-eaten portion of rice, or leftover gravy. Instead of letting these leftovers grow moldy when you inevitably forget about them, you can reduce waste by freeze drying them for a long shelf life. You'll also save fridge space when you move the freeze-dried leftovers to a shelf or cupboard. Garden harvests and bulk groceries can also go bad before you've had the chance to enjoy them, but freeze drying will cut the waste.

Cost-Effective

Inflation, like death and taxes, is a given. Whatever you're spending on food now, chances are you'll be spending double in 10 years. If you freeze dry food now, you'll save on the extra money inflation would have cost you in a couple of years. Plus, when you freeze dry portions, you won't end up with leftovers or spoiled food that only goes into the garbage.

These benefits are making freeze drying a growing trend among home cooks, campers, hikers, small businesses, chain stores, emergency supply stores, and people looking for the convenience of being able to enjoy a tasty, nutritious meal on the go, as well as the sick and elderly who may not have the energy to prepare a full meal from scratch.

Freeze Drying as a Safety Net

Food safety is an issue of growing concern for everyone who watches the news. Political sanctions, riots, and boycotts, natural disasters, war, terrorism, and an unstable job market can cause such upheaval that food may become scarce or unavailable for an unpredictable length of time.

This is where freeze-dried foods can be your life raft. Provide food security for yourself, your loved ones, and your community by having a sufficient stockpile of nutritious food stored for times of need. Imagine the peace of mind that comes with knowing that there will be more than enough food for you, your family, and your pets if anything unforeseen should happen!

Community Freeze Drying Projects

Freeze drying equipment, especially for larger-volume appliances, can be very expensive, and this can be a barrier for many people who can't afford the initial investment. A community (which can be a club, a neighborhood, an extended family, or a group of friends) pulling their financial resources together overcomes the barrier of the initial capital needed. Everyone adding a fraction of the initial cost and sharing the appliance solves the problem. The freeze dryer can pay back everyone's initial investment and even give all the investors a share of the profits if the community sells the freeze-dried food.

Apart from access to a freeze dryer and the possible profit, a community project brings people together around a shared goal. This can strengthen the bonds of family and friendship in a fun way.

Freeze Drying vs. Other Preservation Methods

Freeze drying isn't the only preservation method. Who doesn't have fond memories of Mason jars full of preserved treats at the farmer's market or in grandma's pantry, or the comforting taste of smoked or salted meats? In this section, we'll compare freeze drying to other preservation methods to show why freeze drying comes out top.

Canning

Canned foods are everywhere, in wide varieties, and they are often less expensive than freeze-dried foods. They are convenient, but they're too heavy for backpacking and take up more space than slim freeze-dried packages. Most canned foods contain preservatives, artificial or potentially harmful additives, and added sugar, whereas freeze-dried foods only contain the original ingredients. The canning process also leads to a loss of nutrients—especially vitamins, which are water-soluble—which isn't the case with freeze-dried food. Unlike freeze-dried food, canned food has a mushier or softer texture than when fresh.

Dehydrating

Dehydration is similar to freeze drying in that the moisture content is removed, but, unlike freeze drying, the nutrients, texture, and flavor are lost during the process. This loss, especially of vitamins that are sensitive to heat, occurs due to the high heat used by dehydrating appliances. Another downside is that dehydrated foods only have a shelf life of between four and twelve months (MasterClass, 2022).

Freezing

Frozen foods don't have the moisture removed, and this can cause the nutrient content to degrade over time. Although frozen foods are available in almost every store with a freezer and can be less expensive than freeze-dried foods, they need to be kept constantly frozen and are bulky and heavier than freeze-dried products. If the electricity supply goes down for more than a day due to a disaster, the frozen food would spoil.

Smoking and Salting

Salt is a preservative that draws the moisture out of food, making it difficult for bacteria and mold to grow. Smoking preserves food by drying the moisture out and putting some antimicrobial substances into the food. On the negative side, the food isn't reduced in weight, and many foods simply aren't suitable for smoking or salting. Freeze drying can preserve a wider range of foods, such as desserts and fruits, while also making them lighter and more compact. Salted foods can last months or even years if the salting is done properly (Henney et al., 2010), but the texture can be dry or too salty, and some nutrients may be lost due to a process called salt leaching. Smoked foods can last for a couple of weeks to a few months (Klein, 2021), and the foods have a distinctive smoky flavor and aroma. The heat during the smoking process can destroy some heat-sensitive nutrients, and the texture may be tough. Smoking is often combined with salting for the best results, but neither of these methods is as effective or versatile as freeze drying.

Why Freeze Drying Is Gaining Popularity

Did you know that the first freeze-dried product was instant coffee? Coffee is the perfect example of freeze-dried foods' retention of taste, long shelf life, and light weight. To make a cup of coffee, you just add boiling water—the same as with any other freeze-dried product (although it isn't strictly necessary to have boiling water; any preferred water temperature will do with freeze-dried foods).

We know instant coffee is very popular, but why is freeze drying food becoming more popular than ever? In the previous section, we discovered the advantages of freeze drying and why freeze drying is the best method for preserving food. Let's have a look at more reasons why freeze drying is getting so much attention:

- Freeze-dried foods can **potentially replace the cold chain** of frozen foods. Freezing food uses energy, and this can drive up costs. The food needs to be kept frozen from the freezing plant all along the distribution line and in the homes of the consumers, until the food is taken out of the freezer to be made into a meal. Food that is freeze dried not only eliminates the cold chain but also has less weight and volume, which saves even more money in terms of transportation and storage. This results in food that is generally more affordable and accessible to areas without electricity, such as rural regions in developing countries.
- The **fine dining experience** demands a plate whose aesthetics add to the overall enjoyment of the meal. To this end, gourmet chefs (and home cooks) use freeze-dried ingredients such as crispy herbs and powdered freeze-dried fruits to **enhance flavor, color, and texture** or as an **original, intensely flavored garnish.** Home freeze drying brings fine dining to the casual dinner table.
- Technology is advancing to the point at which space agencies are exploring the possibility of commercial space flights. One of the most important problems of space travel is that any extra weight results in extra fuel cost, and rocket fuel is very expensive. Space agencies such as NASA use freeze-dried food to cut weight without sacrificing nutrients or taste. The advances made by space agencies in freeze drying technology spill over into the commercial market, resulting in **innovations** such as valves in containers that allow water to be added without the need for pots or pans. This is convenient for hikers and emergencies. The more innovations there are, the more the interest in freeze drying grows.

Key Terminology

In this section, you'll find the terminology that you'll likely encounter on your journey to becoming a freeze drying master. You don't have to learn these terms, but reading through them will help you understand the freeze drying process better:

- **Lyophilization** is the scientific word for **freeze drying**. Freeze drying is the method of preserving food by removing moisture through sublimation.

- **Dehydration** is when water is taken out of a substance such as food.
- When you freeze dry a food, the end product can be spongy or solid. This end product is called **cake**. (In this book, we'll stick to the term "product," but you'll probably encounter "cake" in some appliance manuals and cookbooks.)
- As you become more familiar with freeze drying, you might start paying more attention to **porosity**, which is a measure of how many pores (tiny holes) are in the cake. The more porosity, the better the texture will be when the food is rehydrated. Note that the pores can be very tiny, so don't worry if your freeze-dried foods don't look like Swiss cheese—they'll still rehydrate perfectly!
- **Freezing** is simply the process of cooling a substance, like water, until it becomes a solid, like ice.
- **Pre-freezing** is when you speed up the freeze drying process by freezing the food in the freezer first before putting it in your freeze drying appliance.
- Freeze drying uses the principle of **sublimation** to remove moisture from food. When a solid (such as ice) is heated, it usually melts (becomes liquid) and then turns into a vapor (gas). In sublimation, the solid becomes a gas without turning into a liquid first.
- The water vapor that is released during sublimation gets caught and frozen by a special part of the freeze dryer called a **condenser**.
- The water that is chemically part of food (called **bound water**) is removed during the secondary drying stage.
- The movement of vapor from the food into the condenser is called **mass transfer**. The better the mass transfer, the more efficient the freeze drying appliance.
- A **vacuum pump** is the part of a freeze drying appliance that produces low pressure. Liquids boil when atmospheric pressure is equal to vapor pressure. At sea level, this happens for water at 212 °F (100 °C). As the atmospheric pressure lowers, the temperature at which water boils falls. Atmospheric pressure automatically drops the higher up we go, but we don't have to climb Everest to boil water with low heat; we can simply use a vacuum pump to lower the pressure.
- The inside of a freeze dryer where you put the trays is called the **chamber**.
- The **triple point** is the point of low pressure where ice, water, and steam can exist together. If the pressure is lowered below the triple point, liquid water can't exist. Adding energy will then make the ice sublimate into vapor.
- One single complete process where food is freeze dried from frozen to completely dry is called one **cycle**.
- To save energy, some appliances use a **heat recovery system**. This system uses waste heat in another process; for example, "leftover" heat used to defrost water can be used to warm the water.
- The **moisture content** determines how well the food will be preserved. Moisture content simply means how much water is in the food.

- When you want to eat your freeze-dried meal, you add water to it. Adding water is called **rehydration**.
- Industrial or commercial appliances may have **cycle optimization** settings. Cycle optimization is when the freezing and drying steps can be customized for different food types.
- Chefs may choose freeze drying for the **flavor concentration** that it offers. Flavor concentration is the intensified flavor that results from the removal of water without heat.
- You might want to experiment with different **reconstitution methods** such as rehydrating your freeze-dried foods with sauces instead of water.

In the next chapter, we'll discover how freeze drying works. We'll also debunk myths and discover how to prepare food for freeze drying without harmful bacteria hitching a ride.

CHAPTER 2
HOW FREEZE DRYING WORKS

This chapter is all about the actual process of freeze drying. We'll explore how freeze drying works and look at the stages of freeze drying. Then, we'll separate the facts from the myths regarding freeze drying and find out how to prepare food for freeze drying in the safest, most hygienic way.

How Does Freeze Drying Work?

The science behind the freeze drying process may sound complicated at first, but once you understand that it is simply about using temperature and pressure, the process becomes very straightforward.

You encountered sublimation in the terminology section of the previous chapter. Sublimation, which is when water goes directly from ice to vapor, is the core principle of freeze drying. It allows the dehydration of foods without breaking molecular bonds, keeping the texture, taste, and nutrients intact.

By freezing the food, then removing the water through sublimation, then drying the food further to remove bound water, fresh food is transformed into a dry food with many pores. The pores facilitate quick and efficient rehydration, and the lack of moisture ensures a long shelf life. All you have to do to rehydrate your freeze-dried food is to add a liquid, such as water (hot, boiling, or cold), juice, or broth. Stir and wait a short while for the food to absorb the liquid.

The Phases of Freeze Drying

If you don't have an appliance with preset settings, your first step would be to find out what your food's freezing point is. Because the freezing point of water is 32 °F (0 °C), we expect the freezing point of all foods to be the same, but in practice the freezing point can be much lower. To freeze a complete meal or foods without a known freezing point, you can start by setting your appliance at 32 °F (0 °C), then going progressively lower by 9 °F (5 °C) at a time and checking each time if your food is frozen through. Once you've figured out the freezing point, write it down to save time next time.

Some appliances have a setting where the user has to input the lowest permitted pressure (vacuum setting). You can find the appliance's optimal lowest permitted pressure in the appliance manual or on the manufacturer's website. Don't be tempted to set it to the lowest pressure (vacuum) possible, because if the pressure is too low, there will be such a great amount of vapor that the entire drying process will take what seems like forever.

Before any process starts, your food should be at room temperature, which is scientifically assumed to be 68 °F (20 °C), and at the atmospheric pressure at sea level (1 bar).

The first phase is to **freeze** your food to below the food's specific freezing point. This can be done by pre-freezing in the freezer or in the freeze drying appliance itself. An industrial appliance usually freezes food to −40 °F (−40 °C). Food that isn't completely frozen can boil in a vacuum, and that would spoil the process. Freeze dryers can usually freeze food fairly quickly. The faster the food freezes, the fewer overly large ice crystals form. Ice crystals that are too large can damage the texture.

During the second phase, the pressure in the chamber is lowered to about 0.01 mbar, creating a vacuum. In the low pressure of the vacuum, the ice of the frozen food will sublimate at a low temperature. The appliance heats up the chamber to the temperature where sublimation takes place, and the ice transforms into vapor. This removes most of the water in the food in a process called **primary drying**. Primary drying can be a slow process.

In this second phase, primary drying is followed by **secondary drying**. Secondary drying is also called desorption and occurs when the appliance gradually increases the temperature and lowers the pressure in the chamber. This is done to make sure that as much bound water as possible gets removed from the food. After secondary drying, the product will be completely dry and will have a long shelf life.

The water vapor from the ice gets **collected** in the condenser. Condensation is a process you see often in your home, especially in the bathroom and kitchen after taking a shower or boiling a pot. When water vapor contacts a cold surface, the vapor turns into droplets. The condenser in the freeze dryer is very cold, usually about −85 °F (−65 °C). The water vapor from the food contacts the freezing condenser and, instead of forming droplets, forms ice crystals. At the end of the cycle, the appliance warms the condenser and lets the ice sublimate. The resulting water gets pumped away. If a large amount of ice accumulates on the condenser, you might have to physically remove it.

Lastly, the appliance brings the chamber **back to atmospheric pressure** so that the food inside can be safely removed.

If you want your appliance to last and function at its best and your food to be as hygienic as possible, you can include **cleaning** as a final step.

Common Myths vs. Facts

There are many myths about the freeze drying process in the culinary world. In this section, we'll do a little investigating and find out the truth about freeze drying.

Myth: Freeze drying is the same as dehydrating.

Fact: Dehydrating also removes moisture from food, but that is where the similarity ends. The dehydrating process only involves heating the food to take the moisture out; in other words, the moisture is simply evaporated. There is still around 5–10% water left in the product after evaporation, which is more than enough for microorganisms and enzymes to stay active. Dehydration will help preserve food, but not for nearly as long as freeze drying. The freeze drying process is more sophisticated. It preserves the qualities and nutrients of the food by sublimation so that the water can be removed at a low heat.

Myth: Freeze-dried foods have a long shelf life due to preservatives.

Fact: No preservatives are used in freeze drying because the microorganisms that cause food to spoil can't grow without moisture.

Myth: Freeze-dried foods never go bad.

Fact: Although the shelf life of freeze-dried foods can be decades, eventually the food may spoil. Whether or not the product spoils, and when, depends mostly on the food itself, how it is packaged, and the conditions under which the product is stored. Another factor in spoilage is water activity. This is a measure of how much water is available for the growth of mold, bacteria, and yeast. Even a very dry food can spoil if there is more than 0.6% water activity.

Myth: The freeze drying process is a simple procedure and shouldn't take this long.

Truth: To freeze dry efficiently, the freeze dryer has to start with a frozen food item. Fast freezing will result in small ice crystals, which make it difficult for vapor to pass through. The slower the freezing process, the larger the ice crystals and spaces for vapor, but if the ice crystals are too large, the cells in the food can get damaged. Then sublimation has to occur to remove the water without boiling the food, followed by secondary drying, which has to be done gradually to remove the bound water. Secondary drying can take hours, or in some cases days, to remove as little as 1% bound water. These are highly technical processes that can ruin the food if rushed.

Myth: A colder condenser will speed up my freeze dryer.

Truth: The drying process depends on water vapor leaving the chamber and going to the condenser. This can be sped up if there is a higher vapor pressure difference between the food and the condenser. Since it is the pressure difference and not simply the temperature that matters, having a colder condenser won't make much of a difference.

Myth: Once you've figured out the perfect cycle, you can use it for all products.

Truth: If the foods you freeze dry have similar drying times, this approach can work, but if you want the best results, you have to adjust your timing to each individual product.

Myth: Your body can't digest freeze-dried food.

Truth: Because freeze-dried food doesn't contain the preservatives or synthetic additives found in other preservation methods such as canning, your body will digest freeze-dried food better! As an added bonus, freeze-dried foods are higher in nutrients too.

Myth: Freeze drying is best left to professional food scientists and large factories.

Truth: Anyone with a freeze dryer can successfully freeze dry any food that is suited for the freeze drying method. You can easily freeze dry at home and have the same nutritional value, shelf life, and overall quality as any well-known brand.

Myth: All freeze drying appliances are the same; only the price differs.

Truth: Choosing the right freeze dryer is a critical part of the journey toward becoming a freeze drying master. This is because the appliances differ in many ways to serve particular needs. A freeze dryer in a chemistry laboratory won't have the same design as an industrial freeze dryer in a food processing factory. In the next chapter, we'll explore the differences between freeze dryers in more detail to help you choose the one that will suit you best.

Myth: Anyone can sell freeze-dried food.

Truth: There are food safety regulations to ensure that consumers get freeze-dried products that conform to health and quality standards. If you or your community project want to sell your freeze-dried products, you'll have to obtain a Food Sales Retail License and a Food Handler's License. There are states that also require a Cannery License (in this case, "cannery" refers to preserved foods in general, not necessarily just those in a can).

Safety Considerations

As you discovered in the myths vs. facts section above, dried foods with more than 0.6% water activity can be susceptible to bacterial, yeast, and mold growth. Even freeze-dried foods can be at risk of becoming contaminated with these pathogens. Fruits and vegetables can become contaminated with *Listeria* and *Salmonella*, and meats are at risk of contamination with *Listeria*, *Salmonella*, and *E. coli*. Freeze drying doesn't kill microbes, so the best way of making sure your product is safe is to eliminate these pathogens during the preparation stage. Water activity meters can help you check that the food is dry enough to be absolutely safe.

Keep in mind that rehydration puts moisture back into the food, and moisture means potential microbial growth. When you rehydrate a freeze-dried food, it doesn't have a long shelf life anymore. If you don't eat all of the rehydrated food right away, you should either throw out the leftovers or freeze them as soon as possible. Rehydrated freeze-dried foods are no longer preserved. They are perishables and should be treated as such. On the other hand, if you open a freeze-dried food package but do not rehydrate it, the food can last for six months to a year depending on the food's exposure to heat, oxygen, light, and moisture.

Keep your appliance as sanitary as possible through proper cleaning. Shelves and trays with food stuck to them aren't just bacterial breeding grounds but can also contribute to uneven heating during the freeze drying process.

To sum up, you can keep your freeze-dried food contaminant free by following these steps:

- Before slicing vegetables or fruit, rinse them under running water. You can use a vegetable brush (cleaned after each use) to scrub away soil if needed.
- Prepare food with even, thin slices to ensure even drying.
- Don't cross-contaminate. Store and prepare all raw meats separately from other foods.
- All kitchen utensils and countertops must be cleaned thoroughly after use.
- Wash your hands before and after touching food.
- Food that dries unevenly can have pockets of moisture where microbes can grow. Check that your food is completely dry before packaging it.

Freeze Drying Without an Appliance

In this book, it is assumed that you have a freeze dryer or will purchase one. If you don't have a freeze drying appliance, you can still freeze dry foods at home. You will probably not end up with a product that has the same decades-long shelf life as you would with an appliance, but it is worth a try if you are willing to experiment. There are two ways in which you can freeze dry at home without an appliance: with a freezer or using dry ice.

Freeze drying with these methods has some drawbacks:

- Be aware that since you can't control the pressure and temperature as precisely with a DIY method as with a freeze drying appliance, your results are likely to be inconsistent.
- There is a fair chance the food may not be completely freeze dried, which will reduce its shelf life.
- You may save money, but you definitely won't save time.

Using Your Freezer (Preferably a Deep Freezer)

Start with foods that freeze dry easily such as peppers, bananas, and berries. If you are a beginner, you might not want to start freezer freeze drying with meats.

After you've washed your food, cut it into thin, even chunks or slices so that the moisture can get out easier. Lay the sliced food in a single layer, with no pieces touching each other, on a baking tray that fits in your freezer. Put the tray in your deep freezer or regular freezer and be patient. The food will start freezing within hours, but the sublimation can take weeks since you don't have the advantage of a vacuum.

After about two or three weeks, you can start checking if the food has been completely freeze dried. Take a piece of food from the tray and let it sit out until it is room temperature. If your food stays the same color, it means that the freeze drying process is complete and the food can be placed in an airtight container. Food that changes color (the food usually darkens) means that the food should stay in the freezer for longer. Another sign that the food is done is if the texture is brittle. If you can snap or crumble it easily with your fingers, the food is freeze dried.

Once your food is done freeze drying, you should store it in an airtight container such as a ziplock bag and keep it somewhere cool, dry, and dark.

Freeze Drying With Dry Ice

The advantage of using dry ice is that it is much faster than using your freezer. To use this method, you'll need a Styrofoam cooler and a fair amount of dry ice. The ideal time to freeze dry with dry ice is when the humidity in your area is very low, since high humidity will slow down the process.

Start by slicing your washed food into thin, even slices. Unlike the freezer method, you won't use trays but will instead place the slices into unsealed airtight freezer containers or bags. Keep the bags or containers unsealed until the food is completely freeze dried, at which point you'll seal them for storage.

The bags go into the cooler. Ideally, the cooler should be double the size or larger than the bags or containers. Cover your bags with the dry ice (one pound of food needs about one pound of dry ice) and wait. Don't close the lid of your Styrofoam container to eliminate the possibility of it exploding. You'll have to wait at least 24 hours (or until the dry ice is gone) for the food to be totally freeze dried. Use the same color test as with the freezer method to determine if the food is done or needs to go back in the dry ice.

Dry ice can be tricky to work with safely. Follow these guidelines to take the danger out of your project:

- Transport and keep your dry ice in a Styrofoam container only. Other materials, such as glass or metal, can become brittle and shatter from the severe cold unless they are specifically rated for extreme cold. Don't put the dry ice in your freezer or fridge since it can damage the appliances' electronics.
- Keep the dry ice in a well-ventilated place. Unsuitable places for dry ice include walk-in freezers, vehicles, closets, and hallways.
- Never touch dry ice without using leather, thermally insulated, or thick oven gloves. Cold can burn too, and touching dry ice with bare skin can cause serious burns.
- When your food is completely freeze dried, you have to dispose of the dry ice. The best place for disposal is outside and out of reach of animals or children. Leave the lid of the Styrofoam container open for the dry ice to sublimate safely into the air.
- Never throw the dry ice down the drain, in your garbage bin, or anywhere in your home where plumbing is used, such as the toilet or sink. The dry ice will ruin your pipes.

In the next chapter, we'll evaluate different types and brands of freeze dryers to help you choose the one that will make your freeze drying dreams come true.

CHAPTER 3
CHOOSING THE RIGHT FREEZE DRYER

You know what you want to do with a freeze dryer, and perhaps you already have some ingredients and recipes ready. Then you go to the store and are confronted by rows upon rows of freeze dryers, each with a spec sheet as long as your arm. The sales person isn't much help, and it's clear you're being steered toward the biggest, most expensive appliance. Should you choose the appliance that looks as if it can land on Mars and needs an engineering degree to operate, or will the humble little two-shelf do?

This chapter will help you make the decision that is best suited to your wallet, needs, and plans.

Difference Between Home and Commercial Freeze Dryers

Freeze dryers have different designs, functions, features, and capacities. These differences become important when you're picking an appliance to suit your freeze drying needs. The ideal freeze dryer should accommodate needs such as auto-cleaning or manual cleaning, the size of the chamber, the number of shelves, and the ability to fine-tune the temperature or vacuum (pressure).

Bigger isn't always better, since some appliances offer larger batch sizes but compromise on quality performance. The differences between home and commercial appliances involve more than size. Let's take a closer look at these differences.

Features

Home freeze dryers focus more on ease of use than precision. Unlike commercial appliances, home freeze dryers usually have only two or three buttons, and most can't store data. They may not have all the features of a commercial appliance, but they get the job done.

Commercial appliances have more to offer. There are controls to enable the selection of shelf temperature and pressure (vacuum) ranges for each phase in the cycle, and an adjustable timer. Programmable appliances can store settings for individual ingredients or full meals. Many commercial freeze dryers also offer a downloadable record from the pressure and temperature sensors taken in 30-second intervals during the entire process.

The fine-tuning possible with commercial freeze dryers results in a finer-quality product, which is needed in the competitive market. Home appliances produce freeze-dried food that isn't quite as top quality but will offer more or less the same shelf life and preservation of texture, nutrients, and taste.

Structure

Home freeze dryers are generally smaller than their commercial counterparts and have more "one size fits all" settings. Commercial freezers are more suited for people who are already familiar with the freeze drying process. Usually, home freeze dryers don't have heat exchangers included in their design. Heat exchangers are expensive, but they can save businesses a lot of money in the long run since they make the freeze drying process more efficient, leading to lower power bills.

Capacity

If you plan on freeze drying less than about 11 pounds at a time, a home freeze dryer is the obvious choice. Commercial dryers can handle much more product, making them the better option if you plan on starting a freeze drying business. Large freeze drying factories use specialized industrial machines that are massive and can handle several tons at a time.

Time

Freeze drying in a home appliance will take approximately 2–3 days per batch, whereas a commercial appliance takes about 24 hours or less to complete a cycle.

Cost

This is the biggest difference of them all. A humble home freeze dryer costs about $2,000 or less. Going the commercial route can cost at least $10,000, and often much more. If you aren't sure if freeze drying is for you, or if you don't foresee opening a freeze drying business in the immediate future, a home appliance will suit you best. If you already have a commercial business and are looking for an upgrade, you might consider an industrial model. Since the operating functions are similar, you can transfer all your presets and other stored data from your commercial appliance to the industrial machine.

Overall Comparison

The table below gives an overview of the use, cost, capacity, and common features of the various types of freeze dryers.

Appliance type	Use	Cost	Average capacity	Features
Home (beginner or budget)	Basic features for home freeze drying beginners	$1,500–$2,000	Up to 1 gallon (3.7 liters)	Easy to operate, manual controls, few automated features
Home (basic model)	Small-batch home food preservation	$2,500–$3,500	1–2 gallons (3.7–7.5 liters)	Few automated features, basic controls

Appliance type	Use	Cost	Average capacity	Features
Home (advanced model)	Suitable for experienced and advanced home freeze dryers and semi-professionals	$3,500–$5,000	2–4 gallons (7.5–15 liters)	More control options and more features than basic models
Commercial (small to medium)	Small businesses and large-scale home use	$10,000–$50,000	10–50 gallons (38–190 liters)	High efficiency, programmable, preset cycles
Commercial (large scale) and industrial	Large-scale production	$50,000–100,000 and above	50 gallons (190 liters) and more	Innovative and automated processes, advanced control and data systems, high efficiency

Overview of Popular Brands

You are more likely to see, and trust, a popular brand than an unknown brand of dubious quality. Whatever the brand you choose, inspect your appliance before buying to see if there are any visible defects, and pay attention to the material from which the appliance is made. Stainless steel is easy to clean and sanitize and will likely last longer than an appliance made from plastic.

Harvest Right

This very reputable brand focuses on home freeze drying appliances that are user-friendly. Even beginner freeze dryers will find the machines easy to operate. Their durable stainless steel appliances are backed up with a good warranty and efficient, accessible technical support. Harvest Right freeze dryers combine reliability, affordability, and excellent quality, and they are very energy-efficient, which means a lower electricity bill.

Vevor

Vevor's appliances aren't top of the range, but they have a wide selection and the quality is very good. The company backs up their claims to quality with a good warranty, and the customer service is excellent. Vevor freeze dryers are ideal for the beginner who is looking for a practical, affordable appliance that is easy to operate.

Cuddon

Although Cuddon is best known for their industrial freeze dryers, they offer a design option where customers can work with a specialist team to design their own home or commercial freeze drying system. Cuddon is also pricey, and their appliances may be too advanced for beginners.

Blue Alpine

Efficiency, affordability, and ease of use are the name of Blue Alpine's game. Their appliances perform well, and the freeze-dried products are of good quality. Blue Alpine freeze dryers are excellent for beginners looking for a mid-range appliance.

Excalibur

Home and commercial freeze dryers are likely to find what they are looking for in Excalibur's large selection of appliances. What makes Excalibur's machines unique is a special feature that facilitates even drying, thus ensuring a product that is uniform and consistent. The company also includes technology that saves energy to do their bit for the environment, which ups the price. On the downside, the technical support is somewhat limited.

GEA

GEA is a big name in industrial-scale freeze drying. They stand out from the crowd by engaging with businesses, guiding and supporting them to achieve maximum efficiency. Their machines are innovative and high quality, which makes them fairly expensive but worth every penny.

Telstar

The fairly expensive industrial freeze dryers from Telstar are efficient and dependable, and constant innovation keeps the machines in demand while also ensuring they remain user-friendly. Telstar's after-sales support is as excellent as their freeze dryers.

New, Used, Refurbished, or Repaired?

Buying brand-new isn't always the right option. You might get the same value for money with a second-hand or refurbished appliance. In this section, we'll take a closer look at the pros and cons of new and used freeze dryers.

New Freeze Dryers

Buying a shiny, brand-new freeze dryer can save you money in the long run. The latest technology is geared toward energy efficiency, which means a lower electricity bill. Since your new freeze dryer will come with a full warranty, you won't have to worry about repair costs for a while.

Many top modern freeze dryers include not only the new appliance shine and smell but also new features that may take a while to learn and master. If you're not into high-tech, an older used model may be more to your liking.

Sometimes, it is simply time for a new freeze dryer. Perhaps you now have space for a larger appliance, or you want a new color, or you're tired of constant breakdowns and leaks. When the time is right, do a little research before you buy. Look at the latest features in the newest models and pay extra attention to power usage and efficiency. Make sure your new freeze dryer is user-friendly with intuitive settings and controls.

When buying a new freeze dryer, you'll get a full manufacturer's warranty. If you plan to use the freeze dryer often, and it is within your budget and the dealer has the option available, consider taking an extended warranty. An extended warranty gives you coverage for repairs or returns for longer than the standard warranty time.

Another advantage of new freeze dryers is that good, reputable dealers will deliver and install them for free, or at a minimal cost.

Used Freeze Dryers

Freeze dryers can be very expensive, and if you can't afford a model that's perfectly suited to your needs, you can buy a used appliance, which is more budget-friendly. If you are a born haggler, you might be able to bring the price down further! (Most stores have a fixed price policy. It is better to haggle when buying directly from the seller.)

There is a wider selection of used than new appliances available, since most stores and retailers only stock the latest models. If you shop for a used appliance via the internet, you might find bargains on "outdated" models and lesser-known brands. With more choice, you're more likely to find exactly what you're looking for at a price that suits you.

A used appliance isn't necessarily moonshine and roses. You might encounter issues such as the following:

- less durable and more clunky designs
- unknown amount of previous use
- unknown previous maintenance

- unknown damage
- unknown working order
- you can't take it back if it's broken
- it may be stolen
- it may be too old for replacement parts to be available if repairs are needed
- no warranty and no guarantees
- DIY installation
- no free delivery

Do your homework on the appliance model before buying. Make sure you know what to look for when checking if the appliance works before handing over your money. If you are satisfied that the freeze dryer is in working order and will continue to work smoothly for at least the next year or two, you have a bargain!

With the possibility of a bargain, you might be wondering where you can find a good freeze dryer. Use the internet and local newsletters to find free giveaways or affordable secondhand appliances, and put up "used freeze dryer" requests in your local shops.

When you buy a used appliance privately from someone, ask for a demonstration first. Don't hand over a cent until you've seen it working properly with your own eyes.

Keep in mind that appliances wear out, and a used appliance will already have some wear. It is a bit of a gamble how long the appliance will keep working.

Refurbished Freeze Dryers

If you've decided to buy a used freeze dryer, you might also consider a refurbished one. A refurbished appliance is an appliance that was sent back to the manufacturer or retailer, who then sent it to their repair shop. Sometimes, an appliance works perfectly but was damaged in terms of appearance, such as a scratch or a chip, and the cosmetic damage has been repaired. The appliance goes back on the shelf when it is completely fixed and tested and will usually have a limited warranty. Because the appliance was tested for full functionality and has the safety net of a warranty, it is a safer option than buying a used freeze dryer with unknown issues.

The downside is that you don't know exactly what was fixed. The fix might have hidden an underlying defect that will need continual repairs. A refurbished freeze dryer's limited warranty is seldom valid for more than a year, after which you will have to cough up the cash for any repairs.

Repaired Freeze Dryers

Instead of buying a new appliance, you have the option of giving your current one a makeover. Here are the pros and cons of repairing your current freeze dryer:

The Pros

- If your appliance only needs a few repairs, it will cost less than buying a new or even a used one.
- It is more eco-friendly and sustainable to reduce waste through repair than to use resources to manufacture new appliances.
- You already know your appliance's settings, controls, and timing. This knowledge helps you get consistently good results every time you freeze dry.
- Many of us are sentimental about gifts or objects that have special fond memories attached. If your freeze dryer was a gift or gives you the warm, fuzzy feeling of happy memories, you'd probably be happier keeping and repairing it for as long as possible.

The Cons

- The repair shop might not give you a warranty, or at best will give you a limited warranty.
- Your trusty old repaired freeze dryer won't have the latest technology that optimizes energy use and offers fine-tuning of settings.
- Keeping your appliance and putting it on life support through repairs will eventually reach its limit. The time will come when the repair costs are greater than the price of a new appliance.
- There's nothing like the convenience of touch controls, smart presets, data storage, and automatic operations. Repairing an older model keeps you from enjoying these latest conveniences.
- Repairs may take longer than expected. The repair shop may have to order parts and, before you know it, you've been freeze dryer free for weeks and have to pay extra for the special order.
- Chances are good that you'll need repairs after your original warranty has expired. This means that you'll have to pay for the repairs out of pocket. Repairing is a good option if you only need to replace a part or two or have a minor issue that needs fixing.

How Do I Know Which Appliance Is Right for Me?

We've discussed the pros and cons of new, used, refurbished, and repaired freeze dryers, and now you need to decide which one will be best. Here are some ideas to help you choose:

- Consider the purpose of your freeze dryer, and be honest with yourself. If you choose a tiny home freeze dryer but have plans to build a business, you'd be wiser to buy a bigger appliance from the start. On the other hand, if you have big dreams of a freeze-dried food empire but have never freeze dried before, or don't have the time or money to start a business just yet, opt for a home model instead of a commercial or industrial appliance. This will allow you to master the nuances of freeze drying a variety of foods before jumping into big business.
- Decide what your overall budget is (including the warranty) and stick to it. Sales personnel, especially if they get a commission, will try to sell you more expensive models. It is mostly your budget that will steer you toward an appliance you'll be happy with.
- An expensive freeze dryer is only worth its cost if you're going to use it often and maintain it properly. Freeze drying only Thanksgiving leftovers or the occasional leftover dessert can be done more economically with a used appliance.
- Know what kind of plug outlets you have before selecting a freeze dryer size. Look carefully at the appliance's specs for the type of power supply needed, since the larger models may need nonstandard plug outlets.

- Measure the space you have available for a freeze dryer before you go shopping. It might be tempting to buy a larger model, especially if it's available at a special discount, but you can't use it if there isn't space for installation. A freeze dryer is more than just the chamber; it also has an attached pump. Your freeze dryer will be installed off the ground so that it is elevated enough to defrost into a container below it.
- The area where your freeze dryer will go should ideally be in the 45–75 °F (7–25 °C) temperature range. It's okay if you use it up to 90 °F (32 °C), but you may sacrifice optimal performance.
- Choose food-safe deodorizers for the freeze dryer's chamber and trays if you plan to freeze dry garlic and onions.
- Lastly, keep in mind that you need to budget for more than a freeze dryer and some ingredients. To freeze dry food, you'll also need packaging or storage containers such as Mason jars or vacuum-sealing bags, tray liners, and oxygen absorbers.

Now that you've chosen the perfect freeze dryer, it's time to start using it. Join me in the next chapter for tips on how to select and prepare foods for the best freeze drying results.

CHAPTER 4
SELECTING AND PREPARING INGREDIENTS

Now we get to the nitty-gritty: the food. In this chapter, we'll explore which foods make the best freeze-dried products, which foods are guaranteed to be a flop, how to pre-treat foods for the professional touch, and where to source your food.

Best Foods for Freeze Drying

In the world of freeze drying, not all foods are equal. The moisture, oil, fat, and sugar content will determine if the food ends up with a long shelf life and reconstitutes well when dehydrated. Here are foods that are ideal for the freeze dryer:

- water-rich fruits, including bananas, pineapple, peas, apples, melons, pears, berries, and passion fruit
- legumes such as peas, lentils, and tofu
- vegetables such as beets, carrots, leafy greens, asparagus, broccoli, parsnips, and corn
- mushrooms
- baked goods such as cookies and bread, to enjoy as a crunchy, original snack
- candy, including ice cream, gummy bears, Jell-O, marshmallows, Skittles, and desserts
- herbs and spices
- sourdough starter
- liquids such as brewed coffee, tea, fruit puree, and fruit juice (Note that coffee beans aren't suited for freeze drying. Solid beans are too thick for proper moisture removal and the oil content will interfere with the taste. Your freeze-dried whole beans will taste like whatever was in the dryer before them.)
- sliced boiled eggs and scrambled eggs
- full meals such as pies, casseroles, stews, chili, and pasta dishes
- meat (raw or cooked), but trim off the excess fat first
- rice and grains, although they may lose texture when rehydrated
- chocolate bars gain a lightness and intense flavor, but the shelf life isn't very long

Foods to Avoid

The foods in this section can't be effectively freeze dried due to their high fat content or less than ideal sugar and water balance. You can still freeze dry foods with a high fat content if you can remove the excess fat before freeze drying, such as pouring out the fat from a pan of fried bacon, but keep in mind that high-fat foods tend to have a much shorter shelf life than other freeze-dried foods. It is best to preserve these foods with methods other than freeze drying:

- meat with a high fat content (including bacon and sausage)
- high-fat dairy such as butter, full-cream milk, high-fat cheese, and yogurt (they tend to become crumbly when freeze dried since the balance between proteins, fats, and water gets disrupted)
- very-high-moisture produce such as iceberg lettuce, grapes, cucumbers, and watermelon (the texture might change in the freeze-dried product since it is difficult to remove all the water, making canning or dehydration a better preservation option)
- nuts and nut and seed butters
- soft cheeses (the moisture content is too high)
- raw eggs, since they are prone to bacterial contamination
- mayonnaise and sauces containing raw eggs
- seafood (except white fish and salmon), as it tends to spoil quickly, and specialized equipment is needed to freeze dry it successfully

- jellies and jams, which are more suited to canning than freeze drying
- very salty or spicy food, since the flavor intensifies during freeze drying
- syrup, including honey (the high sugar content leads to a product that is sticky and messy)
- pure chocolate, since the cocoa butter is oily, which will spoil the texture when freeze dried (You can freeze dry food that has a little bit of chocolate as an ingredient, but it will only have a shelf life of a month or two.)
- dry soup or broth bones, because the thickness makes it near impossible to remove all the water
- foods with alcohol as an ingredient, since alcohol has a different freezing and sublimation point than water
- crackers, chips, and fries
- soups and sauces, which will be messy and lumpy when rehydrated unless you use a fair amount of thickener in the pre-treatment stage

Pre-Treating Herbs and Fresh Spices

It isn't a good idea to pick herbs and spices from the garden and pop them directly in the freeze dryer. The herbs may have bacterial and fungal hangers-on, which can lead to a product that won't last long on the shelf and may even cause sickness when eaten. Pre-treating your herbs gets rid of the microorganisms and inactivates the enzymes in the herbs that can affect the quality of the freeze-dried product.

Here are the steps for proper herbal pre-treatment:

1. Start by sorting healthy herbs from those with obvious damage or plant diseases. Bruised leaves should also be discarded. The better the herbs you start with, the better your end product will be.
2. Next, wash your herbs under running water to remove soil and similar contaminants. The freeze-dried herbal products will also look better when they've been washed first.
3. Get rid of microorganisms that can spoil the shelf life, such as yeast, bacteria, and mold, by soaking the herbs in a special sanitizer. **Only use food-grade sanitizers!**
4. Inactivate the enzymes by blanching the herbs. To blanch, dip your herbs briefly in a pot of boiling water or steam them. Note that different types of herbs have different blanching times, and the ideal temperature can also vary.
5. To speed up the drying time and ensure more even drying, chop or slice the herbs. This process will also help the freeze-dried product to rehydrate better.

Pre-Treating Meat

High fat content is the enemy of freeze-dried meat. Very fatty meat can take days to freeze dry (which will give you a shock when the power bill arrives), and the shelf life will be much shorter than that of a low-fat freeze-dried meat. Here are some tips to help you get the most out of your freeze-dried meat:

- When you pre-cook meat before freeze drying it, use a meat thermometer or make several cuts to ensure the meat is thoroughly cooked, otherwise you might end up with a bacteria-contaminated product.
- Beef, pork, and game freeze dries fine after the fat and bones have been taken out and the meat has been sliced thinly, with a maximum thickness of 1 inch (2.5 cm). Any meat thicker than that will become hard and extremely tough when rehydrated. Ground beef rehydrates better if you make freeze-dried patties with a maximum thickness of 1/2 inch (13 mm).
- Prepare chicken for the freeze dryer by deboning it, removing the skin, and trimming off any visible fat. The skin, bones, and fat don't have to be discarded; you can use them to make a nutritious broth.

- Fish is best cooked before freeze drying. It may also be easier to remove the bones after the fish has been cooked. It doesn't make much of a difference if you leave the head, skin, and tail on during the freeze drying process.
- If meat is very marbled (has streaks of fat inside), it isn't practical to simply cut the fat off. The solution is to cook the fat off the meat beforehand.
- Remove all bones from the meat before putting it raw or cooked into the freeze dryer.
- You'll get the best results if you slice your meat into pieces of even thickness and size and put the slices on the tray so that they don't touch.
- Ground beef also freeze dries well, especially if you cook the fat out beforehand. You can spice the ground beef before freeze drying it, but some recipes call for specific seasonings that may clash with the pre-freeze drying additions.
- After the freeze drying cycle, break or cut a piece of meat in half to check for moisture. If it isn't completely dry or still has cold spots, put it back in your appliance for another hour or two.
- Remember to label your freeze-dried meat as raw or cooked, and include which spices (if any) you used.

Pre-Treating Vegetables and Fruits

Pre-treating vegetables is easy and well worth it. Here's how you do it:

- Wash your veggies and fruits first. If you bought them from a store, there may be ripening agents, wax, or pesticide residue on their surface, and veggies from your garden may have bits of soil sticking to them that should be rinsed off properly.
- Foods such as apples and pears tend to brown after a while when exposed to air. You can prevent this discoloration by rubbing a little lemon juice over the slices or soaking the slices in a bath of diluted lemon juice. A dip in ascorbic acid also works well to keep the original color.
- Onions, tomatoes, leeks, and peppers don't need blanching, but other vegetables do. The best method is to blanch your veggies in a solution with a ratio of 1/4 teaspoon of ascorbic acid to 1 quart (950 ml) of water. Use 2 gallons (8 liters) of water per pound (450 kg) if you are blanching leafy greens, and 1 gallon (4 liters) per pound for all other produce. Steam works well too. Because blanching facilitates the removal of water through a softened cell structure, it speeds up the freeze drying process. Be careful to not over- or under-blanch since that will result in an unpleasant taste and texture differences after freeze drying. After you've blanched your fruits and vegetables, drain them before putting them on your drying trays.
- Slice berries and grapes to allow water to be released, otherwise it will take forever to remove the moisture through the skin. Bigger fruits should also be cut, although it isn't necessary to cut them very thinly, and you can get away with just cutting any small fruits

or berries in half. Thicker slices will still dry. You don't have to peel the skin off fruit, but remember to lay the fruit skin-side down on the tray. The same goes for vegetables. If you don't want to remove the peel, slice the vegetables and put them peel-side down on the tray.

How to Blanch

Blanching is so easy! All you have to do is boil your water and ascorbic acid mix (or just water, if you prefer) in a pot. Put your sliced veggies or fruit in a wire basket and then lower the basket into the pot (the easiest way), or throw them directly into the boiling liquid. The liquid should start boiling again within a minute if the ratio of liquid to produce is correct.

Start the clock when the liquid returns to boiling. Keep the produce in the liquid only as long as the recommended time (comprehensive lists of blanching times are only an internet search away). When the blanching time has finished, remove the produce right away and cool it quickly by dunking it in ice water. The cooling period is the same amount of time as the boiling time. Drain the produce. Use a fresh mix of water and citric acid (or just fresh water, if preferred) for each batch.

To blanch using steam, you'll need a large pot and a strainer or wire basket. Boil enough water to produce steam, but leave enough space that the strainer or basket will be at least 3 inches (8 cm) above the water level. Put the sliced produce in a single layer in the basket or strainer and lower it into position with the basket or strainer handles outside of the pot. Cover the pot and start the clock. When you've reached the recommended steaming time, take the produce out and cool it quickly in ice water for as long as you steamed it, then remove it and let it drain.

Sourcing the Ingredients

Where you get your ingredients from can affect your budget, the nutrient content of your product, the final texture and taste, the shelf life, and possibly the appearance too. In this section, we'll examine the pros and cons of each sourcing method to help you decide on a supplier, whether you're freeze drying for home use or are growing a business.

If you're planning a freeze drying business, it might be best to source in bulk or from a store to facilitate a uniform, consistent product. There's a market for organic, homegrown, and homemade products as well. Be aware of any regulations regarding home-sourced foods in your state.

Homegrown and Homemade

When it comes to natural, full-bodied taste and nutrient content, nothing beats homegrown. If you don't have your own garden, you can find fresh-from-the-soil produce in farmer's markets or local community projects. If you grow your own food, you can choose to go organic without having to pay extra for the privilege of pesticide-free, all-natural good food. Another advantage of homegrown is that you can grow the varieties you like best to ensure you have your favorites available. And unlike stores, which use artificial ripeners, you can harvest when your fruit and vegetables are completely ripe, which means optimum vitamin content.

The best part of homegrown ingredients and homemade meals is the freshness. The flavor is better and the nutrient content optimal. Homemade foods can be made exactly to your taste and standards. The produce may vary greatly in size and appearance, though. If you source from your own garden, you'll have to decide between pesticides or organic and be willing to take losses if nature sends too much or too little rain.

Homemade foods give you control over the ingredients and kitchen conditions. You can add spices to your individual taste and leave out unwanted artificial additives. Above all, you have the assurance that your food has been prepared in a (hopefully) clean environment. Not all store kitchens are up to your cleanliness standards, and who knows how strictly the store enforces health regulations?

Store-Bought

Nutrient quality isn't always the best in store-bought fruits and vegetables, even though the appearance is uniformly good. This is because most stores buy crops before they are fully ripened to compensate for the ripening that takes place in transit. All too often, the ripening occurs only in outside appearance and taste but not peak nutrient content.

Produce starts losing nutrients right after harvesting. If the temperature, light exposure, storage time, and packaging aren't optimal, even more nutrients get lost. Imported food can take weeks to get to stores, and it is seldom eaten on the same day it hits the shelves or your fridge.

If you buy store-bought prepared food (such as canned soup to freeze dry as is or as an ingredient), you save the time and energy of making the soup yourself, but you pay for the convenience with potentially unhealthy additives. The extra sodium, sugar, preservatives, colorants, and artificial flavorings just don't produce the same quality product as homemade or garden grown.

The produce used by stores usually consists of specific varieties bred to look the same and have longer shelf lives than garden varieties. The food looks good, but it may not be as flavorful as garden varieties.

Store-bought isn't all negative. You have the convenience of simply opening a can or packet to enjoy a familiar and predictable taste and quality. Homegrown isn't always practical or possible, and store-bought can be an ideal option if you need ingredients that are otherwise unavailable. Store-bought is a great time saver and can occasionally work out less expensive than homemade.

Bulk Buying

Wholesalers make their profit by selling large amounts of items at a low profit margin. They keep their prices low to encourage retailers, and sometimes home buyers, to buy from them. They don't need to make a huge profit on each item since they make their money with turnover. This means that you'll pay less for items when buying in bulk than you would for the same items at your local retail store.

Around 10% of a product's price is its packaging (Habek, 2023). It costs more to package items individually than in bulk, which means the manufacturer saves money and can sell the items more cheaply to the wholesaler. These packaging savings get passed to the buyer, which can be you if you buy in bulk.

Buying in bulk saves you money at the checkout and in gas, since you cut down on trips to the grocery store. You're also less likely to spend out of budget on impulse buys.

Some wholesale stores require a membership fee, but the fee is minimal compared to the savings. Considering that inflation goes up and almost never down, you'll save money buying in bulk now. In five years' time, when you're still using the bulk canned ingredients, you can think back to the good old days when a can of peas didn't cost $20.

Despite the many advantages, bulk buying isn't always the best solution. Be aware that buying in bulk requires extra storage space at home, and if you buy perishables in bulk, you may need an extra freezer. If you don't freeze dry perishables as soon as possible, they might spoil, which means your money will go straight in the trash can.

Brush up on your mental math skills or carry a calculator with you when bulk buying to determine the unit price. Sometimes, what seems like a bargain because you get several items in one package is more expensive per unit than your local grocery.

CHAPTER 5
THE FREEZE DRYING PROCESS STEP-BY-STEP

You have chosen the perfect appliance, selected your ingredients, pre-treated them if necessary, and are now ready to pop them into the freeze dryer. This chapter will guide you through the entire process, step-by-step. Here we go!

Preparing the Freeze Dryer

You have chosen the prefect freeze dryer for your needs, and it has been delivered. Now what? Open the box, plug it in, and put in your trays loaded to the brim with food ready to be freeze dried? Not so fast! You have to set up your freeze dryer first.

Setting Up

Let's start with the assumption that your appliance is still in the box and your dealer didn't include installation, or you bought a used freeze dryer. Take the packing list (a list of everything in the box) out and start unpacking the box's contents. Make sure everything in the packing list was in the box, and if there is a component missing, contact your dealer immediately.

Place your new machine in a cool space with at least 6 inches (15 cm) clearance on either side and 3 inches (8 cm) clearance at the back, and elevated to leave space for water drainage. If the freeze dryer's drain outlet is high enough off the ground for a bucket to be placed beneath it, you can leave it on the ground.

Your model may require you to add oil manually to the vacuum pump. If your instructions tell you to do so (in which case, the manufacturer usually includes the oil), open the oil cap and fill with oil slowly until you reach the recommended oil level (usually mid-level). Close the cap.

Connect the pump's hose to the pump and the vacuum port on the freeze dryer, and fix both ends securely in place with hose clamps. Check the instructions to see if you should also open or close any valves.

Plug the vacuum pump into the freeze dryer. This plug is usually at the back of the freeze dryer. There will be a drain valve on the freeze dryer. Connect your drain hose there and secure it with a clamp. The other end of the hose goes into a bucket, which usually isn't included with the freeze dryer.

Plug your appliance directly into the wall outlet, unless you have an industrial freeze dryer or the instructions tell you otherwise. If possible, have your freeze dryer close enough to the wall outlet that you don't have to use an extension cord, because a cord may influence the operating voltage. Switch on the vacuum pump. The pump is automatically controlled by the freeze dryer, which means you can leave it switched on.

Switch the freeze dryer's power on. Ignore the temptation to play with your new appliance and instead let it sit undisturbed for 24 hours. After the waiting period, you can check for water (liquid or ice) in the chamber and around the door. They should be dry. Unless your freeze dryer's instruction manual says otherwise, you are now set up and ready to start freeze drying.

Test Run

It is a good idea to have a test run to ensure everything is working as it should and to absorb the new-machine smell. Use cheap food that you won't miss when you discard it afterward. Dip some slices of bread in water and run your freeze dryer.

Loading Trays Properly

Being a freeze drying master means knowing the finer nuances of the process. Loading the trays for the best results is an art form in itself.

Silicon and Parchment Liners

Unless you enjoy scrubbing trays, you'll want to cover your trays with removable liners. You have a choice between silicon and parchment, and each type has its own pros and cons.

Parchment, also called baking paper, is a specially treated paper with nonstick and heat-resistant properties. Unlike ordinary paper, it won't burst into flames in your oven. It is sold in rolls for you to cut to your preferred size or as pre-cut sheets, and it is disposable, with some types even compostable. The downside of parchment paper is that you can use the lining only once or twice.

Silicon liners aren't absorbative like parchment. Any grease or moisture will stay on the liners, which can make removing certain foods a messy affair. Silicon is dishwasher-safe and reusable, though. Silicon liners can be too insulating, which interferes with drying times, but they help provide more even heat distribution.

Bulk Density

Bulk density is a measure of how dense your food is. This comes in handy when you have a commercial or industrial freeze dryer and have to calculate how much you can safely load on a tray. Since it is difficult to take accurate measurements of irregularly shaped food, the easiest way is to put the food into a square or rectangular container. Measure the container's length and width and how high the food reaches inside. If you can lay your food out directly in the tray, you can use the tray's measurements, but the height shouldn't be over 0.8 inches (20 mm) because that is the maximum height of food on the tray for efficient freeze drying.

Once you have these measurements and the weight of the food, you can enter the data into an online bulk density and tray load calculator. You can fine-tune your data by adding the food's moisture percentage (if known) and your freeze dryer's manufacturing model. The result of the calculations will tell you how heavily you can load a tray and more or less how much your freeze-dried product will weigh. Knowing the bulk density and maximum tray load is important if you want to maximize efficiency and cut down on electricity use.

Load All Trays

Your freeze dryer contains several temperature sensors. Loading all the trays means the sensors can give more accurate readings, which helps the electronics in the dryer maintain an even temperature over all the trays. If some trays are left empty, this can lead to uneven temperatures, which can cause uneven drying.

That said, there are some people who swear by freeze drying candy only in the middle trays. When you have more experience with your particular appliance, you'll be able to tell if your freeze dryer has a "sweet spot" for certain types of food.

Drying Time

You aren't a freeze drying master, or even a freeze drying Average Joe, if you don't take recommended drying times seriously. Since drying times can vary from hours to days, patience is key.

The following factors play a role in determining drying time:

- Slices that are **thin and even** dry faster and more evenly. Also, put the food on the tray in a single layer and don't let pieces overlap.

- The **type** of food determines how fast it will dry because of the variation in **moisture content and density**. The denser the food, the longer the wait. Higher moisture content means the appliance will take longer to remove all the moisture.
- The **initial temperature** plays a crucial role in the drying time. The colder the food is when the drying starts, the more quickly it will dry. This is because less energy is required to bring the food to sublimation. You can shave more time off by pre-freezing the food. If your food is frozen solid right through, you can skip your appliance's freezing phase and go directly to the drying (sublimation) phase.
- The **more food** you are drying, the longer the drying time.
- You may find that the drying time is longer in the dead of winter or on humid summer days. This is because the appliance has to use more energy to remove water when the **ambient temperature and humidity** are high.

Fine-tuning your freeze drying by using custom settings for specific foods will make the process more efficient, which will shorten the drying time.

Techniques of the Masters

Every art form and trade has some secrets that separate the casual amateur from the true master. Level up your freeze drying game with these tips:

- During humid days or when freeze drying high-moisture foods, place some silica gel packets or buckets near your trays to dehumidify and decrease the moisture.
- If your meat isn't very tender, marinate it after freeze drying to infuse it with taste and tenderness, or tenderize it with a tenderizing mallet. In other words, rehydrate it with a marinade instead of with water.
- Never increase the recommended temperature to speed up the drying time. The product will lose nutrients and the texture can be compromised.
- If you don't have enough of a certain type of food to fill all the trays, you can load your trays with different foods that have the same drying time.
- Prolong the life of your freeze dryer by installing a surge protector. This will protect the delicate sensors and electronics from power spikes resulting from power outages and interruptions. But check with the manufacturer first, because some appliances are sensitive to the slightest current changes and a surge protector may interfere with the delicate electronics.
- Don't neglect the maintenance of your freeze dryer. Clean the vacuum pump, check all the hoses, filters, seals, and oil wells for leaks, and remove ice buildups.

When Is the Freeze Drying Process Done?

If your food isn't completely freeze dried when the recommended drying time ends, your product will spoil quickly because the remaining moisture will become a kindergarten for bacteria. As you become more experienced with freeze drying, you'll develop a "feel" for the perfect drying times, but until then, this section will guide you.

Use Your Senses

You can eyeball a sample to see if the process is done. Snap or cut a freeze-dried food in half, or in thirds if possible, to check for moist spots. Feel if the sample is cold in places. Any residual moisture or cold means the food needs more drying. Once you're familiar with how a specific freeze-dried food feels, you can also use texture to determine if it's done. Freeze-dried foods are brittle and crumbly. Using your senses is subjective and it is easy to make mistakes, especially if you are inexperienced. For business purposes, it is wise to use more scientific methods to comply with industry regulations.

Be Scientific

Water has weight, and this water weight gets removed during freeze drying. You can use specialized scales that are able to withstand the low pressure and freezing temperatures in the chamber to track the weight of your product. If the product is losing weight, the drying process is still ongoing. When the weight remains constant, all the water has been removed and the process is done. There are methods to analyze the moisture content during the process, such as Karl Fischer titration and spectroscopy, but these methods are mostly used in laboratories and industry.

Knowing the correct cycle time for each type of food, how to prepare food, and how to correctly load it on the trays will result in a predictable process time. If you do everything by the book, you can set your timer and be sure that the product will be perfectly freeze dried when the cycle ends.

High-end freeze dryers have pressure, mass and heat flow, and temperature sensors that update in real time. Mass and heat flow measurements get taken with special sensors that show how fast vapor is being removed from the food and how the temperature of the food is changing as a result.

When the drying process begins, the food will be frozen and will then stay cold due to the evaporation during sublimation. The food will thus be colder than the trays. It remains colder throughout sublimation, until the temperature gradually starts to rise as sublimation slows down. When the trays have the same temperature as the product, it means there's no more evaporative cooling underway and the entire drying process is complete.

Sophisticated pressure gauges that are affected by vapor show when the process is done by using a convergence point. When the gauges reach this point, it means there is no more vapor being released and the product is as dry as possible. Some appliances detect the end of the drying process by closing a valve between the condenser and the chamber. Water vapor will influence the gauge, showing that the process is still ongoing while the pressure is rising. After the reading, the valve is opened again.

Drying Times

Here are the **approximate** drying times for some common foods (assume all the food types are thinly and evenly sliced):

Product	Total cycle time (from freezing to drying) in hours
Apples	24–28
Corn	24–28
Peas	20–26
Asparagus	20–24
Ground beef	26–30
Precooked beef	22–30
Turkey	20–26
Lasagna	36–48
Grated cheese	20–25
Pineapple	48–52
Berries	48–52
Blanched raw potato	32–36
Bananas	25–27
Soup	40–48
Candy	12–20
Tomatoes	26–34

Moisture Content

You've seen moisture content mentioned several times in this book, and you may be wondering how moist foods really are. The table below lists some common foods and their moisture content. The moisture is mostly water:

Food	% moisture
Apples (with skin)	85
Berries	90
Tomatoes	94
Onions	90
Corn	77
Bananas	76
Ground beef	68
Cooked or scrambled egg	74
Poached chicken breast	70

Pampering the Machine

The better you treat your freeze dryer, the longer and more efficiently it will serve you. Following the recommended treatment will also ensure that your warranty isn't voided and any repairs remain the manufacturer's responsibility. Here's how to treat your freeze dryer:

- Unless you enjoy getting electrocuted, don't take the side panels off, and definitely don't run the appliance without these panels. Don't stand in a puddle of water or let the plugs get wet. You can touch exposed wires when the freeze dryer is unplugged, but you'll get the shock of your life if you try the same thing when it's plugged in.
- Some freeze dryer manufacturers recommend that you don't use extension cords or surge protectors. Anything that can interfere with the finely tuned electrical and electronic system, no matter how small the interference, can damage your appliance.
- Use proper hose joints and hose clamps. Should anything go wrong with your freeze dryer, the manufacturer can claim that you used damaging equipment or interfered with the machine if they see duct tape or other DIY fixes. Then you'll have to pay for the

repairs. The same goes for plugging anything but the vacuum pump into the vacuum pump outlet.

- If you use chemicals that can harm the machine, such as organic solvents, abrasive cleaning products, bleach, acids, or ammonia, your warranty won't cover repairs. Even the vapors of these chemicals can cause damage. Only clean with warm water and mild detergents such as dishwashing liquid. Hand-wash the shelves, since shelf units are generally not dishwasher-safe.
- Scratches make your freeze dryer look old and tired. Preserve its good looks by using only soft cloths and never anything that's abrasive or bristly to clean it.
- Impatient people beware! If you override the freeze dryer's automatic cycle to skip any parts of the cycle, you might damage the appliance. Remember that modern freeze dryers run on sensitive electronics.
- The drain tube is an ideal breeding ground for microorganisms such as mold and bacteria. Pour some warm soapy water down the drain line regularly to keep it hygienic and clean.
- Don't vent your vacuum chamber while the drain hose is still in water in the bucket.
- Take care of the most important machine (you) by not sleeping in the same room as your freeze dryer. Operate your appliance only in an area with good ventilation. Don't store flammable liquids or vapors in the same room as your freeze dryer.
- Before you start a fresh batch of product, make sure your drain valve is closed and that the rubber around the chamber door is clean to ensure a proper seal.
- Have you ever touched a cold surface with damp hands or licked frozen metal? If you have, you'll know why it isn't a good idea to touch the cold parts of your freeze dryer unless your hands are absolutely dry.
- Don't block the air vents. These vents stop the dryer from overheating.
- It will cost you a pretty penny to replace the parts in the thermal cutoff, which will blow if you defrost the appliance with a blow torch (even a tiny one used to make crème brûlée) or a hair dryer.
- Before any maintenance or cleaning, unplug your freeze dryer.
- You can change the oil in your vacuum pump. Your device manual will tell you how frequently you should drain the oil and replace it with new or filtered oil.
- If you aren't going to use your freeze dryer for at least a couple of weeks, turn it off. Use a soft cloth to dry it inside. Keep the inside of the chamber ventilated by leaving its door open.
- Modern freeze dryers record the room temperature when the appliance is running a cycle. If you operate the freeze dryer in an area warmer than a certain maximum listed in the owner's manual (Harvest Right lists 105 °F/40 °C, for example), your warranty is automatically voided.

In the next chapter, we'll examine the best ways to package and store your freeze-dried products for long-lasting freshness, flavor, and nutritional value.

CHAPTER 6
PACKAGING AND STORAGE FOR A LONG SHELF LIFE

Now that you know how to put your food through the freeze drying process until it is completely dry, we can move on to packaging and storage methods. When this is done correctly, your food can last for so long that your as yet unborn grandkids will be able to eat it after they graduate from college. Well, almost.

Packaging Options

Every type of packaging has its pros and cons. Let's explore them to find the perfect packaging for your freeze-dried food.

Mylar Bags

Mylar bags, also called pouches, are strong, light, and long-lasting. They keep air and humidity away from the product, and they will work even harder to keep your freeze-dried food edible if you add oxygen absorbers.

Always use food-grade Mylar bags and check the rating. They should be able to handle boiling water.

This storage option seals your product in an airtight bag, where it is safe from humidity and air. Nutrients and flavor are well preserved. As an added bonus, vacuum-sealed Mylar bags don't take up much storage space. On the downside, vacuum-sealed bags aren't as effective as other methods for very long-term storage.

To take full advantage of this packaging method, always check that the bags are completely sealed. The smallest gap will let moisture and air in to spoil the product. Only use bags designed for vacuum sealing, and look for quality even if it costs a little more. Good-quality bags will be puncture resistant, opaque (don't let light through), BPA free, odorless, and rated for long storage periods. Your extra investment will be worth it.

There are different Mylar bag designs. Stand-up pouches look good on a shelf (good for sales), and the layers of plastic and aluminum give them extra resistance against light and punctures. Pillow pouches look like pillows, and they are usually filled with inert nitrogen gas to keep oxygen out. These pouches are also very resilient. Gusseted pouches can store more food than you'd guess at first glance because they have gussets on the sides and bottom. When the bottom is extended, the pouch will also stand upright.

You can also use buckets with an airtight seal around the lid, or, if you have the equipment, you can store freeze-dried food in a can.

Rehydration is easy: Just add water and stir. Reseal with the zip and wait until the water has been absorbed.

Mason Jars

What could be easier than opening a Mason jar filled with freeze-dried delights, pouring a little water in, screwing the lid back on, and shaking the jar? That's really all it takes to rehydrate freeze-dried food with this storage method. Mason jars are durable, versatile, and reusable. They look inviting and comforting on a pantry shelf. The thick glass is fairly strong and, unless exposed to extremes of temperature, won't crack easily.

Despite all the advantages, Mason jars aren't always the perfect packaging. They aren't always completely airtight (unless you use a jar vacuum sealer gadget) and they let light in, which why it is imperative to store them in a dark corner. The transparency isn't necessarily bad, since you can keep an eye on your product to watch for spoilage.

Make your Mason jars even better by putting an oxygen absorber on top of your product before you screw on the lid, and use a vacuum sealer if you have one. Don't screw the lids on with white-knuckle force because this can damage the threads on the lid or glass. Just tight is tight enough.

Vacuum or Nitrogen?

To preserve your freeze-dried food with the longest shelf life possible, you can either remove all the air from the packaging (vacuum packaging) or fill the packaging with nitrogen gas (nitrogen packaging). Vacuum packaging is less costly than nitrogen packaging since you don't need to buy nitrogen gas, and the process entails simply sucking the air out. However, a package filled with nitrogen can keep products fresher for longer and preserve a crispy texture, which is why potato crisps are sold in nitrogen-filled pillow packaging. Nitrogen-filled packages take up more space than vacuum packages, though. Whichever method you choose, rest assured that your food's shelf life will be extended because microorganisms, humidity, and oxygen can't take hold of your product.

Freeze-dried foods will last a long time even if you don't vacuum the packaging or fill it with nitrogen, as long as they are stored in the recommended conditions.

Commercial Packaging Machines

Once your business takes off, you probably won't have time to hand-pack and seal every bag, bucket, or jar. Automatic or semi-automated packaging machines save time and deliver uniformly packaged products. No matter what the specific type, all do the same work. The product gets loaded, then the machine weighs exact amounts and puts the specific amount into a container. The machine will then use heat or pressure to seal the package. Lastly, the sealed packages of freeze-dried food are safely discharged and ready to be sent to stores.

There are many types of packaging machines available. Let's take a brief look at the different types to help you choose:

- **Rotary** packaging machines are fully automatic and able to package a wide variety of freeze-dried products. You put a bulk amount of freeze-dried product in its hopper, and it will fill and seal the packages in a rotary direction.
- An **automatic conveyor belt multi-packaging** machine can fill and seal cans, jars, and bags. This machine is ideal if your business sells freeze-dried foods in a variety of packaging. Automatic machines can do all the work without any humans helping.

- **Semi-automatic** packaging machines can weigh and fill packaging. One or more humans have to load the machine, put the packaging in place, and discharge the filled packages.
- **Linear** packing machines for freeze-dried products do the work in a straight sequence. The product is loaded, then weighed, then the packages are filled and finally discharged in a single, easily observable line.

Packaging machines can be further divided into **specialties**. There are packaging machines specifically for stand-up, gusset, and pillow pouches. When deciding on a packaging machine, be guided by the type of packaging that's best for your product and whether or not you want the process to be automated or have human interaction.

Ideal Storage Conditions

The ideal storage temperature ranges between 50 and 70 °F (10–21 °C). It is best if you can store your freeze-dried products somewhere with a consistently even temperature.

Light and storage don't go together because the UV rays in sunlight can degrade the food and the packaging. Store your freeze-dried foods in cupboard or in a room without direct sunlight.

If you store your freeze-dried food in an area that is humid, such as the basement, it might absorb some of that moisture. Moisture is to microorganisms what cheeseburgers and pizza are to humans: It makes them grow and expand. Microorganisms can give you food poisoning and reduce the shelf life of your freeze-dried product.

Air, and specifically the oxygen in air, can make its way into a freeze-dried product and cause it to lose nutrients, flavor, and appearance.

Oxygen Absorbers

Oxygen absorbers are little packets containing a mixture of powdered iron and charcoal or sodium. When the packet comes into contact with air, it triggers a chemical reaction where the oxygen from the surrounding air gets absorbed to form iron oxide inside the packet. Yes, you're right—iron oxide is common old rust. The rust forms very slowly and won't affect or discolor the food since it is contained in a special packet. When the oxygen is removed, nitrogen (and a tiny, tiny percentage of carbon dioxide) is left. Nitrogen is inert, which means it doesn't interact with the compounds in your product.

Absorbers are used for more than just removing the oxygen needed for microorganisms to grow. Larger organisms such as insects can't feast on your freeze-dried goodies should they manage to find a way into the package, since they too need oxygen to breathe. The absorbers prevent fats and oils from breaking down and going rancid, because without oxygen, fats can't oxidize. An oxygen-free container will also help preserve the compounds in foods responsible for their specific color, flavor, and aroma. The oxygen-free environment will keep certain vitamins intact too.

Some brands call their absorbers O_2 absorbers or oxygen scavengers. Oxygen absorbers aren't the same as silica gel packets, which absorb moisture only. Usually, an oxygen absorber is enough to ensure maximum shelf life since the freeze-dried product is already free of moisture, but if you live in a very humid climate, you might consider adding a silica gel packet too.

Pro tip: Don't use oxygen absorbers in containers of food that hasn't been freeze dried. If you keep candy, fruit, or other high-sugar edibles in a Mason jar and add an absorber, it can lead to a sticky mess.

Labeling Done Right

Labeling is more than sticking on a piece of paper with "freeze-dried food" written on it. Here are some tips on how to label like a pro:

- Don't stick a label over a label. The newest label may not stick as permanently as you'd like, and then the product can be misidentified by the original label. This can happen easily if you reuse packaging such as Mason jars. (Yes, I know you wash the jars thoroughly and rinse them with boiling water to kill microorganisms before putting your freeze-dried food into them, but the labels don't always come off easily, and you might be tempted to double-label.)
- Foods that have been pre-prepared with heat, such as scrambled eggs, boiled pasta, or roasted beef, must have labels that show that they have been cooked. Label your raw meat as well.
- If you sell your products, your label should include the production date, any possible allergens, and a use-by date, which is calculated from the estimated shelf life.
- Freeze-dried food that contains the following allergens should have them listed on the label: dairy, shellfish, eggs, non-gluten-free wheat, milk, soy, nut butter and nut milk (whole nuts can't be freeze dried, but cookies that contain peanut butter can), and coconut.
- Rehydrated food can spoil quickly, and your label should recommend consumers to use the food within hours of rehydration or within two days if refrigerated.
- Sticky labels aren't for everyone. Tie a card containing the food labeling information to your Mason jars with string or elastic to add some creativity. Removing the cards is much easier than scraping off sticky labels, even if you're clever and use a hair dryer to loosen the glue and take the residue off with rubbing alcohol on a rag.

Why Rotate?

Stock rotation, including of the freeze-dried food in your pantry, is done so that you use the oldest products first. This is to prevent the older products from going past their safe shelf life while you keep consuming the newer products all the time. Rotation allows your pantry to stay full of products that will keep their nutritional value the longest. Whenever you rotate your products, you also get the chance to visually inspect them for any damage to the packaging that can spoil the contents and for any food that has gone bad.

Make it a habit to check the labels on your products and put the oldest ones in the front and the newest ones in the back. This ensures an efficient rotation with minimal effort. If you have a business, make this a daily habit, and remove all freeze-dried food past its recommended shelf life from your stock.

Has It Gone Bad?

Despite taking all the precautions and following instructions to the letter, your freeze-dried product may spoil before the shelf life has expired. This is how you can tell that a product is better suited for the garbage than a dinner plate:

- If the product has an unpleasant smell, it is probably spoiled.
- Break off a piece of the product and press it between your fingers. A texture that is spongy, not brittle is a warning that it shouldn't be eaten.
- Discard any product that shows discoloration. If the texture doesn't look right, or if you see even the faintest speck of mold, toss it into the bin.
- If the product has a mushy texture or remains hard and dry after you've rehydrated it, discard it.
- If your product looks, smells, and feels fine but the first bite has you pulling a face, spit out the bite and don't eat the rest.

Rehydrating

You can measure the weight of your food before and after freeze drying to determine the precise amount of water needed for rehydration. The water required for optimal rehydration is the difference between the weight before and after freeze drying. Freeze drying removes water, so when you rehydrate, you simply put the water back.

The water weight doesn't have to be replaced with ordinary water. Use fruit juice, milk, broth, soup, or sauce if it suits your taste.

Ideally, you should eat freeze-dried food within 24 hours after opening the bag or jar. If you don't rehydrate the opened food but seal it again in an airtight container (and keep the container away from light and high temperatures), the food can last a further week. The reduction in shelf life after opening is due to the absorption of atmospheric moisture.

It is possible to refreeze dry rehydrated food, but it can result in a mushy product that has lost its nutrients. A refrozen dried food also will have a shorter shelf life than a product that has only been freeze dried once. The best way to determine which of your leftovers survive a re-freeze drying is trial and error.

Rehydrate your raw freeze-dried products with cold water. Use hot water to rehydrate products that were blanched or cooked before freeze drying. If you're using boiling or very hot water, you can wrap the food in foil to keep the steam in for faster rehydration. Boiling water will rehydrate freeze-dried food three times faster than cold water.

You can also rehydrate cooked or blanched food with steam, but there's a good chance the food will have a rubbery texture.

Be patient with fruits and veggies that were freeze dried with the skin still on, such as green beans and corn. They might need to be soaked for an hour or two to rehydrate and soften.

One expert suggests spraying water on delicate foods to preserve their appearance. If you like your herbs, berries, and mushrooms to look good after rehydrating, spray them gently, wait two or three minutes, and respray as needed. Keep respraying for as long as the food needs to fully rehydrate, which can be as long as 20 minutes (*Rehydrating Freeze Dried Foods*, 2024).

When you have to rehydrate without knowing the exact water weight you should add, start by adding small amounts of water and waiting a couple of minutes for the food to absorb it fully. Keep adding small amounts and waiting until the food is just right. Too much water will make your rehydrated food a mushy swamp.

Add a long-handled spoon to your kitchen drawer. It will come in handy when you stir the food while it's rehydrating.

Shelf Life Comparison

Knowing the estimated shelf life of your freeze-dried foods will enable you to efficiently rotate your products, plan your emergency stock, and put your mind at ease that you aren't eating spoiled food. Let's compare the shelf lives of popular freeze-dried foods:

- Freeze-dried fish can stay happily on your shelf for 25 years, but the quality may be compromised in the last 10 years. You might be concerned about these dates when you see commercial freeze-dried seafood with a two-year recommended shelf life, but this is done only to ensure top quality and eliminate any risk of contamination. Improperly freeze-dried seafood is notorious for harmful bacteria, and the sellers want to reduce the risk of lawsuits.
- Your boiled or scrambled freeze-dried eggs will keep on the shelf for 5–10 years. After 5 years, the quality starts going downhill a bit.
- Meat that is raw, deboned, and lean will last about 15 years. Precooked meat can last a year or two longer. Freeze-dried meat is best if used before 10 years of storage. After that, it will still be edible and safe, but the quality may not be as good.
- Vegetables have a wide shelf life range. Most veggies remain edible and tasty for more than 20 years. Top quality is up to about 10 years, after which they slowly lose nutrients.
- Candy contains sugar, which can preserve freeze-dried candy comfortably for 30 years. It may not be as fresh and yummy in the last 5 years as it was in the first 25, but it will still be irresistible.
- If your product contains yeast, it won't last as long as unleavened products.

To find the shelf life of a specific food, refer to the table below:

Freeze-dried food	Shelf life in years
Fruit and berries	20+
All-purpose, unbleached, and whole-wheat flour	10–15
Vegetables	25
Eggs	5–10
Legumes	25
Millet	25
Pasta	10–20
Popcorn	30
Cornmeal	20–25
Granola	1
Salt, honey crystals, and sugar	No upper limit
Potatoes	20
White rice	30
Rolled and hulled oats	30
Cocoa powder	10–15
Flax	10–12
Instant milk	25
Shredded cheese	25
Soybeans	10–15

CHAPTER 7
TROUBLESHOOTING AND GOOD ADVICE

This chapter is all about hunting down the causes of freeze drying problems and correcting them. If you are new to freeze drying, it would be wise to read through all the potential issues to prevent them. Many of the fixes are part of a basic maintenance program, which means that many issues can be avoided by taking good care of your freeze dryer. You'd be surprised how many problems can be avoided by proper cleaning, loading foods evenly in trays, and avoiding overloading.

Common Issues

Issue: The pressure in the chamber doesn't drop as low as it should.

Solution: Your vacuum pump may be faulty. Even a microscopic hole in the vacuum hose can lead to a loss of vacuum. If there is a problem with the vacuum or its hose that you can see with the naked eye, you can contact the manufacturer for a replacement part (let the manufacturer or dealer replace the part if it is still under warranty). If you can't find the problem, contact the dealer or manufacturer.

The problem might also be caused by moisture or other contaminants in the vacuum pump's oil. If you suspect that this is causing problems, you can change the oil (do it three times in a row to remove all contaminants) or use a flushing oil. Read your owner's manual to find out how often you're supposed to change the oil, and make this part of your regular maintenance routine.

If neither an oil change nor a new hose helps, the problem might be with the freeze dryer itself. Try replacing the rubber seal (gasket) around the chamber door. Should the low vacuum strength persist, the problem may be a faulty selector knob or valve or, less likely, a leak somewhere in the manifold, and a trained technician should take a look.

Issue: The vacuum works fine, but the chamber doesn't get cold enough.

Solution: Pay attention to when the temperature drop is insufficient. If it happens during a defrosting cycle, the problem is most likely a stuck defrost valve. If it isn't the valve, the problem lies with the refrigeration system itself. Either way, let your warranty take care of the repairs; otherwise, if your warranty has expired, you can unstick the valve by unplugging your appliance and trying to move it (very gently!) to loosen any debris. Should this not work, you can gently tap the valve to get rid of debris or bits of ice.

If your chamber doesn't reach freezing temperatures and the defrost valve isn't stuck, clean any ice from your condenser and ensure your freeze dryer has enough clearance around it to facilitate good ventilation.

Issue: The inside of my freeze dryer has an icy buildup.

Solution: Very long cycles can lead to ice buildup. A very humid environment and overloading can also lead to ice buildup. Clean the ice, and try a lighter load next time.

On rare occasions, food contains so much moisture that the ice on the condenser spreads to the trays in the chamber. The freeze dryer can't tell the difference between ice in food and ice on the trays and will sublimate the tray ice. Should this happen, you can take the trays out and place them in your freezer to stay cold, defrost the ice buildup in the chamber and condenser, return the trays, and let your freeze dryer complete the cycle.

Issue: My freeze-dried food loses quality after only a few months. Isn't freeze-dried food supposed to last for years?

Solution: Use oxygen absorbers to make sure your food remains perfectly preserved. Even though the moisture has been removed, the oxygen present in the food can lead to spoiling. This is because the enzymes in food react with the oxygen in the air. In nature, these enzymes are necessary for ripening and rotting. By depriving the enzymes of oxygen and water, they can't decompose the food.

Sometimes it happens that most of the product on a tray freeze dries perfectly, but a few morsels (usually those that are cut more thickly or unevenly) may not be completely dry. These ever-so-slightly moist pieces can rehydrate, giving microorganisms enough moisture to thrive, which means everything in the package will be rotten.

Issue: My appliance takes much longer than the recommended drying time to dry the food.

Solution: Check for ice buildup on the condenser and leaks in the vacuum seal. These problems can cause an overly long drying time by insulating heat. Your freeze dryer can also take a longer time to dry if your appliance is in an area warmer than about 90 °F (32 °C). A fan blowing on the appliance will help cool it down. A long drying time can also be due to the food itself. Foods containing sugary water such as oranges can take longer to dry.

Issue: I've had my freeze dryer on for days but the food is nowhere near dry.

Solution: There might be a problem with your freeze dryer's heater. If you're lucky enough to be under warranty, let the technicians fix it. For a DIY fix, you can check the shelving unit's overload switch, which may have tripped, and you should ensure that the heater's wiring is still firmly connected. Should the problem persist, it may be an issue with the heat relay. Your manufacturer can guide you to do a heat relay reassignment.

Issue: My freeze dryer is making funny noises.

Solution: Listen carefully—the sound is most likely coming from your vacuum pump. Check the oil and make sure the visible components of the pump are free of debris and ice. If this doesn't quiet things down, you probably have worn-out parts that need replacing.

If you can't find the solution in your freeze dryer's manual, contact your manufacturer's technical support division for help. Trying to fix it yourself can void the warranty, so leave it to the trained technicians.

Issue: My freeze dryer simply doesn't work when I switch it on.

Solution: Although this advice may sound silly, check that the appliance is plugged in properly. Even if you plugged it in perfectly, you may have stepped or pulled on the cord without knowing, or the plug might not be making proper contact. The next things to check are the circuit breakers and fuses. The chamber door must be firmly closed too, or the sensors will pick it up and the appliance won't start.

Issue: My products dry unevenly. Some are completely dry, but others on the same tray are still moist inside.

Solution: Fine-tune your shelf temperature by adjusting it to fit the foods you're freeze drying, and pack your trays with thin, even slices that don't touch each other. A little space between the foods allows better airflow and heat transfer. Don't load food higher than tray height at maximum.

Issue: My electricity bill is so high when I use my freeze dryer that I suspect it drains the power of my entire neighborhood!

Solution: Unfortunately, many freeze dryers use a lot of energy, and this translates into high electricity costs. You can keep your bill lower by freeze drying multiple trays in the same cycle, doing regular maintenance, cleaning off any excess ice, ensuring that there are no leaks in the gasket or hoses, checking the insulation, or upgrading to a newer model that is more frugal with electricity.

Issue: Oil sprayed out of my vacuum pump!

Solution: If the fittings and caps of your vacuum pump aren't tightly closed, the vacuum hose isn't snug over both ends, the pump has too much oil, the door gasket has debris, a crack, or a misalignment, or the drain valve isn't closed, your vacuum pump can become a little fountain of unpleasant surprises.

Issue: My product doesn't look anything like the food I put in. The shape is distorted.

Solution: This issue often arises with fruits. In a previous chapter, you learned that fruits should be sliced and placed skin-side down. This will help prevent the shape distortion because you're providing a pathway for the water to escape. Foods such as frozen fruits with skin have a massive pressure difference between their inside and outside during freeze drying; this difference can cause a mini fruit explosion in your chamber, which ruins the shape.

It may also be that the sublimation stage heated the food too quickly or stopped too soon, so the secondary drying phase started before it should have done. When this happens, your product can shrink or bubble. In the freeze drying industry, this is called product collapse and occurs due to melting. Prevent this from happening again by reducing the chamber temperature during sublimation and letting sublimation run for longer. Turn the vacuum pressure up a bit, and don't let your product heat to more than 41 °F (5 °C).

Issue: My meat freeze dried well, but when I rehydrated it, it was tough and leathery.

Solution: Your freeze-dried meat was probably not ground, diced, sliced, cubed, or shredded. The thicker the meat, the longer the process, and meat doesn't do well if the process is prolonged.

Good Advice for Top Freeze Drying

Let's sum up the good advice from previous chapters and the solutions to common issues in a tidy package. If you follow the recommendations discussed in this section, you'll save time, money, and your nerves.

Regular Maintenance on a Real Schedule

Don't get lazy! Regular maintenance doesn't mean wiping down a tray or two when you remember to do so. You need a schedule where you do the following after every or after every second batch:

- Clean the trays.
- Check the gaskets.
- Check if the hoses and wires are tightly connected.
- Remove ice buildup.
- Empty the water bucket. Don't let the hose sit in water.
- Keep an eye on your vacuum pump. Depending on the model, you may have to top up the oil after every batch. Never overfill the oil well.

Draw up a list of everything you have to do on your maintenance schedule, and print it or write it out with boxes you can tick when the tasks are completed. Write the date next to it. This way, proper maintenance becomes a habit, and you'll have a maintenance schedule to show the manufacturer or dealer if they need it when repairs have to be done.

Quality In, Quality Out

Marinades and sauces make food taste great, so you might be tempted to freeze dry low-quality food since you can fix it with other ingredients later. Don't. It never works. Even the gravy made by an Italian grandmother who's slaved in front of a stove approved by Gordon Ramsay himself won't be able to turn a tough cut of meat into a soft delight. The marinades, sauces, broths, and juice you use to rehydrate or enhance the flavor will only enhance what is already there. It can't impart taste to the tasteless or a nice texture to the edible version of a brick. The better quality your ingredients, the better the results when you rehydrate.

Getting Chilly

Whether you pre-freeze in your freezer or let your freeze drying appliance do the freezing, don't underestimate the importance of this crucial phase. Make sure that the food is properly frozen before you start the sublimation process. If your food isn't completely frozen, your drying time will take longer and the end result will be not a perfectly preserved freeze-dried food but something you'd have to force yourself to eat.

After buying perishable foods, refrigerate them within the hour if they have been exposed to temperatures of 90 °F (32 °C) or hotter. Whatever the temperature, they should be in the freezer or fridge within two hours.

Defrosting for Pre-Treatment

Use your fridge, not your countertop, for defrosting since bacteria start multiplying above 40 °F (4 °C). Put the food to be defrosted in a container on the lowest shelf. If you don't get around to freeze drying this food within a day or two (keeping it in the fridge all the time), you can still safely refreeze it, but the product will be of slightly lower quality. Red meats can stay defrosted in the fridge for three to five days before they have to be freeze dried, eaten, or refrozen.

Defrosting in the fridge can take a very long time. A quicker method is to submerge a non-leaking (preferably sealed, but unsealed is okay) bag containing the frozen food in cold tap water and leaving it there. As soon as the food is defrosted, it should be cooked right away. Food that has been defrosted in cold water should be cooked before refreezing or freeze drying.

Microwave-thawed food should also be cooked right after defrosting, whether you want to refreeze or freeze dry it.

Hot Stuff

When you precook, use a thermometer to be certain that your food has been cooked to a high enough temperature to kill harmful microorganisms. The thermometer should go in where the food is at its thickest, and it shouldn't touch gristle, fat, or bone.

You can cook with a microwave too. Read food labels carefully for instructions. Sometimes, the instructions tell you to let the food rest for a certain time after microwaving. This allows the colder areas inside the food to absorb heat from the warmer areas so that the food can cook through.

Recipes and package instructions will tell you if a food should be stirred or not while cooking. Not following these instructions can result in an unwanted texture or burned food.

The table below shows the recommended minimum internal temperatures for food safety when cooking:

Food	Minimum internal temperature
Eggs	Cook until both whites and yolks are firm
Egg dishes such as quiche	160 °F (71 °C)
Raw ham	165 °F (74 °C), and let it sit for 3 minutes after cooking
Game, such as venison and rabbit	160 °F (71 °C)
Fish	Cook until the flesh is opaque and flakes easily with a fork, or 145 °F (63 °C)
Meat	145 °F (63 °C), and let it sit for 3 minutes after cooking

Sausage and ground meat	160 °F (71 °C)
Poultry	165 °F (74 °C)
Vegetarian and meat casseroles	165 °F (74 °C)

A Good Start

The best start to the freeze drying process, apart from selecting good-quality ingredients, is the correct pre-treatment. Take the time to blanch, slice, grate, shred, and dice if you want to be proud of the final product. The correct pre-treatment is the difference between a freeze drying hobbyist and a master.

Clean Your Food

Food with soil or other contaminants will result in an inferior product:

- Rinse produce before preparations such as cutting and peeling. Fruits and veg should be rinsed under running water. The water is enough; don't add other cleaning products. You can add a little salt to a container of water for a final sanitary rinse, and use a vegetable brush to scrub away dirt or soil if needed.
- After rinsing, use a clean cloth to dry the produce.
- Unless you're going to use the produce right away, store it in a container with a label marking it as already washed.
- Don't wash seafood, eggs, or meats (including poultry).

Spreading Germs

Prevent cross-contamination that may lead to food poisoning by avoiding contact with potentially contaminated food. This is how:

- Don't use the same chopping board, dishes, knives, and other utensils for raw and cooked food. Clean the chopping board, utensils, and dishes after each use, using hot water and dish soap.
- When storing food in the fridge or freezer, keep the food in sealed bags or containers with closed lids, and never store raw food above cooked or otherwise prepared food.
- Use a different cleaning cloth for countertops, tables, and cutlery. Keep these cloths clean with regular washes and sanitize them by rinsing with boiling water. Kitchen cloths should never ever be used interchangeably with cloths to clean other areas such as bathrooms.

- Speaking of cloths, it is more sanitary to let your dishes air dry than drying them with a cloth, since the cloth may pick up a contaminant and spread it to other dishes and utensils.
- It is gross to store food on the floor, even if it is in containers.
- Your cleaning supplies, chemicals, and nonfoods don't belong in your food storage area.
- Please wash your hands after you've eaten, smoked, touched an animal, sick person, or garbage, blown your nose, or visited the bathroom. Wash your hands before and after you prepare food or take care of a wound.
- Wash your hands for at least 20 seconds and clean your palms, your fingers, the back of your hands, between your fingers, and your wrists. Use a clean nail brush to clean under your fingernails. If you have a cut or other wound on your hands, put on a double layer of rubber gloves.
- Take the time to dry your hands properly afterward with a clean hand towel, and don't use that same towel to dry your dishes or clean surfaces.
- The handwashing basin is for hands only, not for washing dishes or defrosting.
- Eggs go in the main section (not the door) of your fridge in their original container.
- When you go food shopping, use a different cart for eggs, raw meat including poultry, and seafood, or place them away from the other foods in your cart. Don't put these foods in the same bag as other foods.

Now that you know freeze drying theory, it is time to put it into practice. The "Recipes" section at the end of the book includes many easy recipes for high-quality freeze drying, while in the next chapter, we'll explore ideas for freeze drying candy, using freeze-dried foods as gifts, making herbal remedies, and setting up a freeze drying business venture.

CHAPTER 8
GETTING CREATIVE

The better you know your craft, the easier it is to get creative with it. You've gained enough knowledge in the previous chapters that you can use the ideas in this chapter as a springboard for your own freeze drying experiments and plans.

Freeze-Dried Candy

Freeze drying candy is all the range among those with a sweet tooth and a sense of adventure. The process changes the texture into a crunchy, light treat with a concentrated taste. When you freeze dry candy, remember that one batch is never enough. The more the better!

This original and fun way of experimenting with candy leaves you with a product that can be eaten as is or used as a sweet, colorful topping on cupcakes, birthday cakes, and ice cream. Like other freeze-dried products, you'll also enjoy the benefit of a long shelf life, which is great if you aren't all that into candy but want some at hand for visitors or the occasional craving.

Chocolate-based and high-sugar candy won't give you a good-quality product. You can successfully freeze dry candy that contains only a little bit of chocolate, but it will last only a few months even if you package and store it as recommended.

The best candies for freeze drying are marshmallows, gummies, and those with a fruity or sour base such as Skittles.

Here are some tips to get the best results when freeze drying candy:

- Facilitate a more even and thorough drying by breaking larger candies into small pieces.
- Prevent the frustration of candy cleanup by using a tray liner.
- Place the candies in a single layer with spaces between them on your freeze dryer tray.
- If you preheat your chewy and hard candies before starting the freeze drying process, it might improve the texture of the product. In a 110 °F (45 °C) oven, warm these candies on a baking tray until they are just turning soft, then put the slightly softened candy onto the freeze dryer tray. If your oven can go to such low temperatures and has the space, you can save some effort by putting the lined freeze dryer tray with the candy directly in the oven for the preheat.
- Most modern freeze dryer models have a special candy setting, but if your appliance doesn't, manually choose 0 °F (−18 °C) for the freezing cycle and 135 °F (60 °C) for the drying cycle.

Gifts

Freeze-dried products and supplies make welcome and original gifts. Freeze-dried goodies in a gift basket are perfect for any occasion. Whether it's a holiday, a birthday, or just because, you can't go wrong with the convenience and flavor of freeze-dried foods and candy.

Here are some ideas for freeze-dried gifts:

- Give an outdoorsy person a gift basket containing easily rehydrated and light freeze-dried meals. One of the drawbacks of camping and hiking is carrying weight around, and

- the recipient will be happy to receive a gift that will literally lift a huge weight off their shoulders.
- A gift basket containing healthy freeze-dried snacks is a suitable treat for any gym junkie or fitness lover.
- Help a busy parent with a gift basket containing freeze-dried meals and treats. A night off from cooking after work will be greatly appreciated!
- Make a gift basket a little more personal and thoughtful by tying a handwritten card to a Mason jar or bucket or pasting a special note to a Mylar bag. Always tie or paste; never make a hole in packaging to thread a ribbon or twine through, since any puncture lets air and moisture in, which will mess up the shelf life.
- Surprise someone with a sweet tooth with a treat basket full of freeze-dried candies and fruits.
- A colleague or loved one who loves cooking will be over the moon to receive a gift basket containing a selection of freeze-dried ingredients.
- Home freeze drying hobbyists and masters will appreciate gifts such as Mylar bags, Mason jars, tray liners, and food thermometers.

Herbal Remedies and Teas

Whether you use herbs medicinally, as a food flavoring, or as a garnish, you'll be glad to hear that herbs can be successfully freeze dried. Let's take a look at some popular herbs you might want in your pantry:

- A cup of **chamomile** tea can soothe frayed nerves, treat nausea, and ease tired and crampy muscles. Chamomile flower is also a good treatment for skin conditions such as rash, acne, and eczema.
- **Peppermint**'s refreshing taste makes it a favorite in herbal teas and as a garnish. Herbal teas containing peppermint are traditionally used to soothe digestive upsets. Peppermint jelly is a condiment that pairs very well with red meats.
- **Lemon balm** repels unwanted insects and chases away feelings of unease, heartache, and general sadness. In a salve, it can treat viral and bacterial skin conditions.
- **Spearmint** is related to peppermint and is medicinally used as a remedy for muscle spasms and cramps. Its menthol content makes it an effective component of cough and nasal congestion remedies.
- **Calendula** is a skin healer that can treat rashes and burns. It is also often used in ointments to treat minor wounds.
- **Lavender**'s scent alone is enough to induce a peaceful sleep, and the aroma brings a timeless, tranquil feel to any room. Since lavender is also edible, it can be used as a flavoring agent in tea and ice cream, and as a garnish.

- ✘ Gargle with **bergamot** to ease a scratchy or sore throat, or use it as a mouthwash to treat gum infections. Applied as a tincture, it can also soothe rashes and minor wounds.
- ✘ **Sage** adds a savory flavor, which means it is an ingredient in many recipes for meat, poultry, soups, beans, and more. Medicinally, it is used to treat menopausal symptoms, digestive upsets, dental plaque, inflammation, and skin inflammations.

Prepare your fresh herbs for freeze drying by washing them, then removing excess water with a salad spinner. You can freeze dry already-frozen herbs, which will keep their flavor after the process but the color will be dulled. Check back to Chapter 4 for more detail about freeze drying herbs.

Remember that freeze-dried foods, including herbs, have a more concentrated flavor than fresh or air-dried, so use a slightly smaller amount of freeze-dried herbs in your cooking than you would otherwise.

Starting a Freeze-Dried Food Business

The market for freeze-dried foods is growing exponentially, providing an opportunity for entrepreneurs. Whether you're considering opening a business as an individual, a partnership, or a community project, there are certain considerations that demand attention before starting your business.

The first question you need to ask yourself is if your business will give you a return on your investment. A return on investment means that a business will make enough profit to pay back the money you spent to start the business. Will the profit cover your freeze dryer, packaging, storage, and distribution costs? And if you hire a helper or two? What about the cost of the foods you want to freeze dry, and renting or buying factory space?

Your profit will rely on factors such as market demand, cost of production, and other expenses such as wages. Make 110% sure that your business will make enough money for it to be worthwhile, or else you'll sit with a money pit that can plunge you into debt fast.

Let's take a closer look at the factors that determine your business' profit potential:

- ✘ Putting a **price** on your freeze-dried product is more complex than thinking of a number that appeals to you. Make a detailed list of all the costs involved in the business, such as packaging materials, vacuum sealers, oxygen absorbers, labels, labor, electricity and water, fresh high-quality food, cleaning products, rubber gloves, and others. Then add up the costs and divide the total by the amount of product you can sell. This will give you the production cost per unit, which tells you how much it costs to produce one package of freeze-dried food.

- **Research** other freeze drying business. What are the pricing models and target markets of successful businesses? What do they do right—and what can your business do better? Also research the less successful businesses to learn from their mistakes.
- Know who you are selling to (the **target market**). What would make your target market buy your products instead of the freeze-dried food in the local grocery store?
- Once you know your target market and know why they'll be interested in your product, you have to devise a **marketing strategy**. You'll need to figure out how you'll make people aware of your product and why they should buy it. Where are you planning to sell your product? Will you sell via delivery based on online orders or at the local farmer's market? You can also work with the owners of outdoor, prep and survival, or health stores to stock your product. Are you going to spend money on advertising, and will you advertise on the radio, on TV, or in local newsletters? Will you invest in a professionally designed website for your product? You can let more people know about your product by being visible and active on social media and at trade fairs.
- Find out about the **legislation and regulations** in your state that cover food production, and stick to the rules. The regulations may demand things such as getting relevant permits, having a food sales retail license, including mandatory information on labels, health inspections, and specific packaging and storage.

Is Your Own Freeze Drying Business Worth It?

Your business can make you some serious money or plunge you into debt and despair. Success depends on planning thoroughly, being prepared to take reasonable risks, and having realistic expectations.

Here is some food for thought to help you decide about building a business:

- If your business is successful, you will probably make more money than with a traditional salary.
- You can't predict market competition. For example, if you make freeze-dried meals aimed at busy parents, campers, and the elderly, the convenience and ease of rehydrating a full meal will be a big selling point. Will your business survive if a big brand starts selling a range of ready-made freeze-dried meals at a lower price to your target market?
- While you are building your business, you will likely have to work longer hours than at the office. Are you willing to forego leisure time, weekends and holidays, and time with your loved ones?
- Launching and building a business can be very expensive. Do you have the funds? If you're taking out a loan, do you have a backup plan in case circumstances prevent you from making a payment or two?
- Be honest with yourself. Do you really have the drive to start a business and steer it to become a viable source of income?

The Business Plan

A well-written business plan is your ticket to financing and attracting investors. Financial institutions won't lend you a penny unless they are convinced that customers will want your product and that you'll make enough money to pay back the loan in full.

Your business plan must be an accurate description of your business or business idea. In it should be details of what the business plans to do, what the business needs to complete its projects or achieve its aims, and the projected future of the business.

Include the resources needed and what, if any, resources you currently own, your marketing strategy, current personnel (even if it is only you), if you plan on employing people, and your financial projections.

Our final chapter awaits, where we'll discuss how to make a food storage plan, how to fit freeze-dried food into a busy schedule, freeze-dried experiments, and FAQ.

CHAPTER 9
WHAT NEXT?

Now that you're a freeze drying master, you'll probably be interested in taking your skills further. In this chapter, we'll discuss emergency food supplies for disasters and busy schedules, community resources and online groups, experiments with freeze drying, and some FAQs about freeze drying in general.

Emergency Food Supply

Your freeze drying expertise can provide food security for your family during a disaster or food shortage. Below, we'll look at the preparation of emergency food supplies, but remember that you'll also need an emergency water supply and a method to warm water without electricity or mainline gas to rehydrate cooked meals. A portable propane gas stove or grill and gas bottle, or sufficient gas or wood for the barbeque, will do.

An emergency food supply also comes in useful for non-disaster emergencies, such as unplanned-for guests or when unexpected circumstances leave you in a financial pinch.

Be Prepared

Your emergency kit needs more than freeze-dried food. It should also have a flashlight with extra batteries, a radio with extra batteries, soap and other hygiene items, a first aid kit, a pocketknife, and bottled water. If you have pets, include pet food and water and food bowls. Add a couple of lightweight blankets, and your kit will be good enough to see you through for a while if you have to evacuate.

Planning the Food Supply

Anyone can put a couple of freeze-dried foods on the pantry shelf and hope they'll be okay in an emergency. But you're not anyone; you're a freeze drying master with a flair for planning. Here are some tips to help you put together a food supply that will last for two weeks:

- Make a list of all the freeze-dried and staple foods in your home, including what's in your fridge and freezer. Have columns for the number of items, such as two cans of soup, and the use-by date, such as 2040 for a freeze-dried item. Update this list at least twice per week. This list is the starting point for your planning. You can see at a glance what you'll have available and how long it will last in an emergency.
- Make a list of all the people and pets who will be fed from your supply in an emergency. Do you have enough and, if so, for how long? Does your supply take special needs into account, such as food allergies and diabetic-friendly foods, if applicable?
- Planning is easier if you have a dedicated storage box for your emergency foods. Since freeze-dried foods don't take up much space, you can fit quite a lot in a box. Make a list of everything in the emergency box and update it every time you use or add an item.
- Have a couple of freeze-dried meals in a cupboard for non-disaster emergencies, such as unplanned-for dinner guests or days when you're sick and not able to cook. When you have to rehydrate these meals, make a note to replace them at the earliest opportunity.
- Written lists are most effective. It is unlikely that you'll remember every item of food in your house and when something was eaten or added. Having a clear, regularly updated list will help you keep on top of your supply and plan like a pro.

Community Resources and Online Groups

Have you considered using social media and community resources such as neighborhood get-togethers and farmer's markets to connect with other freeze dryers? Connecting with fellow freeze dryers lets you share and exchange tips and recipes. Being part of a community is fun, educational, and an opportunity to make new friends who share your interests. You'll also get to hear about deals, discounts, workshops, and courses that can help your freeze drying activities.

You can also start your own freeze drying club to connect, mentor, and exchange ideas with freeze drying friends. Here's how you start a club:

- Decide what your club is all about. Is the purpose to have social gatherings where you discuss freeze dryers over rehydrated goodies, or do you envision a more formal meeting where members discuss the technicalities of the freeze drying process and appliances? Do you have any specific goals for the club, such as attracting a sponsor, experimenting with new recipes, or gaining brand visibility for your freeze-dried food business?
- Once you've decided what the purpose of your club will be, you can formulate a mission statement. This is a summary of what the club will offer; for example, "Club Fantastic Frozen exists to exchange information about new developments in the freeze drying world" or "It is the mission of Club Polar-Desert Food to boost the members' freeze drying skills by sharing tips and exchanging recipes."
- Now that you have a reason for the club's existence, consider the long-term elements of your club. Will there be membership fees and, if yes, how will the fees be used to benefit the members? Where and when will your club meet, and are there any special requirements for the meeting place, such as access to a freeze dryer or seating space for a certain number of people? Is the club going to host events such as markets or demonstrations? What will be done or discussed at the club meetings? What are the requirements for joining the club?

The more details you've decided on, the better prepared you'll be for the first meeting. Take the lead or appoint someone to welcome the members, say a joke or two to break the ice, have the members introduce themselves to the group, and get started with what's on the agenda. Perhaps have some rehydrated foods at the ready to demonstrate recipes you're willing to share, or have a representative from a freeze dryer manufacturer give a speech about freeze drying. The possibilities are only limited by your imagination.

As your club grows, you can appoint a chairperson or meeting leader, a deputy chairperson for assisting or leading meetings if the main chairperson is unavailable, a secretary to take minutes of the club's meetings and send out invitations to events, a treasurer to be in charge of the club's finances, and perhaps also a general manager to take care of membership records, advertising, and organizing events.

Experimenting With Freeze Drying

Freeze-dried food is so much more than an emergency or outdoors go-to convenience; it is also used by chefs in high-end dishes and for nonfood items. Experiment with the various uses to make full use of your appliance and skillset.

Freeze-Dried Flowers

Did you know that you can freeze dry flowers and use the product in resin art and jewelry? Experiment with decorative pieces, or make wedding bouquets with freeze-dried flowers as an accent.

To freeze dry flowers, choose flowers that are fresh and at or just before their blooming peak. Check that all the petals are whole and firm. Some flowers, such as irises and tulips, have too much moisture for a good freeze dry, but generally flowers will come out nicely. Size doesn't influence the outcome, so feel free to experiment with anything from the most delicate to the boldest rose.

After cleaning your chosen flowers, ensure the flower will look its best by cutting off any wilted or damaged petals. Flowers freeze dry very well if they've been pre-frozen. To pre-freeze, lay your clean flowers on a lined tray, leaving spaces in between. Pop the tray in your freezer for a couple of hours before they go into your freeze dryer. If you don't have a freeze dryer yet but want to experiment with freeze-dried flowers anyway, use a silica gel packet for dehydration. The product will be similar to one made in a freeze drying appliance, but it won't last nearly as long.

Freeze-dried flowers are very delicate and crumble easily, and they can absorb moisture from a humid atmosphere. Using a spray-on sealant will help the flowers last longer, and if you are a resin artist, the spray sealant will help keep the color intact.

Whatever your plans with freeze-dried flowers, you might not want to use them in a project right away. You can store the flowers in a dark and dry place in an airtight container.

Manuscripts and Artifacts

Wouldn't it be great if there was a way to recover manuscripts, books, photos, video cassettes, textiles, and film that have suffered water damage? Freeze drying can do this!

Such documents and films are first frozen and then freeze dried to remove the moisture that caused the damage. This takes the mushiness away so that they keep their proper structure and do not deteriorate further. Removing the moisture also takes away the ability for mold to multiply. But freeze drying as a restoration method hasn't been perfected yet, although museums, businesses, and archives have used it successfully. Paper made from a mix of various materials can become deformed, since each material has its own absorption rate and the different materials may expand at unequal rates.

Freeze drying is also used on archeological artifacts that are waterlogged when dug up. Such artifacts, if they were made from wood, can be freeze dried with only tiny deformations, thereby preserving the objects for many years to come. A scientific study used half-rotten artifacts from China's Zhejiang University to see if freeze drying could remove the water and stabilize the objects. The scientists found that they got the best results when they presoaked the wooden artifacts in a protective agent such as polyethylene glycol before freezing (Shaozhi et al., 2016).

Frequently Asked Questions (FAQs)

Although the previous chapters contain all the information you need to be a freeze drying master, there may be some questions left.

Question: Can I freeze dry cannabis?

Answer: If it is legal in your state, yes. Pay attention to all regulations, especially if you plan to sell your product. Freeze-dried cannabis will preserve the potency much better than other methods such as drying only. This is because the freeze drying process doesn't break down the delicate molecules of CBC, THC, and others. The intact terpenes combined with the loss of moisture will give you a product that may be more potent and have a more intense aroma and flavor. To freeze dry cannabis, follow the same directions as for other herbs.

Question: Do I need a special license to sell freeze-dried food from my home?

Answer: Some states consider certain foods to be "cottage food," which you may sell from your home. With cottage foods, there are regulations about how much you can sell and to whom. For example, some states allow you to sell your freeze-dried food directly to people in your community but not to retailers or restaurants. You might not necessarily be allowed to sell all your products but only certain kinds of freeze-dried veggies. Regulations regarding cottage food vary from state to state, and you can find the relevant regulations on the website of your State Department of Agriculture.

Note that even if you're allowed to sell your freeze-dried products from home, there are other regulations you'll have to comply with, such as labeling and packaging requirements. Your state may also impose an annual sales limit, and even if you operate from your own home, your state may require you to register your operation as a business. Like any other business, you have to comply with all tax regulations.

Question: How do I stay up to date with freeze-dried food trends?

Answer: Keep an eye on forums and groups where freeze dryers, chefs, retailers, and restaurateurs chat. If you see specific foods, such as health foods, ethnic cuisine, or experimental fusions, stirring up a buzz, jump on the trend.

Question: What would make potential buyers want my freeze-dried food?

Answer: Offer prospective buyers a choice of freeze-dried foods, such as a variety of fruits, or ready-made meals in a regular and vegetarian option. This way, your products will appeal to more people. Always stick to strict hygiene regulations, and brag about it on the label. If you use only the highest-quality ingredients, say so on the packaging. Let your packaging catch the eye of buyers with easy-to-read labels and attractive designs.

Question: Do you have any tips for expanding my freeze-dried food business?

Answer: When your freeze drying business is doing well enough that you can consider expansion, you have to do your homework first. The following tips will guide you to the information you need to prepare for an expansion:

- Keep up with trends, as described in a previous question. Then look at your current line of products to see how you can incorporate a trend by making small changes. For example, if smoked bacon is trending, use it as an ingredient in your ready-made meals. If a certain herb is trending for its health benefits, use it in your foods. Make sure you advertise the new ingredient on your packaging.
- Use surveys to find out what your potential customers want that they aren't getting from other freeze-dried products. For example, if the survey tells you that people want more freeze-dried candy with sugar alternatives, incorporate that in your product line.
- If you have a taste for novelty, consult chefs to develop new recipes that will make your brand unique. A partnership with a chef allows you to have new flavors without a trial-and-error process that may cost you a small fortune.
- Before investing in a new product line, let people try it first. Have someone hand out bite-sized samples at events, and listen to the feedback. Adjust your recipes as needed before rolling out a thousand packaged products that no one wants.
- As your business grows, you may not be able to keep up with production demands if you, or a helper, do everything by hand. Should you have the money and your business is doing very well, consider investing in a commercial or industrial automated packager. Find out what regulations are required for you to supply retailers and restaurants. Once you have all the needed licenses, approach stores and restaurateurs with samples of your products.
- Have a high-quality website for your business where clients can see what you have on offer and where they can place online orders. A professional web designer can have your site looking top class and fully functional.

Question: Other than plants, documents, and wooden artifacts, what else can I freeze dry?

Answer: You can freeze dry biological specimens. Preserve that pretty butterfly wing you discovered in the garden or the dead starfish you found on the beach, or extend the shelf life of cosmetics such as lotions, perfumes, and shampoo by freeze drying them.

Question: How much oxygen absorber is right for my food?

Answer: Generally, 300–500 cc of absorber per gallon (3.8 liters) will lower the oxygen content to near zero.

Question: How much electricity will my home freeze dryer consume?

Answer: A small home appliance can use 1,000–1,500 W per hour. To keep your appliance as electrically efficient as possible, do regular maintenance. A machine that isn't well maintained can use more than 1,500 W per hour. Of course, the larger the freeze dryer, the more electricity it will use.

Question: Apart from the freeze drying appliance, packaging, and electrical costs, what else do I need to budget for?

Answer: You can probably install and maintain a small household freeze dryer yourself, but commercial and industrial models should be installed and maintained by professionals, and this isn't always included in the sales price. Business-class freeze dryers might also need special plumbing and electrical work.

Question: I like to pre-freeze food before putting it in the freeze dryer, but I worry about freezer burn. How to I deal with freezer burn?

Answer: Freezer burn is identified by dry, tough patches on the food's surface, a layer of white frost inside the packaging, hardness and a leathery texture, and grayish-brown areas of discoloration.

Prevention is better than cure. Avoid freezer burn by not thawing then refreezing, not storing food in the freezer long-term, and not keeping the freezer door open for long periods.

If you do have freezer-burned food, you can cut the burnt portions off and eat the rest, since freezer burn isn't a contributing factor toward food poisoning. Freezer-burned food often has a distinctive odor, which you can mask with aromatic herbs such as garlic in your cooking.

It is a myth that ice crystals on or in the food means the food is freezer burned. If the color, texture, and smell haven't changed, the food is just frozen and not freezer burned.

Let's go the conclusion for a brief overview of what you've learned in this book.

CONCLUSION

Freeze drying is a practical art, which means the best road to mastery is practice. Experiment with ingredients, try new recipes, explore different styles of cuisine, and have fun. The key to getting the most out of freeze drying isn't to polish your machine and show visitors how it still has its plastic wrap on, but to dive in and use it as much as possible.

Looking back through the chapters, you'll realize how much you've learned. We started with the basic concept and looked at the benefits of freeze drying, the role of freeze drying as a safety net, community projects allowing anyone to freeze dry, and the terminology used by freeze dryers.

Then, you learned exactly how freeze drying works, and we separated the myths from the facts. This, together with the safety considerations, gave you the same knowledge of the process as a representative of a freeze drying company. You might even consider applying for a job at such a company and impressing the boss with your knowledge and practical experience.

You learned what to look for in a freeze dryer and how to choose the appliance that will suit your needs, budget, and dreams. Knowledge takes the guesswork out of choosing a new, used, refurbished, or repaired appliance, and you can now make a clear-headed decision because you know the pros and cons of each option. The more you know what you want and why, the easier it will be to buy a freeze dryer that will kick off your journey to producing perfect products every time.

A high-quality product demands high-quality ingredients, and you learned which foods will yield a good product and which foods to avoid. Pre-treatment isn't a mystery anymore, and you know the pros and cons of buying in bulk, from a store, or growing your own plant-based ingredients. Freeze drying, like all other endeavors, hinges on the concept of getting out what you put in, and that means not only good ingredients but also good knowledge of food and proper care of your appliance.

We followed the freeze drying process step-by-step, so you can prepare the food and the machine correctly, know the tricks of correct tray loading and timing, and tell when the process is completely done. You also learned how to clean your appliance for hygiene and maintenance without voiding the warranty.

Packaging and storage are an integral part of guaranteeing a long shelf life, and you now know precisely how to keep your product under ideal conditions. Labeling and rotating stock correctly will enable you to keep track of your freeze-dried products at a glance.

In the troubleshooting section, you learned about the fixes you can do yourself and those better left to a professional. By reading through the possible problems, you also learned how to avoid them. Paying attention to troubleshooting will help you get the most out of your appliance and have your freeze dryer last for many years.

The "Recipes" section that follows gives you a good starting point to make your own freeze-dried meals and treats, as well as convenient freeze-dried pet treats and meals for outdoor excursions. The given recipes have all been tested, and they freeze dry and rehydrate well. Use them as is, or as inspiration to try out your own favorite recipes. As long as you remember the pre-treatments and which foods are suitable or not, your own recipes will be fine.

However, freeze drying is more than preserving food. The other uses, such as freeze drying candy, flowers, and documents, allow you to blend your creativity and imagination with your freeze drying skills and give you ideas for using freeze-dried products as gifts. Your skill set now additionally includes how to freeze dry herbal items and how to start a freeze-dried food business.

Through participating in community projects and online groups, you can learn more, become aware of trends, or partner with chefs to produce your own unique product line. You learned how to keep your finger on the pulse and what regulations you have to comply with if you start selling your product.

Now that you have enough knowledge of freeze drying to be not only a master but a guru if you so choose, use your knowledge in everyday life. You can provide food security for yourself and your loved ones and build up an emergency food supply to carry you in times of need. Show off your freeze drying flair on special occasions, such as a full freeze-dried haute cuisine meal with dessert at Thanksgiving or birthdays.

Once mastered, freeze-dried food can also become a source of income. You can become a business owner or a paid consultant. Your mastery will enable you to start a club or community project where freeze drying will be a common bond to draw new friends into your circle.

You already have the knowledge; the actual freeze drying is up to you. Whatever your plans with your freeze dryer, may you have success and also enjoy freeze drying as a creative outlet.

Recipes

Welcome to the recipes section of this book! Here, you'll find both recipes for dishes that can be successfully freeze dried and recipes that use freeze-dried ingredients. From main meals to snacks, and from side dishes to desserts, there's something for everyone—including your pets and your home!

HERBS, SPICES, AND SEASONINGS

HERBS AND SPICES

Ready-to-Use Oven-Roasted Garlic

Roasted garlic is perfect for adding flavor to any dish. This recipe will help you roast and prepare garlic for freeze drying or immediate use.

Ingredients:

- olive oil
- 1 head garlic
- salt and pepper

Directions:

1. Prewarm the oven to 400 °F (200 °C).
2. Remove the top 1/3 of the garlic head.
3. Cut a small square piece of aluminum foil.
4. Place the garlic in the center of the foil square.
5. Drizzle olive oil over the garlic and sprinkle evenly with salt and pepper.
6. Wrap the garlic in foil then bake for 40–45 minutes in the oven.
7. Take the garlic out of the oven and allow it to cool for a few minutes.

8. Peel the garlic cloves and finely mash them in a small bowl until they form a smooth paste.
9. Set aside.

Freeze drying instructions:

1. Arrange the garlic on freeze dryer trays lined with parchment paper and silicone mats to ensure optimal drying, then freeze the trays until solid.
2. Place the trays in the freeze dryer and process according to the machine's instructions.
3. Once the process is complete, remove the garlic and store in airtight containers in a dark, cool place.

To reconstitute:

1. Measure the quantity of freeze-dried roasted garlic needed.
2. Add warm water to cover the garlic and soak for about 5 minutes.
3. Mash or stir to combine and soften.
4. Use immediately.

Source: *Roasted Garlic*, 2023

Smoky Paprika

Give your meats, sauces, and stews that extra special smoky flavor with this homemade freeze-dried paprika!

Ingredients:

- 10–12 bell or sweet peppers
- olive oil for grilling or 1 tbsp liquid smoke (depending on your chosen method)
- salt and pepper to taste

Directions:

1. Select your preferred method to infuse smoky flavor into the peppers:
    - Liquid smoke: Evenly coat the peppers with liquid smoke using a brush.

- Grilling: Coat the peppers evenly with olive oil, then sear them on a scorching grill for 5–7 minutes until their skins blister and blacken.

2. Let the peppers cool completely.
3. Remove the skins—peel off charred layers if grilled—then discard the seeds and slice the peppers into thin strips.

Freeze drying instructions:

1. Lay the pepper slices in a single layer on trays lined with parchment paper or silicone mats, ensuring they don't touch, then freeze them overnight.
2. Place the trays in the freeze dryer and start the drying cycle.
3. Grind the freeze-dried peppers into fine powder.
4. Sift the powder for a finer texture (optional).
5. Store the paprika in a vacuum-sealed bag or airtight jar in a cool, dark place.

Source: *Freeze-Dried Paprika Recipe*, 2024

SEASONINGS

Tzatziki Seasoning Blend

This homemade tzatziki mix uses freeze-dried ingredients for a fresh, bold flavor. Convenient and long-lasting—just add yogurt for a creamy, tangy sauce that's perfect for dipping, spreading, or topping.

Ingredients:

- 2 1/2 cups full-fat Greek or regular yogurt
- 1/4 cup freeze-dried chopped cucumber
- 1 1/2 tsp freeze-dried garlic powder
- 1 tbsp freeze-dried crushed dill weed
- 2 tsp freeze-dried lemon powder

- 2 tsp freeze-dried onion powder
- 1 tbsp freeze-dried spearmint
- 1 tsp salt
- 1 tsp black pepper

Directions:

1. Combine all the dry ingredients in a sealed container, then secure the lid and vigorously shake to make sure everything is mixed well.
2. To create tzatziki, add yogurt to the tzatziki seasoning and mix well. Store the mixture in the fridge for about 2 hours to enhance the flavors.

Source: *Freeze Dried Tzatziki Seasoning Mix, 2024*

Classic Burger Spice

Take your burgers up a notch with this hamburger seasoning! Your burgers are guaranteed to be infused with a touch of smoky flavoring—perfect for grilling or pan-frying.

Ingredients:

- 1 tbsp paprika
- 2 tsp freeze-dried garlic (blended into a powder)
- 1 tsp freeze-dried onion (blended into a powder)
- 1/2 tsp pepper
- 1 1/2 tsp salt

Directions:

1. Combine all the ingredients in a small bowl and mix thoroughly until evenly blended. Generously coat your favorite burgers with this seasoning blend for enhanced flavor.

Freeze drying instructions:

1. Arrange the garlic, pepper, and onions on trays lined with parchment paper and silicone mats, then process as per your freeze dryer's instructions.
2. Once the process finishes, transfer the contents to a sealed container to preserve the freshness for future use.

Source: *Hamburger Seasoning Recipe*, 2023

Onion Soup Seasoning

Unlock rich flavors with this homemade onion soup mix! It's is perfect for adding a burst of deliciousness to your soups, dips, and recipes.

Ingredients:

- 1 tsp freeze-dried parsley
- 1/4 tsp freeze-dried garlic powder
- 1 1/2 tbsp freeze-dried onion powder
- 1 tbsp freeze-dried beef broth
- 1/3 cup freeze-dried white onion
- pinch black pepper
- 1/2 tsp celery salt

Directions:

1. Combine all the ingredients thoroughly in a small bowl then store the blend in an airtight container, clearly marked with the preparation date. This homemade onion soup seasoning remains fresh for up to a year. You can use this soup mix as you would one packet of dry onion soup mix purchased at the store.

Source: *Onion Soup Mix*, 2023

SAUCES, DRESSINGS, PUREES, AND SIDES

SAUCES

Naturally Sweet Applesauce

Enjoy the natural taste of apples with no added preservatives or sugar. Enjoy it as a snack, dessert, or meal addition.

Ingredients:

- apples
- cinnamon (optional)

Directions:

1. Wash, peel, and remove the cores from the apples, then dice them finely. If you prefer a chunkier texture, don't peel the apples.
2. Put the prepared apple pieces in a large pot with some water to stop the apples sticking to the bottom of the pot.
3. Heat the apples with a pinch of cinnamon (if using) over a medium-high flame until boiling, then lower the heat and cover the pot. Stirring occasionally, simmer the apples for 20–30 minutes.
4. When the apples soften enough to break apart easily with a fork, remove them from the heat. Then, mash the cooked apples using a potato masher or fork. For a silkier texture, blend them with a standard or immersion blender.
5. Let the applesauce cool, then store or freeze dry.

Freeze drying instructions:

1. Line the trays with parchment paper or silicone mats.
2. Place spoonfuls of the applesauce on trays to dry into powder, or use molds for bite-sized pieces.
3. Weigh the trays with applesauce and record the weight.
4. Follow your freeze dryer's instructions.
5. After drying, weigh the trays again. The weight difference indicates how much water to add to reconstitute.

To reconstitute:

1. Add the recommended amount of hot water.
2. Stir and let it rest for a few minutes until reconstituted.

Source: *Homemade Applesauce,* 2025

Marinara Homestyle Sauce

Rich and bursting with flavor, this homemade marinara sauce will soon become a favorite. Easy to make and perfect for pastas, dips, or any Italian-inspired dish!

Ingredients:

- 1 cup chicken broth
- 3/4 cup olive oil
- 2/3 cup diced onion
- 1 tsp garlic salt
- 2 crushed garlic cloves
- 1/2 cup chopped fresh parsley
- 2 cans (12 oz each) tomato paste
- 4 cans (14.5 oz each) stewed tomatoes
- 2 tsp dried oregano
- 1/2 tsp black pepper
- 1 tsp salt

Directions:

1. Combine the garlic, oregano, parsley, pepper, salt, garlic salt, stewed tomatoes, and tomato paste in a food processor and blend until smooth.
2. Warm the oil in a large pan over medium heat, then sauté the onion for 2 minutes.
3. Stir in the blended tomato sauce and chicken broth.
4. Stirring occasionally, simmer for about 30 minutes until thick.
5. Remove from the heat, store, use, or freeze dry.

Freeze drying instructions:

1. Evenly spread the cold marinara sauce across 4 freeze dryer trays lined with parchment paper or silicone mats.
2. Place in the freezer overnight.
3. Begin a frozen batch in your freeze dryer.
4. When the machine notifies you, insert the trays of sauce. Remove when done.
5. Continue to batch.
6. For long-term preservation, seal the freeze-dried sauce in Mylar bags with an oxygen absorber.

To reconstitute:

1. Mix 4 oz water with 1/2 cup of powder to rehydrate.

Source: *Marinara Sauce Recipe*, 2024

Sugar-Free BBQ Sauce

Enjoy this tangy BBQ sauce made without added sugar—perfect for a healthier twist on a classic favorite!

Ingredients:

- 2 tbsp apple cider vinegar
- 1 tbsp coconut oil
- 1 diced onion
- 1 tsp chili powder
- 6 oz tomato paste
- 1 tsp powdered mustard
- 3 crushed garlic cloves
- 1 tbsp soy sauce
- 1 tsp Stevia or Truvia
- 1 tsp oregano
- 2 cups chicken stock
- 1 tsp cumin
- salt and pepper to flavor

Directions:

1. Over medium-high heat, in a saucepan, heat the coconut oil.
2. Add the diced onion and garlic; cook until soft.
3. Stir in the tomato paste, mustard powder, cumin, oregano, and chili powder. Cook for 1–2 minutes.
4. Pour in the chicken stock, apple cider vinegar, and soy sauce; stir well.
5. Add the Stevia or Truvia to balance the flavors, plus the salt and pepper.
6. Simmer the sauce, stirring frequently, until it thickens—about 20 minutes. Taste and, if needed, adjust the seasoning.
7. Allow the sauce to cool completely before handling or storing.

Freeze-drying instructions:

1. Spread the cooled sauce evenly in a thin layer on freeze dryer trays lined with parchment paper or silicone mats.
2. Place the trays in the freeze dryer and run the freeze-drying cycle according to your machine's instructions until the sauce is completely dried and brittle.
3. Once done, remove the freeze-dried sauce and store in an airtight container or vacuum-sealed bag to keep moisture out.

To reconstitute:

1. Measure the amount of freeze-dried sauce you want to reconstitute.
2. Add warm water gradually to the freeze-dried sauce—start with about half the volume of sauce you want to rehydrate.
3. Stir well and let it sit for a few minutes to absorb the water.
4. Add more water as needed until you reach your desired consistency.
5. Heat gently if desired, and stir before serving.

Source: Harvest Right, 2017a

Creamy Parmesan and Tomato Sauce

This creamy Parmesan and tomato sauce is easy to whip up in your kitchen and is great for pasta, pizza, and more.

Ingredients:

- 2 tbsp sour cream powder
- 1/2 cup of tomato sauce mix
- 1/3 cup grated Parmesan cheese
- 1 cup tomato dices
- 2 cups water

Directions:

1. Add the water to a medium-sized saucepan, then add the tomato sauce mix.
2. Over medium heat, whisk the water and sauce, mixing until smooth.
3. Add the tomato dices and simmer for 2 minutes.
4. Stir in the sour cream powder.
5. Fold in the grated Parmesan.
6. Stir until the sauce turns creamy and the cheese has melted.
7. Remove the sauce from the stove and allow it to cool.

Freeze drying instructions:

1. Spread the sauce thinly on freeze dryer trays lined with parchment paper or silicone mats.
2. As per the machine's instructions, freeze dry.
3. Store in airtight containers.

To reconstitute:

1. Mix the freeze-dried sauce with 3–4 times its weight in water.
2. Stir gently and allow to rest briefly.
3. Heat (optional).
4. Serve.

Source: *Thrive Life, n.d.-b*

DRESSINGS

Tangy Herb Dressing

You can whip up a delicious dressing anytime with this bold freeze-dried herb mix. Packed with creamy flavor, it's the perfect treat for your taste buds.

Ingredients:

For the herb mix

- 1/2 tsp freeze-dried chives
- 1 tsp freeze-dried dill weed
- 1/2 tsp freeze-dried parsley
- 1/4 tsp freeze-dried onion powder
- 1/2 tsp freeze-dried garlic powder
- 1/4 tsp fine sea salt
- 1/8 tsp cracked pepper

To make the dressing

- 1/2 cup buttermilk or milk
- 1/2 cup mayonnaise
- 1–3 tsp lemon juice, to taste
- 1/2 cup sour cream

Directions:

For the herb mix

1. Mix all the herb mix ingredients together in a small bowl, and transfer to a sealed jar or airtight container.

To make the dressing

1. Combine the milk, sour cream, and mayonnaise until the mixture is smooth.
2. Incorporate the herb mix and blend well until combined.
3. Add lemon juice to taste.

Source: *Ranch Dressing Mix*, 2024

PUREES

Baby's Favorite Food

Skip those store-bought jars and prepare homemade baby food. Freeze-dried baby food lasts up to 25 years and is ideal for emergencies or travel.

Ingredients:

Consider using ingredients like:

- sweet potatoes
- carrots
- bananas
- blueberries
- pumpkin
- apples
- strawberries

Directions:

1. Wash and peel the chosen fruit or vegetable.
2. Dice into small, even pieces.
3. Steam or boil the pieces until soft.
4. Allow to cool slightly.
5. Puree the cooked pieces until smooth, using a blender or food processor.

Freeze drying instructions:

1. Evenly layer the puree on parchment- or silicone-lined trays and freeze dry until fully crisp, according to your machine's instructions.
2. Place the freeze-dried puree in a sealed, airtight container or a vacuum-packed bag to preserve its freshness.
3. To serve, rehydrate with water, breast milk, or formula to your desired consistency.

Source: *Freeze Dried Baby Food*, 2023

Year-Round Pumpkin Puree

Want to enjoy pumpkins all year round? Pumpkin puree is great for baby food or even a dessert.

Ingredients:

- pumpkins, halved with seeds removed
- sugar (optional)
- cinnamon (optional)

Directions:

1. Warm the oven to 350 °F (180 °C).
2. Arrange sugary, cinnamon-dusted, or plain pumpkin halves cut-side down on a baking tray.
3. Bake the pumpkin until the flesh is soft and easily pulls away from the skin. This should take anything from 45 to 60 minutes.
4. Remove from the oven.
5. Scoop out the soft inside and blend before use.

Freeze drying instructions:

1. Follow the machine's guidelines carefully. Accurately weigh the pumpkin before and after processing to determine the amount of water required for reconstitution.

To reconstitute:

1. Add the recommended amount of hot water.
2. Stir and let it rest for a few minutes until reconstituted.

Source: *Freeze Dried Pumpkin Puree, 2023*

SIDES

Classic Butter Herb Stuffing

Buttery herb stuffing made easy, with parsley, rosemary, and sage for crispy, fluffy bites. Prep ahead, freeze dry, and enjoy!

Ingredients:

- 3 cups diced sweet onion
- 6 crushed garlic cloves
- 1 cup unsalted butter
- 18–24 oz bread cubes (1.5 loaves, toasted or stale)
- 2 1/2 cups vegetable or chicken stock
- 2 cups diced celery
- 1 1/2 cups cranberries
- 1 1/2 tbsp parsley
- 1 1/2 tbsp rosemary
- 1 1/2 tbsp sage
- 2 large eggs
- kosher salt and pepper

Directions:

1. Toast or dry the bread cubes to make breadcrumbs.
2. Set the oven to 350 °F (180 °C) and lightly oil a baking dish.

3. Melt the butter over medium heat, then cook the celery, garlic, onions, and cranberries with salt and pepper until softened and the cranberries start to burst—about 8–10 minutes.
4. Add the herbs and cook for 1 more minute.
5. Pour 1 cup of stock into the pan, then pour it over the breadcrumbs and mix well.
6. Beat the eggs with the remaining broth, then thoroughly combine with the breadcrumbs.
7. Put the mixture into the baking dish and bake for 45 minutes, or until the center reaches 160 °F (70 °C). If the top browns too quickly, cover it with foil to prevent burning.

Freeze drying instructions:

1. Cool the stuffing completely.
2. Evenly spread the stuffing on parchment- or silicone-lined trays, then weigh each tray.
3. Run the freeze dry cycle following your machine's instructions.
4. After freeze drying, weigh the trays to determine the water needed for rehydration, then seal the stuffing in Mylar bags with oxygen absorbers.

To reconstitute:

1. Add 0.75 oz (about 22 ml) of water per gram of freeze-dried stuffing. Let the water absorb fully, then warm the stuffing at 350 °F (180 °C) for 10–15 minutes before serving.

Source: *Buttery Herb Stuffing*, 2024

SOUPS AND BROTHS

SOUPS

Beefy Bean Taco Soup

Packed with taco and ranch seasoning, ground beef, beans, corn, and tomatoes, this dish is a quick, hearty meal that's perfect for any night. Top with sour cream and cheese for ultimate comfort.

Ingredients:

- 1 lb lean ground beef
- 1 can (15 oz) kidney beans with liquid
- 1/2 chopped yellow onion
- 2 cans (14.5 oz each) Italian stewed tomatoes
- 1 package taco seasoning
- 1 can (15 oz) corn, including liquid
- 1/2 package dry ranch seasoning
- 2 cans (14.5 oz each) diced tomatoes
- 1 can (15 oz) pinto beans with liquid
- 6 cherry tomatoes, halved, for garnish (optional)
- choice of herbs, for garnish (optional)
- 1 tsp pepper
- 1 tsp salt

Directions:

1. Over a high heat and in a large pot, brown the chopped onion with the ground beef. This should take 3–5 minutes.
2. Add the rest of the ingredients (except the garnish).
3. Thoroughly mix the ingredients, bring the mixture to a vigorous boil, then reduce the heat and gently simmer for 15 minutes.
4. Add salt and pepper to taste.

5. Garnish with the cherry tomato halves and herbs (optional), and top with cheese and sour cream if desired.
6. Serve.

Freeze drying instructions:

1. Pour the soup evenly onto trays lined with parchment paper or silicone mats; they should be no more than 3/4 full.
2. Weigh and note down the weight of the trays of food.
3. Follow the freeze dryer instructions.
4. Once you've finished the freeze drying process, re-weigh the trays. The weight difference shows how much water you need to add to bring it back to its original state.

To reconstitute:

1. Add the recommended amount of hot water.
2. Stir and let it rest for a few minutes until reconstituted.

Source: *Taco Soup*, 2023

Cheesy Basil Potato Soup

Warm your tummy with this scrumptious potato soup whenever you like. This healthy, flavor-packed soup is bound to become one your ultimate favorites.

Ingredients:

- 4 chicken stock cubes
- 3/4 cup butter
- 2 cups milk
- 1 cup diced celery
- 1 cup diced carrots
- 12 oz processed cheese
- 3 cups cubed potato
- 3/4 cup flour
- 3 cups water
- 1/2 cup chopped onion
- 1 tsp basil
- 2 cups heavy cream

Directions:

1. Combine the potato, water, stock cubes, onion, carrots, and celery in a pot and simmer over medium heat for 15 minutes.
2. Over medium-high heat, in a saucepan, melt the butter, then add the flour and milk; combine until smooth.
3. Add the contents of the saucepan to the vegetables. Combine well and make sure there are no lumps.
4. Add the basil, cheese, and heavy cream.
5. Simmer gently over low heat until the soup thickens and the cheese fully melts, then remove from the heat and serve.

Freeze drying instructions:

1. Let the soup cool completely.
2. Pour the soup evenly onto trays lined with parchment paper or silicone mats.
3. Weigh and note down the weight of the trays of food.
4. Follow the freeze dryer instructions.
5. Once you've finished the freeze drying process, re-weigh the trays. The weight difference shows how much water you need to add to bring it back to its original state.

To reconstitute:

1. Add the recommended amount of hot water.
2. Stir and let it rest for a few minutes until reconstituted.

Source: *Cheesy Potato Soup*, 2023

Creamy Potato Ham Soup

This creamy soup is a tasty and comforting meal that's perfect for any day. Packed with tender ham and hearty potatoes, it's easy to make and delicious.

Ingredients:

- 1/3 cup chopped onion
- 5 tbsp butter
- 2 tbsp chicken stock
- 5 tbsp all-purpose flour
- 3 1/4 cups water
- 2 cups milk
- 3 1/2 cup diced potato
- 3/4 cup diced cooked ham
- 1/3 cup diced celery
- salt and pepper to taste
- herbs of choice to garnish (optional)

Directions:

1. Add the onion, celery, ham, potatoes, and water to a large pot.
2. Over medium heat, bring the ingredients to a boil and cook until the potatoes are soft. This should take 10–15 minutes.
3. Stir in the chicken stock and add salt and pepper to taste.
4. Melt the butter over low-medium heat in a separate saucepan.
5. Add the flour to the melted butter and whisk for about 1 minute until thick.
6. Gradually add the milk while stirring continuously until the mixture thickens—about 4–5 minutes.
7. Pour the milk mixture into the vegetable pot, stir thoroughly, and warm until heated.
8. Serve, garnished with herbs (optional).

Freeze drying instructions:

1. Let the soup cool down.
2. Line freeze dryer trays with parchment or silicone mats, then spread the contents evenly over them.
3. Weigh and note down the weight of the trays of food.
4. Follow the freeze dryer instructions.
5. Once you've finished the freeze drying process, re-weigh the trays. The weight difference shows how much water you need to add to bring it back to its original state.

To reconstitute:

1. Add the recommended amount of hot water.
2. Stir and let it rest for a few minutes until reconstituted.

Source: *Ham & Potato Soup*, 2023

Chicken Enchilada Bowl

When the crisp fall air rolls in, nothing beats a warm bowl of soup. This easy-to-make soup delivers bold flavors and cozy vibes in every savory bite.

Ingredients:

- 2 cups shredded cheese
- 8 oz diced cream cheese
- 1 cup heavy whipping cream
- 2 cans (15 oz each) white beans, drained and rinsed
- 6 cubed deboned skinless chicken thighs
- 1 can (28 oz) green enchilada sauce
- 3 cups chicken broth
- 4 oz salsa verde
- 1 tbsp cornstarch
- salt and pepper

Toppings:

- 1 cup sour cream
- 1 sliced avocado
- 1 bunch chopped cilantro

Directions:

1. Add the salt, pepper, beans, chicken, salsa verde, and enchilada sauce to a slow cooker.
2. Cover and cook on:
   - high: 3 hours
   - low: 6 hours
3. Blend the cornstarch into the cream.
4. Add the cream cheese, shredded cheese, and whipping cream to the crockpot and mix well.
5. Cover and cook for 30 more minutes until the cheese melts.
6. Serve, garnished with avocado slices, cilantro, and sour cream.

Freeze drying instructions:

1. Evenly spread the mixture on parchment- or silicone-lined trays.
2. Weigh and note down the weight of the trays of food.

3. Follow the freeze dryer instructions.
4. Once you've finished the freeze drying process, re-weigh the trays. The weight difference shows how much water you need to add to bring it back to its original state.

To reconstitute:

1. Add the recommended amount of hot water.
2. Stir and let it rest for a few minutes until reconstituted.

Source: *Crock Pot Green Enchilada Chicken Soup*, 2023

Chicken and Spinach Soup

Whether you need a fast, nourishing meal or want to stock your pantry with wholesome options, this soup delivers every time.

Ingredients:

- 1 cup diced bacon
- 2 cups shredded sharp cheddar, plus extra for topping
- 1 chopped yellow onion
- 2 minced garlic cloves
- 2 large diced carrots
- 4 cups shredded cooked chicken
- 6 cups chicken broth
- 2 cups baby spinach
- 2 tsp parsley
- 2 diced celery ribs
- 2 tbsp unsalted butter
- 1 package dry ranch dressing
- 8 oz cream cheese, cubed
- 1 cup sour cream
- 1 tsp black pepper
- salt and pepper
- chopped green onion, for garnish

Directions:

Stovetop method

1. Fry the bacon in a large skillet over medium-high heat; drain and set aside.
2. Sauté the butter, carrots, celery, and onion in the pot for 5 minutes until soft.
3. Stir in the garlic and cook for an additional minute.
4. Stir in the broth, bacon, chicken, ranch, parsley, pepper, cream cheese, and sour cream; cook until the cream cheese melts.
5. Stir in the spinach and cheddar; cook until the spinach wilts and the cheese melts, then season with salt and pepper.
6. Serve immediately, topped with chopped green onions and extra sharp cheddar.

Slow cooker method

1. Cook the bacon and sauté the vegetables and garlic as above.
2. Transfer the veggies to a crockpot with the broth, bacon, chicken, ranch, parsley, pepper, cream cheese, and sour cream.
3. Cook on low for about 3 hours, stirring after 2 hours.
4. Add the spinach and cheddar; cook until the spinach is soft and the cheese melted, then season with salt and pepper.
5. Serve as above.

Freeze drying instructions:

1. Spread the soup evenly on trays lined with parchment or silicone mats.
2. Weigh and record the tray weight with the soup.
3. Follow the freeze dryer instructions.
4. After drying, weigh the trays again. The weight difference shows how much water to add for rehydration.

To reconstitute:

1. Add the recommended amount of hot water.
2. Stir and let sit for a few minutes until fully reconstituted.

Source: *Crack Chicken Soup*, 2023

Golden Turmeric Turkey Noodle Soup

Fast to make but slow-cooked flavor! This hearty soup is packed with wholesome goodness—perfect for cozy comfort or a nourishing meal that hits the spot every time.

Ingredients:

- 2 tbsp olive oil
- 6 cloves crushed garlic
- 1 tsp turmeric
- 2 bay leaves
- 3 sticks celery
- 3 large diced carrots
- 8–10 cups chicken or turkey broth
- 4–5 cups cooked shredded turkey
- 2 cups egg noodles
- 1 large onion, diced finely
- salt and pepper, to taste
- 4 halved boiled eggs, for garnish (optional)

Directions:

1. Warm the olive oil in a large pot over medium heat, then add and sauté the celery, onions, and carrots until soft—about 5 minutes.
2. Stirring continuously, add the turkey, bay leaves, garlic, and turmeric and continue cooking for about 2 minutes.
3. Include the broth and bring to a boil.
4. Lower the heat and allow the mixture to simmer.
5. Remove the bay leaves.
6. Add the egg noodles and continue cooking until they're tender but still firm. This should take anything from 2 to 8 minutes.
7. Once the noodles are cooked, remove from the heat.
8. Serve, topped with halved boiled eggs (optional).

Freeze drying instructions:

1. Spread the mixture evenly on parchment- or silicone-lined trays, then weigh and record each tray's weight.
2. Follow the freeze dryer instructions.
3. Once you've finished the freeze drying process, re-weigh the trays. The weight difference shows how much water you need to add to bring it back to its original state.

To reconstitute:

1. Add the recommended amount of hot water.
2. Stir and let it rest for a few minutes until reconstituted.

Source: Harvest Right, 2017b

Cheddar Lover's Broccoli Soup

Warm up with this soup, which is ideal for cold evenings. Prepare a large batch, freeze it, and add hot water later for a quick, cheesy meal. Here's how to make and store it!

Ingredients:

- 1/4 cup all-purpose flour
- 2 cups chicken stock
- 2 cups milk
- 1/2 chopped onion
- 1/4 cup melted butter
- 1 cup thinly cut carrot strips
- 1 stalk thinly sliced celery
- 2 1/2 cups grated cheddar cheese
- 1 tbsp butter
- 1 1/2 cups chopped broccoli florets
- salt and pepper

Directions:

1. Place a skillet with 1 tablespoon of butter over medium-high heat and melt the butter.
2. Cook the chopped onion in the pan for 5 minutes.

3. When the onion becomes soft, remove it from the heat.
4. To make the base, over medium-low heat in a large saucepan, whisk the 1/4 cup melted butter and flour.
5. Continue whisking for 3–4 minutes.
6. To stop the flour from burning, add 1–2 tablespoons of milk if needed.
7. Slowly whisk in the remaining milk and the chicken stock.
8. Increase the heat until the mixture simmers.
9. Cook the mixture for 15–20 minutes until it has thickened.
10. Now add the carrots, broccoli, celery, and sautéed onions to the mixture and simmer until the veggies are tender. This should take about 10–15 minutes.
11. Add the cheese and stir continuously until it melts, then season with salt and pepper.
12. Allow the soup to cool down.

Freeze drying instructions:

1. Line trays with parchment or silicone mats and evenly spread the soup over them.
2. Weigh and note down the weight of the trays of food.
3. Follow the freeze dryer instructions.
4. Once you've finished the freeze drying process, re-weigh the trays. The weight difference shows how much water you need to add to bring it back to its original state.

To reconstitute:

1. Add the recommended amount of hot water.
2. Stir and let it rest for a few minutes until reconstituted.
3. You can add a little more or less water to get the consistency you want.

Source: *Cheddar Broccoli Soup*, 2024

Lemon and Herb Chickpea Soup

Bursting with oregano, rosemary, and zesty lemon, this comforting protein-packed soup is perfect for a cozy dinner or a refreshing lunch. A bright, flavorful feast you're bound to love!

Ingredients:

- 1/2 cup olive oil and 2 extra tbsp, divided
- 2 garlic cloves
- 3 cups vegetable stock
- 1 large red onion
- 1 bay leaf
- 2 lemons, juice of
- 2 celery sticks, chopped
- 1 tsp minced rosemary
- 1 tbsp oregano
- 1 carrot, chopped
- 1 lb dry chickpeas or 2 cans (14 oz each) chickpeas
- fresh parsley (optional)
- salt and pepper, to taste

Directions:

1. In a large pot over medium-high heat, warm 1/2 cup olive oil.
2. Fry the onion until it softens—about 1–2 minutes.
3. Add and sauté the garlic for 30 seconds until aromatic.
4. Add the celery and carrot with the bay leaf, oregano, and rosemary. Stir well.
5. Then add the chickpeas and vegetable stock. Stirring well, bring to a simmer.
6. Reduce the heat and simmer, covered, for 25–30 minutes, then remove from the heat.
7. Add the lemon juice, the additional 2 tablespoons of olive oil, and the chopped parsley (optional).
8. Stir well. If you feel that the soup is too thick, add additional vegetable stock. Alternatively, if you want to thicken the soup, use a wooden spoon to crush some of the chickpeas.
9. Add salt and freshly ground pepper to taste.
10. Serve with bread.

Freeze drying instructions:

1. Pour the soup onto trays lined with parchment or silicone mats, then weigh and record each tray's weight.
2. Follow the freeze dryer instructions.
3. Once you've finished the freeze drying process, re-weigh the trays. The weight difference shows how much water you need to add to bring it back to its original state.

To reconstitute:

1. Add the recommended amount of hot water.
2. Stir and let it rest for a few minutes until reconstituted.
3. You can add a little more or less water to get the consistency you want.

Source: *Greek Chickpea Soup With Lemon*, 2024

Rosemary and Sage Butternut Soup

This rosemary and sage butternut soup topped with toasted pepitas and parsley offers pure comfort in every spoonful. A perfect fall favorite!

Ingredients:

- 3 lbs peeled, seeded, and cubed butternut squash
- 1 large yellow onion
- 2 tbsp olive oil
- 3–4 cups vegetable broth
- 3 garlic cloves
- 1 tsp grated ginger
- 1/2 tbsp rosemary
- 1 tbsp sage
- 1/2 tsp salt
- pepper

For serving

- toasted pepitas
- chopped parsley

Directions:

1. Warm the oil in a large pot over medium heat.
2. Add the onion, a few grinds of pepper, and the salt. Sauté until tender—about 5-8 minutes.
3. Add the squash and cook, stirring occasionally, until it softens—about 8-10 minutes.
4. Add the garlic, ginger, rosemary, and sage and cook for about 1 minute until fragrant.
5. Add 3 cups of broth and bring to a boil.
6. Lower the heat and simmer the squash for 20-30 minutes until soft. Remove from the heat and let cool slightly when tender.
7. Blend the soup until smooth, adding more broth if it's too thick.
8. Season to taste.
9. Serve hot with parsley, crusty bread, and pepitas.

Freeze drying instructions:

1. Line trays with parchment or silicone mats. Spread the soup evenly across them.
2. Weigh and note down the weight of the trays of food.
3. Follow the freeze dryer instructions.
4. Once you've finished the freeze drying process, re-weigh the trays. The weight difference shows how much water you need to add to bring it back to its original state.

To reconstitute:

1. Add the recommended amount of hot water.
2. Stir and let it rest for a few minutes until reconstituted.

Source: *Butternut Squash Soup*, 2024

Vegan Veggie Soup

This warm blend of fresh vegetables and herbs is perfect for a healthy, comforting meal anytime.

Ingredients:

- 3 tbsp olive oil
- 2 large potatoes, diced into 1-inch pieces
- 1 diced red bell pepper, seeds removed
- 4 cups vegetable broth
- 1 large sweet onion
- 3 peeled, chopped carrots
- 4 cloves garlic
- 1 bag (12 oz) frozen corn
- 3 chopped celery stalks
- 1 tsp oregano
- 1 tsp fresh ground pepper
- 1 tsp salt

Directions:

1. Warm the olive oil in a large pot over medium-high heat.
2. Add and sauté the onion, celery, and bell pepper until tender—about 5–7 minutes.
3. Add and then sauté the garlic, oregano, salt, and pepper for 1 minute.
4. Add the potatoes, carrots, corn, and broth.
5. Turn the heat down and let the soup simmer for 30–40 minutes until the veggies are tender.

Freeze dry instructions:

1. Cool the soup, then lay it thinly on parchment- or silicone-lined trays for freeze drying.
2. Freeze dry according to the machine's guidelines, then seal securely with oxygen absorber packets.

To reconstitute:

1. Add 3–4 times hot water to freeze-dried soup by weight.
2. Stir and let sit a few minutes.

Source: Harvest Right, 2018

BROTHS

Nourishing Veggie Broth

Packed with the fresh flavors of garden vegetables, this broth is perfect for soups, stews, and sauces. Simmer fresh veggies to release their rich taste, then freeze dry the broth to keep its flavor and nutrients.

Ingredients:

- 1 onion
- 1 leek
- 2 cloves garlic
- 2 parsnips
- 3 carrots
- 1/2 celery stalk and leaves
- 1 turmeric root
- 2 root parsley
- handful of parsley (optional garnish)
- 2 bay leaves
- 1/2 kohlrabi
- pepper or peppercorns, to taste
- 2 oz salt

Directions:

1. Wash all the vegetables well.
2. Chop the vegetables so they fit into your pot.
3. Put the vegetables in a large pot.
4. Add the bay leaves, pepper, and salt.
5. Add 10–12 cups of water, cover, and cook gently for 1 hour.
6. Remove from the heat and strain the stock to separate (then discard) the peppercorns and vegetables.
7. Serve garnished with parsley.

Special note:

Adjust the ingredients according to the vegetable scraps available or your preferred vegetables. Consider options such as:

- garlic skins and ends
- onion skins and ends
- fennel fronds
- leek tops
- herb stems
- mushroom stems
- corn cobs
- carrot tops
- scallion roots and tops

Avoid veggies that might make your broth bitter, like:

- broccoli
- cabbage
- cauliflower

Freeze drying instructions:

1. Freeze dry per the machine's instructions, using trays lined with parchment paper or silicone mats.
2. Pour the mix evenly onto the trays.
3. Weigh and note down the weight of the trays of food.
4. Follow the freeze dryer instructions.
5. Once you've finished the freeze drying process, re-weigh the trays. The weight difference shows how much water you need to add to bring it back to its original state.

To reconstitute:

1. Add the recommended amount of hot water.
2. Stir and let it rest for a few minutes until reconstituted.

Source: *Vegetable Broth*, 2024

STEWS AND CASSEROLES

STEWS

Rosemary Beef Stew

This hearty beef stew is packed with tender meat and nourishing vegetables that offer you the perfect nourishing meal.

Ingredients:

- 2 lbs beef chuck, cut into cubes
- 1 chopped yellow onion
- 1 chopped pepper
- 4 quartered yellow potatoes
- 3 tbsp olive oil
- 32 oz beef broth
- 4 sliced carrots
- Italian seasoning
- 4 crushed garlic cloves
- 2 rosemary sprigs
- 2 tbsp Worcestershire sauce
- 3 chopped celery stalks
- 4 tbsp flour
- parsley (to garnish)
- 2 tbsp tomato paste
- 1 tsp garlic powder
- 1 tbsp salt

Directions:

1. Mix the Worcestershire, salt, and flour.
2. Coat the beef cubes in the seasoned flour.
3. Sear the beef in 2 tbsp olive oil in batches; set aside.
4. Cook the garlic, celery, and onion in the remaining oil until soft.
5. Add the garlic powder, tomato paste, and Italian seasoning; cook briefly.
6. Add the beef broth, beef, pepper, and rosemary; cook on low heat for 30 minutes.
7. Add the potatoes and carrots, then simmer for 1 hour.
8. Serve garnished with parsley.

Freeze drying instructions

1. Spread the cooled stew evenly in a thin layer on freeze dryer trays.
2. Freeze dry according to your machine's instructions.
3. Store the freeze-dried stew in vacuum-sealed bags with oxygen absorbers or in airtight containers.

To reconstitute:

1. Put the freeze-dried stew in a bowl.
2. Add 3–4 times as much warm water as the stew weight.
3. Stir and wait a few minutes for it to soak up the water.

Source: Kathleen, 2025

Smoky Bean and Quinoa Stew

Enjoy this hearty stew packed with protein, veggies, and bold spices. It's warm, nutritious, and perfect for any meal!

Ingredients:

- 1 can (15 oz) black beans, drained and rinsed
- 1 cup rinsed quinoa
- 2 tbsp olive oil
- 1 diced bell pepper
- 1 can (15 oz) diced tomatoes with juice
- 2 cloves crushed garlic
- 1/2 tsp chili powder
- 1 diced celery stalk
- 2 cups fresh or frozen corn
- 1 finely chopped onion
- 1 diced carrot
- 1/2 tsp oregano
- 1 tsp cumin
- 4 cups vegetable broth
- 1 tsp smoked paprika
- juice of 1 lime
- salt and pepper
- lime and fresh cilantro for garnish

Directions:

1. Warm the olive oil in a large pot over medium heat.
2. Add the onion and cook for about 5 minutes until partly see-through.
3. Add the celery, bell pepper, carrot, and garlic and cook until the vegetables begin to soften. This should take about 5 minutes.
4. Combine the chili powder, cumin, oregano, smoked paprika, black pepper, and salt.
5. Stir to evenly coat the vegetables with the spices.
6. Add the vegetable broth and bring to a boil.
7. Reduce the heat to a simmer and add the quinoa, then simmer until it's fully cooked and the stew has thickened—approximately 20–25 minutes.

8. Add the diced tomatoes and black beans to the pot, then stir well.
9. After 18 minutes, add the corn.
10. When the corn is heated and the quinoa cooked, add the lime juice.
11. Stir, then remove from the heat.
12. Garnish with cilantro and lime wedges, then serve.

Freeze drying instructions:

1. Put the cooled stew evenly on trays lined with parchment paper or silicone mats.
2. Weigh the trays with the food.
3. Note down the weight.
4. Follow your freeze dryer's directions to process.
5. After drying, weigh the trays again. The weight difference is the amount of water needed to rehydrate.

To reconstitute:

1. Add the recommended amount of hot water.
2. Stir and let it rest for a few minutes until reconstituted.

Source: *Smoky Quinoa and Black Bean Stew*, 2023

Country-Style Chicken Stew

A hearty chicken stew packed with veggies and rich flavor—perfect for a satisfying meal any day.

Ingredients:

- 2 peeled, cubed potatoes
- 3 diced medium tomatoes
- 2 tbsp cooking oil
- 1 chopped onion
- 1.5 cups water
- 17 oz chicken pieces
- 3 tbsp dry minestrone soup mix
- 1 chopped green pepper
- 2 cups frozen mixed vegetables
- your choice of herbs (optional)

Directions:

1. Cook the green pepper and onion in the oil over medium heat until soft, then brown the chicken for 5 minutes.
2. Combine the diced tomatoes, assorted vegetables, and potatoes in a pot with the water. Heat until boiling, then lower the temperature and cover, allowing it to simmer gently for 30 minutes.
3. Mix the soup mix with a little warm water to form a paste, then stir into the stew.
4. Simmer for 5 more minutes.
5. Serve, garnished with herbs (optional).

Freeze drying instructions:

1. Spread the cooled stew evenly in a thin layer on freeze dryer trays lined with parchment paper or silicone mats.
2. Freeze dry following your machine's instructions.
3. Keep the freeze-dried stew in airtight or vacuum-sealed containers.

To reconstitute:

1. Place the freeze-dried stew in a bowl.
2. Slowly pour in hot water, stirring until smooth. Allow to rest briefly to fully absorb the liquid.

Source: *Chicken and Vegetable Stew*, n.d.

CASSEROLES

Sausage and Hash Brown Casserole

This cheesy casserole is loaded with sausage, hash browns, and veggies—perfect for a satisfying breakfast or even a brunch!

Ingredients:

- nonstick cooking spray
- 1 cup cheddar cheese
- 1/2 diced small onion
- 1 cup béchamel sauce

- 2 cups milk
- 1/2 cup sausage
- 1/2 cup red bell peppers
- 1 cup powdered scrambled eggs
- 1/2 cup green chili peppers
- 1 bag (30–32 oz) frozen shredded hash browns, thawed

Directions:

1. Spray a 9- by-13-inch baking pan with nonstick cooking spray.
2. Prewarm the oven to 350 °F (180 °C).
3. Cook the hash browns until golden brown in a greased pan.
4. Arrange the hash browns evenly in the greased baking dish.
5. Cover the hash browns with the onion, red peppers, sausage, and green chilies.
6. In a mixing bowl, whisk the milk and scrambled egg mix together.
7. Whisk the béchamel sauce into the milk and egg mixture, then pour it over the mixture in the baking dish.
8. Sprinkle the cheese over the top and put in the oven uncovered.
9. Bake for 35–45 minutes, then let rest for 5 minutes before serving.

Freeze drying instructions:

1. After baking and cooling the casserole completely, cut it into smaller pieces or portions for even drying.
2. Arrange the pieces in a single layer on freeze dryer trays lined with parchment paper or silicone mats, spacing them evenly apart.
3. Weigh the portions before freeze drying for accurate rehydration later.
4. Place the trays in your freeze dryer and start the cycle according to your machine's instructions.
5. Afterward, seal the freeze-dried casserole in airtight containers or vacuum bags with oxygen absorbers to preserve the quality.

To reconstitute:

1. Weigh the freeze-dried casserole pieces you want to rehydrate.
2. Add hot water equal to about 60–70% of the weight of the freeze-dried casserole.
3. Stir well and let it sit for several minutes to absorb the water and soften.

Source: Thrive Life, n.d.-c

Mozzarella and Sausage Pizza Casserole

A cheesy, hearty casserole loaded with sausage, pepperoni, and fresh veggies. Easy to make and full of classic pizza flavors in every bite!

Ingredients:

- 1 can (15 oz) crushed tomatoes
- 1/2 cup shredded Parmesan, divided
- 3 minced garlic cloves
- 1/2 cup fresh mozzarella pearls
- 3 cups shredded mozzarella cheese, divided
- 2 tbsp olive oil
- 1/3 cup pickled banana peppers, divided
- 2 tsp dried oregano
- 1/2 cup chopped red onion, divided
- 3 pepperoni slices, divided
- 1 can (28 oz) crushed tomatoes
- 1 lb pork sausage
- 1/2 cup sliced black olives, divided
- 1 chopped green bell pepper, divided
- 16 oz pasta
- salt

Instructions:

1. Warm the oven to 350 °F (180 °C).
2. Over high heat, bring salted water to a boil in a large pot.
3. Add the pasta and cook until just tender, then drain and set aside.

4. Heat 2 tablespoons of oil in a large pan over medium heat, then brown the sausage for 7 minutes.
5. Add and sauté the garlic for 2 minutes.
6. Stir in the oregano and crushed tomatoes; simmer uncovered for 5 minutes.
7. Season with salt and mix in the cooked pasta.
8. Layer half the pasta mixture in a 9- by-13-inch dish, then sprinkle with 1/4 cup Parmesan and 2 cups shredded mozzarella.
9. Spread with half the diced red onion, chopped bell pepper, banana peppers, and black olives, then top with half the pepperoni slices.
10. Add the remaining pasta mixture, 1/4 cup Parmesan, and the remaining shredded mozzarella.
11. Finish by layering the remaining pepperoni, banana peppers, bell pepper, red onion, and black olives, and the mozzarella pearls.
12. Bake until golden and bubbling—about 30 minutes.
13. Remove from the oven, then serve.

Freeze drying instructions:

1. Spread the casserole evenly on trays lined with parchment or silicone mats.
2. Weigh the trays with food and note the weight.
3. Freeze dry according to your machine's instructions.
4. After drying, weigh the trays again; the weight difference is the water needed for rehydration.

To reconstitute:

1. Add hot water equal to the weight difference noted.
2. Stir and allow to hydrate for several minutes.
3. Adjust the amount of water if needed for your preferred consistency.

Source: *Pizza Casserole*, 2023

Ultimate Cheeseburger Mac Casserole

Enjoy all the flavors of a cheeseburger in a creamy, cheesy pasta bake that's easy to make and perfect for any night!

Ingredients:

Casserole ingredients

- 1 lb 90% lean ground beef
- 3 cups whole milk
- 12 oz (about 3 cups) grated sharp cheddar cheese, divided
- 8 slices American cheese
- 1/4 cup all-purpose flour
- 1 tbsp yellow or Dijon mustard
- 3 tbsp unsalted butter
- 2 tsp Worcestershire sauce
- 1 lb dried elbow macaroni
- 2 tbsp grilling seasoning
- 1 tsp kosher salt, plus more for pasta water
- parsley for garnish (optional)

Topping ingredients

- 1/2 tsp salt
- 1 tbsp butter
- 2 tbsp sesame seeds
- 1 cup breadcrumbs

Directions:

1. Warm the oven to 425 °F (220 °C).
2. Over medium-high heat, bring a large pot of water, seasoned with salt, to a boil.
3. Boil the macaroni for 7–8 minutes until just cooked.
4. Drain the macaroni and put aside.
5. Brown the ground beef in a large Dutch oven over medium heat for 7–8 minutes. Drain with a slotted spoon onto a paper-towel-lined plate and set aside.
6. Melt the butter in the Dutch oven's beef drippings over medium heat.
7. Whisking continuously, add the flour and cook for 2 minutes, then slowly whisk in the milk.
8. Whisking continuously, cook for about 5 minutes until bubbly and thick, then reduce to a low heat.
9. Whisk in 2 cups of cheddar cheese plus the grilling seasoning, Worcestershire sauce, salt, and mustard until the cheese is melted and everything is well combined.
10. Stir in the macaroni and beef.
11. Top with the remaining cheddar cheese.
12. Arrange the cheese slices evenly to create a complete layer over the casserole's surface.
13. Make the topping: Stir together the salt, butter, sesame seeds, and breadcrumbs in a small bowl.
14. Evenly cover the pasta with the mixture.
15. Place in the oven and bake for 15–18 minutes until golden brown.
16. Remove from the oven and allow the dish to cool for 5 minutes.
17. Serve, garnished with parsley (optional).

Freeze drying instructions:

1. Evenly distribute the cooled casserole on trays lined with parchment paper or silicone mats.
2. Weigh the trays with the food.
3. Note down the weight.
4. Follow your freeze dryer's directions to process.
5. After drying, weigh the trays again. The weight difference is the amount of water needed to rehydrate.

To reconstitute:

1. Add the recommended amount of hot water.
2. Stir and let it rest for a few minutes until reconstituted.
3. A little less or more of the recommended amount of water can be added so you get your desired consistency.

Source: *Cheeseburger Casserole Recipe*, 2023

Creamy Spinach and Cheese Casserole

Cheesy and packed with spinach, this casserole is comfort food at its best. Topped with crispy fried onions and a hint of lemon zest, it's the perfect dish to wow your family and friends!

Ingredients:

- 3 tbsp butter
- 1 cup crushed fried onions, divided
- 1 1/2 cups shredded Gruyère cheese
- 3 tbsp flour
- 1/2 cup breadcrumbs
- 2 bags (each 9 oz) fresh spinach
- 3 crushed garlic cloves
- 2 tbsp olive oil
- 1 1/2 cup milk
- 2 oz cream cheese
- 1/3 cup grated Parmesan
- zest of 1 lemon
- salt and pepper, to taste

Directions:

1. Warm the oven to 350 °F (180 °C).
2. Combine the breadcrumbs with 3/4 cup fried onions in a small bowl. Put aside.
3. Over medium heat, heat a Dutch oven or a large skillet and then add the olive oil.
4. In batches, if needed, add the spinach, stirring occasionally for about 5 minutes until wilted.

5. Put the wilted spinach into a heat-safe bowl and put aside.
6. In the same pan, add the butter and let it melt until golden.
7. Stir continuously with a wooden spoon for 2 minutes, slowly adding the flour and garlic.
8. Whisk in the milk, pepper, and salt, then, stirring often, cook for about 5–7 minutes until the mixture thickens.
9. Once the mixture has thickened, turn the heat to low.
10. Next, stir in the cream cheese until it has fully mixed in.
11. Making sure that the cheese is well combined before adding the next batch, add the Gruyère in three batches.
12. Next, stir in the Parmesan. The mixture will be thick.
13. Stirring until well combined, place the wilted spinach along with its juices into the cheese sauce.
14. Add the remaining 1/4 cup fried onions.
15. Place the spinach and cheese mix into an 8- by 8-inch baking dish.
16. Sprinkle the breadcrumbs and fried onion over the cheese and spinach mixture.
17. Bake for 30–35 minutes until the topping turns golden, then remove from the oven and let cool for 10 minutes.
18. Top with lemon zest before serving.

Freeze drying instructions:

1. Spread the cooled casserole evenly on parchment- or silicone-lined trays.
2. Weigh the trays with the food.
3. Note down the weight.
4. Follow your freeze dryer's directions to process.
5. After drying, weigh the trays again. The weight difference is the amount of water needed to rehydrate.

To reconstitute:

1. Add the recommended amount of hot water.
2. Stir and let it rest for a few minutes until reconstituted.
3. It's important to note that a little less or more of the recommended amount of water can be added so that you get your desired consistency.

Source: *Spinach Casserole Recipe*, 2023

Creamy Chicken and Bacon Casserole

Warm up with this easy tender chicken and crispy bacon casserole. Perfect for those busy nights!

Ingredients:

- 8 oz cooked rotini pasta
- 1 diced onion
- 1/2 cup chopped green onions, plus extra for garnish
- 4 cups chopped rotisserie chicken
- 6 slices bacon, chopped
- 4 oz drained diced pimientos
- 3 cups shredded mozzarella, divided
- 4 minced garlic cloves
- 1 oz dry ranch seasoning packet
- 2 cup milk
- 8 oz cubed cream cheese

Directions:

1. Warm the oven to 375 °F (180 °C).
2. Heat a pan over medium and fry the bacon. Stirring often, cook the bacon until crispy.
3. Drain the bacon with a slotted spoon and leave the drippings in the pan.
4. Add the garlic and onion to the pan drippings and, stirring often, cook for approximately 5 minutes.
5. Whisk together 1 cup mozzarella with the milk, ranch seasoning, and cream cheese until smooth, then remove from the heat.
6. Combine the ranch dressing, chicken, pimientos, half the green onions, and the cooked pasta in a large bowl.
7. Mix well and put the mixture into a 13- by 9-inch casserole dish.
8. Cover with the bacon and top with the remaining mozzarella and green onions.
9. Place the casserole dish in the oven and bake for 25–30 minutes until the top is crispy and golden brown in color.
10. Remove from the oven and allow it to cool down slightly.
11. Before serving, top with more green onion.

Special note:

To add vegetables to this casserole:

1. Stir 4 cups of spinach into the chicken.
2. Stir in 2 cups of broccoli florets during the final minutes of cooking the pasta.

Freeze drying instructions:

1. Spread the casserole evenly on parchment- or silicone-lined trays.
2. Weigh the trays with the food.
3. Note down the weight.
4. Follow your freeze dryer's directions to process.
5. After drying, weigh the trays again. The weight difference is the amount of water needed to rehydrate.

To reconstitute:

1. Add the recommended amount of hot water.
2. Stir and let it rest for a few minutes until reconstituted.
3. It's important to note that a little less or more of the recommended amount of water can be added to get your desired consistency.

Source: *Chicken Bacon Ranch Casserole, 2023*

Cheddar-Topped Green Bean Bake

Try this casserole with tender green beans, a rich mushroom sauce, and a crunchy fried onion topping. This is a comforting dish that will be welcomed all year round.

Ingredients:

- 1 cup shredded cheddar cheese, divided
- 1 can (10.5 oz) condensed cream of mushroom soup
- 1 can (6 oz) french-fried onions
- 2 cans (14.5 oz each) green beans, drained

Directions:

1. Prewarm the oven to 350 °F (180 °C).
2. In a large microwave-safe bowl, mix the condensed soup together with the green beans.

3. Place the bowl in the microwave and microwave on high for 2–3 minutes.
4. After heating, transfer the mixture to a baking dish and spread it evenly across the base.
5. Sprinkle the onions and cheese over the top to cover the mixture.
6. Place the baking dish in the oven; bake for approximately 10 minutes until the onions are starting to brown and the cheese has melted, then remove from the oven.
7. Serve.

Freeze drying instructions:

1. Spread the bake evenly on parchment- or silicone-lined trays.
2. Weigh the trays with the food.
3. Note down the weight.
4. Follow your freeze dryer's directions to process.
5. After drying, weigh the trays again. The weight difference is the amount of water needed to rehydrate.

To reconstitute:

1. Add the recommended amount of hot water.
2. Stir and let it rest for a few minutes until reconstituted.
3. It's important to note that a little less or more of the recommended amount of water can be added to get your desired consistency.

Source: *Best Green Bean Casserole*, 2023

Squash and Ricotta Casserole

Cozy up with this tasty casserole! Rich, savory, and irresistibly satisfying, this dish will delight your palate.

Ingredients:

- 1.5 cups dry short-grain rice
- 3 cups vegetable or chicken broth
- 1 small butternut squash, peeled and diced into 1/4-inch pieces for even cooking (about 4–5 cups)
- 1 tsp salt
- 1/4 tsp ground nutmeg
- 1 1/2 cups shredded mozzarella
- 1 1/2 cups ricotta cheese
- 5 cups chopped spinach
- 1 tsp minced freeze-dried sage
- sage leaves for garnish (optional)

Directions:

1. Preset the oven temperature to 400 °F (200° C).
2. Heat 2 tablespoons of water in a large skillet over medium heat, then add the chopped spinach.
3. Use tongs or a wooden spoon to toss and turn the spinach until it wilts.
4. Once the spinach has wilted, remove it from the heat and set aside to cool.
5. Add the salt, ricotta cheese, nutmeg, sage, and spinach to a large bowl. Use a spatula or wooden spoon to stir and mix the ingredients.
6. Combine the rice and butternut squash in a 2- or 3-quart baking dish and stir thoroughly.
7. Next, dollop the ricotta cheese mix evenly on top of the rice and squash it into the baking dish.
8. Add the broth.
9. Stir all the ingredients together to mix well.
10. Seal the baking dish with foil.
11. Place the dish in the oven to bake until all the rice is cooked and all the liquid is absorbed. This should take about 40–45 minutes.

12. Once cooked, take the baking dish out the oven, remove the foil, and sprinkle with the mozzarella cheese.
13. Uncovered, put the casserole back into the oven until the cheese has melted and is slightly golden. This should take 5–10 minutes.
14. When the cheese has melted, remove the casserole from the oven and let it cool slightly.
15. If you like, add sage to the casserole:
    - Warm the olive oil in a pan over a medium-high flame.
    - Fry the fresh sage leaves for 3–5 minutes until golden (don't burn).
    - Remove with tongs, drain on paper towel, and sprinkle with salt.
    - Top the casserole with the fried sage before serving.

Freeze drying instructions:

1. Spread the casserole evenly on parchment- or silicone-lined trays.
2. Weigh the trays with the food.
3. Note down the weight.
4. Follow your freeze dryer's directions to process.
5. After drying, weigh the trays again. The weight difference is the amount of water needed to rehydrate.

To reconstitute:

1. Add the recommended amount of hot water.
2. Stir and let it rest for a few minutes until reconstituted.
3. A little less or more of the recommended amount of water can be added to get your desired consistency.

Source: *Butternut Squash Casserole*, 2024

Marshmallow-Topped Sweet Potato Delight

This sweet potato casserole topped with baked golden brown marshmallows is a classic comfort dish. Easy to make and bursting with warm flavors!

Ingredients:

- 1 pack (10.5 oz) mini marshmallows
- 1/4 cup butter or margarine
- 5 sweet potatoes, peeled and sliced
- 3 tbsp orange juice
- 1/2 cup brown sugar
- a dash of cinnamon

Directions:

1. Warm up the oven to 350 °F (180 °C).
2. Cover the sweet potatoes with water in a large pot.
3. Over medium-high heat, bring the sweet potatoes to a boil and cook for around 15–20 minutes until tender.
4. When fully cooked, remove from the heat source, drain thoroughly, and then mash until smooth.
5. Transfer the mashed sweet potato to a large bowl.
6. Add the butter or margarine, cinnamon, brown sugar, and orange juice to the bowl.
7. Using an electric mixer, blend the contents of the bowl.
8. Evenly press the mixture into a 9- by 13-inch pan, then top with mini marshmallows.
9. Bake for 25–30 minutes until the casserole is hot and the marshmallows are crisp and browned.
10. Remove from the oven.
11. Serve.

Freeze drying instructions:

1. Spread the casserole evenly on parchment- or silicone-lined trays.
2. Weigh the trays with the food.
3. Note down the weight.
4. Follow your freeze dryer's directions to process.
5. After drying, weigh the trays again. The weight difference is the amount of water needed to rehydrate.

To reconstitute:

1. Add the recommended amount of hot water.
2. Stir and let it rest for a few minutes until reconstituted.
3. It's important to note that a little less or more of the recommended amount of water can be added to get your desired consistency.

Source: *Sweet Potato Casserole With Marshmallows*, 2023

Cheesy Eggplant Casserole

While dishes like mac and cheese and lasagna are super tasty, there are simple, healthy alternatives. This tasty eggplant dish is easy to make and perfect for freezing ahead of time.

Ingredients:

- nonstick cooking spray
- 3 tbsp olive oil, divided
- 1 medium diced yellow onion
- 1/2 lb lean ground beef
- 1/4 cup panko
- 1 can (28 oz) crushed fire-roasted tomatoes
- 2 1/2 lb eggplants, sliced lengthwise into 1/2-inch-thick pieces
- 3 minced cloves garlic, divided
- 1/2 cup chopped fresh Italian parsley, divided
- 1/4 tsp red pepper flakes
- 3 tbsp chopped fresh basil, divided
- 1 large lightly beaten egg
- 2 1/2 cups shredded Italian blend cheese, divided
- 3/4 cup grated Parmesan, divided
- 15 oz container whole milk ricotta cheese
- 1 tsp Italian seasoning, divided
- 2 3/4 tsp salt, divided
- 1 1/4 tsp ground black pepper, divided

Directions:

1. Preheat the oven to 425 °F (220 °C).
2. Place the eggplant slices on two baking trays and sprinkle evenly with 2 tsp salt. Let sit for 30 minutes.
3. Heat 1 tablespoon olive oil in a pan over medium heat. Cook the onion until golden, 5–7 minutes.
4. Add the red pepper flakes, 1/2 teaspoon black pepper, 1/2 teaspoon 2 tsp salt, 1/2 the garlic, and 1/2 tsp Italian seasoning; cook for 1 minute.
5. Brown the ground beef in the same pan.
6. Stir in the basil and crushed tomatoes; simmer for about 15 minutes until thick. Remove from the heat and stir in 1/2 the chopped parsley.

7. Pat the eggplant slices dry, brush with 2 tbsp olive oil, and sprinkle with 1/2 tsp black pepper.
8. Bake the eggplant for 20–22 minutes until soft and golden.
9. Mix the remaining Italian seasoning, garlic, salt, pepper, and parsley with the panko, egg, ricotta, and Parmesan in a bowl.
10. Spray an 11- by 7-inch dish with nonstick cooking spray.
11. Spread 1/2 cup of the meat sauce evenly in the dish. Layer 1/2 of the eggplant, 1/2 of the ricotta, 1/3 of the meat sauce, and 3/4 cup cheese. Repeat.
12. Top with the eggplant, remaining meat sauce, and cheese blend.
13. Bake for 40–45 minutes until golden and bubbling.
14. Cool for 10 minutes and serve with the remaining basil and parsley.

Freeze drying instructions:

1. Spread the casserole evenly on parchment- or silicone-lined trays.
2. Weigh the trays with the food.
3. Note down the weight.
4. Follow your freeze dryer's directions to process.
5. After drying, weigh the trays again. The weight difference is the amount of water needed to rehydrate.

To reconstitute:

1. Add the recommended amount of hot water.
2. Stir and let it rest for a few minutes until reconstituted.
3. A little less or more of the recommended amount of water can be added to get your desired consistency.

Source: *Eggplant Casserole*, 2023

Creamy Zucchini and Chicken Casserole

Enjoy a cheesy casserole packed with comfort food that's wholesome and delicious! A perfect dinner that everyone will love.

Ingredients:

- 2 lbs skinless, boneless chicken breasts, diced into 1-inch cubes
- 1 cup chicken broth
- 1 large chopped red bell pepper
- 2 large zucchini cut into 1/2-inch pieces
- 3 tbsp butter, divided
- 1 cup whole milk
- 1/3 cup all-purpose flour
- 1 1/4 cups shredded part-skim mozzarella cheese, divided
- 3 oz light cream cheese
- 1/2 tsp salt
- 1/3 tsp ground pepper

Directions:

1. Prewarm the oven to 400 °F (400 °C).
2. Over medium heat, in a large pan, melt 1 tablespoon of butter.
3. Put the chicken in the skillet and cook, stirring now and then, for about 8 minutes until it turns golden brown. Once golden brown, place the chicken in a bowl.
4. Add the bell pepper and zucchini to the pan and, stirring often, cook until the vegetables begin to soften.
5. After preparing the zucchini mix, add it to the bowl with the chicken.
6. Put the remaining butter in the pan, and stir in the flour.
7. Stirring continuously, cook the flour and butter mix for about a minute until the flour starts to brown.
8. Add the milk and broth and, whisking often, bring to a boil.
9. Remove from the heat and add 3/4 cup mozzarella and the cream cheese. Stir until the cheese has melted.
10. Stir in the salt and pepper.
11. Drain any liquid from the vegetable and chicken mixture.
12. Combine the vegetables and chicken with the cheese sauce, then transfer to a 2-quart baking dish.
13. Place the casserole on a foil-lined sheet and sprinkle with the remaining cheese.
14. Place the dish in the oven and bake for about 20–25 minutes until the edges are bubbly and the top is browned.
15. Remove from the oven, and let the dish rest for about 10 minutes before serving.

Freeze drying instructions:

1. Evenly distribute the cooled chicken and zucchini casserole on trays lined with parchment paper or silicone mats.
2. Weigh the trays with the food.
3. Note down the weight.
4. Follow your freeze dryer's directions to process.
5. After drying, weigh the trays again. The weight difference is the amount of water needed to rehydrate.

To reconstitute:

1. Add the recommended amount of hot water. A little less or more of the recommended amount of water can be added so that you get your desired consistency.
2. Stir and let it rest for a few minutes until reconstituted.

Source: *Chicken and Zucchini Casserole*, 2023

MEAT DISHES

CHICKEN

Lemon-Garlic Chicken

This creamy chicken dish combines fresh lemon, rich butter, and savory spices for a delicious taste. You'll want to have more after every bite.

Ingredients:

- 1/2 stick diced butter
- 1/2 tsp cayenne or chili pepper flakes
- 2 tsp chicken stock
- 1 tsp onion powder
- 1/3 cup chicken broth
- 6–8 skinless, boneless chicken thighs or breasts
- zest of 1/2 a lemon; slice the other 1/2 and set aside to use as a garnish
- juice from 1 lemon
- 1 tsp Italian seasoning
- 1/2 tsp paprika
- 4 crushed garlic cloves
- 1 tsp garlic powder
- salt and pepper to taste
- 8 oz fresh mushrooms (optional)
- fresh parsley, for garnish

For the cream sauce

- 1 cup heavy cream
- 1 tbsp cornstarch

Directions:

1. Add the chicken to a slow cooker.
2. In a separate container, blend the optional mushrooms, lemon zest and juice, chicken broth, and stock. Pour this mixture over the chicken.
3. Combine the salt, pepper, onion and garlic powders, paprika, cayenne or crushed red chili pepper flakes, and Italian seasoning in a small bowl.
4. Once mixed, sprinkle the blend over the chicken.
5. Add the crushed garlic and then spread the diced butter on top.

6. Cover the slow cooker and begin cooking:
    - low: 6–8 hours
    - high: 3–4 hours
7. In the last hour of cooking, take out the chicken pieces and put them on a plate.
8. Whisk together the creamy sauce ingredients, then stir the creamy sauce into the juices.
9. Put the chicken back in the crockpot, cover, and cook for another hour.
10. Adjust the seasoning with salt and pepper to taste.
11. Sprinkle the parsley and lemon slices on the crockpot chicken.
12. Serve.

Freeze drying instructions:

1. Pour the chicken dish evenly onto trays lined with parchment paper or silicone mats.
2. Weigh and note down the weight of the trays of food.
3. Follow the freeze dryer instructions.
4. Once you've finished the freeze drying process, re-weigh the trays. The weight difference shows how much water you need to add to bring it back to its original state.

To reconstitute:

1. Add the recommended amount of hot water.
2. Stir and let it rest for a few minutes until reconstituted.

Source: *Crock Pot Lemon Chicken*, 2023

Chicken and White Bean Chili

This is a protein-packed one-pot wonder that's bound to be a crowd-pleaser. Juicy chicken bites, creamy beans, and a blend of flavorful spices come together to create the ultimate comfort meal.

Ingredients:

- 1/2 cup heavy cream
- 1 diced yellow onion
- 2 tbsp crushed garlic
- 2 cans (15.9 oz each) drained white kidney beans
- 3 cups chicken broth
- 1 lb cubed chicken breasts, cut into 1/2–1-inch pieces
- 1 tbsp olive oil
- 1 1/2 cups frozen or canned corn, drained
- 1 can (28 oz) green chilies
- 1/2 tsp chili powder
- 1 1/2 tsp cumin
- 1/2 tsp oregano
- 1 tsp salt
- 1/2 tsp pepper
- chopped cilantro (optional)

Directions:

1. Heat the oil in a Dutch oven over medium heat.
2. Add the onion and chicken; stirring occasionally, sauté until the onion is translucent and the chicken is no longer pink.
3. Sauté the garlic for 30 seconds.
4. Combine with all the ingredients except the cilantro and cream, cover, and simmer gently for 20 minutes.
5. Remove from the heat and stir in the cilantro and heavy cream.
6. Serve with toppings like:
    - avocado
    - cheese
    - sour cream
    - tortilla chips

Special note:

- To thicken the sauce, remove about 1/2 cup of beans, mash or blend them, then add them back into the hot soup and stir.

Freeze drying instructions:

1. Pour the cooled chicken chili evenly onto trays lined with parchment paper or silicone mats.
2. Weigh and note down the weight of the trays of food.

3. Follow the freeze dryer instructions.
4. Once you've finished the freeze drying process, re-weigh the trays. The weight difference shows how much water you need to add to bring it back to its original state.

To reconstitute:

1. Add the recommended amount of hot water.
2. Stir and let it rest for a few minutes until reconstituted.
3. Add a little more or less water to reach the consistency you want.

Source: *White Bean Chicken Chili*, 2025

Smoky Bacon Chicken Chili

Enjoy this comforting chili dish with juicy chicken, smoky bacon, black beans, and bold spices. Cream cheese and mild cheddar cheese make it creamy and indulgent.

Fresh Recipe

Ingredients:

- 1 tbsp onion powder
- 2 1/2 cups chicken broth
- 3 medium boneless skinless chicken breasts
- 1 1/4 cups cooked and crumbled smoked bacon
- 1 tbsp chili powder
- 1 can (10 oz) mild diced tomatoes and green chilies (do not drain)
- 8 oz cubed cream cheese
- 1 oz ranch seasoning mix
- 2 cups fresh shredded mild cheddar and gouda cheese
- 1 can (15.25 oz) southwest corn with poblano and red peppers (do not drain)
- 1 can (15.25 oz) black beans, drained and rinsed
- 1 tsp cracked black pepper
- 1 tsp kosher salt
- 1 1/2 tbsp chopped cilantro (optional garnish)

Directions:

1. Coat the interior of a 5–7-quart slow cooker with nonstick spray, or line it with a disposable slow cooker liner.
2. Combine the onion powder, salt, pepper, chili powder, ranch mix, southwest corn, diced tomatoes with green chilies, and chicken broth in a bowl; mix until well blended.
3. Arrange the chicken breasts snugly along the bottom of the slow cooker, creating a perfect base for your dish.
4. Evenly scatter the black beans over the top of the chicken breasts.
5. Slowly pour the chicken broth mixture to cover the black beans evenly.
6. Over the broth mixture, sprinkle the cooked bacon.
7. Add the cubed cream cheese over the bacon.
8. Cook at a low temperature for 6 hours or on high for 4 hours.
9. Once the chili is done, take out the chicken breasts and shred them with two forks.
10. Stir the broth and cream cheese together until the cheese melts and blends smoothly before adding the chicken back to the slow cooker.

11. Mix in the shredded cheese until it's fully combined.
12. Stir the shredded chicken back into the slow cooker.
13. Garnish with cilantro.
14. Serve.

Freeze Dry Recipe

Ingredients:

- 1 can (15.25 oz) black beans, drained and freeze dried (can use pinto too)
- 3 cups boneless skinless freeze-dried chicken breasts
- 1 tbsp chili powder
- 1 tbsp cracked black pepper
- 1 1/4 cups smoked bacon, cooked and freeze dried
- 3 cups chicken broth (freeze-dried broth powder and water)
- 2 oz freeze-dried cream cheese powder with 1/4 cup water
- 1 tbsp freeze-dried onion powder
- 1 can (10 oz) mild diced tomatoes and green chilies, drained and freeze dried
- 2 cups freeze-dried shredded cheese with 1/8 cup water
- 1 can (15.25 oz) southwest corn with poblano and red peppers, drained and freeze dried
- 1 tsp kosher salt
- 1 tbsp cilantro for garnish (optional)

Directions:

1. Heat the chicken and broth in a pot over medium heat for 5 minutes without stirring.
2. Pour 1 1/4 cups of water over the corn and stir, then add to the pot.
3. Add 1 cup water and mix in the tomatoes.
4. Add 1 cup water and stir in the black beans.
5. Add the salt, pepper, chili powder, onion powder, and bacon. Stir the ingredients gently so that they mix well.
6. Add the shredded cheese.
7. Add the powdered cream cheese and stir for a few minutes.
8. Simmer gently, covered, for 5 minutes.
9. Serve, garnished with cilantro (optional).

Freeze drying instructions:

1. Spread the cooled chicken chili evenly on trays lined with parchment paper or silicone mats and weigh them.
2. Follow your freeze dryer's instructions to process.
3. After drying, weigh the trays again. The weight difference shows how much water to add for rehydrating.

To reconstitute:

1. Add the recommended amount of hot water.

2. Stir and let it rest for a few minutes until reconstituted.

Source: *Crack Chicken Chili*, 2024

Cheesy Chicken Pepper Fajitas

Savor the flavors of sizzling chicken, colorful peppers, and lime in this easy skillet chicken fajitas recipe. Perfectly seasoned and ready in minutes, it's a tasty meal the whole family will love!

Ingredients:

- 12 warmed flour tortillas (8 inches)
- 1/2 tsp ground cumin
- 2 tbsp olive oil, divided
- 1 medium onion, cut into thin wedges
- 1 1/2 lbs boneless, skinless chicken breast strips
- 1 crushed garlic clove
- 1/2 cup salsa
- 1 tsp chili powder
- 1/4 cup lime juice
- 1/2 yellow bell pepper, cut into strips
- 1/2 red bell pepper, sliced
- 1/2 green bell pepper, cut into strips
- 1 1/2 cups shredded cheddar cheese
- 1/2 tsp salt

Directions:

1. Mix 1 tablespoon of olive oil with the chili powder, garlic clove, ground cumin, lime juice, salt, and chicken. Marinate the chicken for 15 minutes.
2. Warm the remaining olive oil in a large skillet over medium-high heat.
3. Sauté the pepper and onion until tender, about 3 minutes, then remove from the pan.
4. Sauté the chicken mixture for about 3–4 minutes, until it's no longer pink, in the same skillet.

5. Stir in the pepper, onion, and salsa, heat briefly, then remove from the stove.
6. Serve with cheese and tortillas.

Freeze drying instructions:

1. Evenly spread the cooked chicken mixture on trays lined with parchment paper or silicone mats.
2. Weigh and note down the weight of the trays of food.
3. Follow the freeze dryer instructions.
4. Once you've finished the freeze drying process, re-weigh and note down the weight of the trays. The weight difference shows how much water you need to add to bring it back to its original state.

To reconstitute:

1. Add the recommended amount of hot water.
2. Stir and let it rest for a few minutes until reconstituted.
3. You can add more or less water to reach the consistency you want.

Source: *Skillet Chicken Fajitas Recipe*, 2023

Chicken Pot Pie

This homey comfort food classic is a must for any freeze-dried pantry, and it can stay on the shelf for 20 years.

Ingredients:

For the crust

- 1 cup cubed cold butter
- 1 tsp salt
- 1 tsp sugar
- 1 cup ice cold water
- 2 1/2 cups flour

For the filling

- 8 cups chopped chicken
- 2/3 cup butter
- 2 cups diced onions

- 2 cups diced celery
- 2 cups diced carrots
- 1 cup flour
- 4 cups beef or chicken bone broth
- 2 cups peas
- 2 cups heavy cream, half and half, or evaporated milk
- salt and pepper, to taste

Directions:

For the crust

1. Crumble the butter, salt, sugar, and flour together until the crumbs are about pea sized. You can do this by hand or in a food processor set to pulse.
2. Feed the cold water into the mixture bit by bit and mix until the dough begins to hold together and appears moist all the way through. Depending on your flour and the ambient temperature, you might need less than a cup of water, so feed the water in slowly.
3. Knead the dough on a floured surface until it forms a cohesive doughball that doesn't stick to the surface.
4. Cut the doughball into four equal pieces and put them in the fridge for 20 minutes.

For the filling

1. Use a large skillet to melt 2 tbsp of butter over medium-high heat.
2. Tip the chicken pieces into the skillet and let them cook almost through, then add all the vegetables (except the peas) and cook further until the vegetables start softening.
3. Spoon the remaining butter into the vegetable and chicken mix and stir until the butter has melted.

4. Lightly sprinkle the flour over the contents of the skillet and stir for about 3–5 minutes to mix the flour in evenly.
5. Mix the cream and broth into the mixture when the flour has turned a golden-brown color. Keep stirring.
6. Add the pepper and salt with the peas to the skillet and keep stirring to let the filling thicken evenly.
7. Once the filling has thickened, remove it from the stove and let it cool.
8. Divide the filling equally into four pie pans.

For the pie:

1. When the filling is done, take the dough out the fridge and roll each piece out to about 1/4 inch (60 mm) thickness. Cover the filling in each pie pan with a piece of rolled-out dough to form the crust. Cut a few slits in each crust to facilitate the release of steam and put in a 375 °F (190 °C) oven for more or less 25 minutes. The pie is ready when the crust covering is fully cooked.
2. Load slices of the pie onto trays and freeze dry. Crumble the product into Mason jars or other packaging, and put an oxygen absorber into the packaging.
3. To rehydrate, add about a cup of boiling water slowly to the package, close the package, and shake it gently. After a few minutes, the chicken pot pie will be ready to serve.

Source: Thomas, 2022

TURKEY

Turkey Meatballs

These tender, flavorful turkey meatballs are perfect for a quick and healthy meal any time. Simple to prepare, and even easier to enjoy!

Ingredients:

- 1 crushed garlic clove
- 2 tsp fresh thyme
- 1 slice whole-wheat bread crumbs
- 1/4 cup grated Parmesan cheese
- 1/4 cup grated onion
- 1 lb ground turkey

- 1 beaten egg
- 1/2 tsp black pepper
- salt and pepper

Directions:

1. Set the oven to 350 °F (180 °C).
2. Combine the ingredients and form into 2-inch balls.
3. Bake for 10 minutes.

Freeze drying instructions:

1. Let the cooked meatballs cool completely and then arrange them in a single layer on freeze dryer trays lined with parchment paper or silicone mats, leaving space between each one.
2. Place the trays in the freeze dryer and start the cycle according to your machine's instructions.
3. Once freeze dried, the meatballs will be light and dry.
4. Store them in sealed containers with oxygen absorbers to preserve their freshness.

To reconstitute:

1. Add the recommended amount of hot water.
2. Stir and let it rest for a few minutes until reconstituted.
3. You can add more or less water to reach the consistency you want.

Source: Harvest Right, 2017a

Liquid-Smoke-Brined Turkey

A flavorful, juicy turkey brined with liquid smoke for a deep, smoky taste. Slow-cooked low and slow for tender, moist meat every time.

Ingredients:

- 2 bags Morton's Tender Quick
- 2 gallons or more of water
- 1 (12 lb) whole turkey
- 1 small bottle liquid smoke
- 1 cup pickling salt

Directions:

1. Place the frozen turkey in a 5-gallon bucket filled with water, ensuring the turkey is fully submerged.
2. Add the salt, liquid smoke, and Tender Quick to the water.

3. Store the bucket outside in the snow or in a garage refrigerator to let the turkey soak for 2–4 days. Larger turkeys may require extra time for the brine to penetrate fully.
4. Preheat the oven to 225 °F (100 °C) when the soaking time is up.
5. Take the turkey out of the brine and pat it dry with paper towels.
6. Place the turkey inside a pan or put the turkey in a roasting pot with a lid.
7. Let the turkey bake for 6–10 hours.
8. After baking, let the turkey rest for 20–30 minutes to allow the juices to redistribute, ensuring moist and tender meat, before carving.
9. Carve and serve.

Freeze drying instructions:

1. Evenly spread the cooled cooked turkey out on trays lined with parchment paper or silicone mats.
2. Weigh and note down the weight of the trays of food.
3. Follow the freeze dryer instructions.
4. Once you've finished the freeze drying process, re-weigh and note down the weight of the trays. The weight difference shows how much water you need to add to bring it back to its original state.

To reconstitute:

1. Add the recommended amount of hot water.
2. Stir and let it rest for a few minutes until reconstituted.
3. You can add more or less water to reach the consistency you want.

Source: *Bucket Brine Smoked Turkey*, 2023

BEEF

Shredded Beef

Tender shredded beef, slow-cooked to perfection with savory onion soup mix and beef broth. Easy to prepare and full of rich flavor, it's perfect for a hearty meal.

Ingredients:

- 2 cans (14.5 oz each) beef broth
- 2 packets (1 oz each) dry onion soup mix
- 2 tbsp olive oil
- 3 lbs boneless beef roast
- 2 cups water
- salt and pepper to season

Directions:

1. Over a medium-high heat, heat the olive oil in a pan.
2. Put the roast in the pan and cook all sides over high heat when the oil is hot.
3. Once the roast is seared, put it in a crock pot and sprinkle the onion soup mix over the roast.
4. Add water and the beef broth and cook:
   - low: 8–10 hours
   - high: 4–6 hours
5. Once cooked, let it cool for about 10 minutes and then shred the roast.
6. Serve.

Freeze drying instructions:

1. Evenly spread the beef on trays lined with parchment paper or silicone mats.
2. Note down the weight of the trays of food.
3. Freeze dry according to the machine's instructions.
4. Once the freeze dry process is complete, note the weight of the trays again. The weight difference is the recommended amount of water that you will need to use to reconstitute the meat.

To reconstitute:

1. Add the recommended amount of hot water.
2. Stir and let it rest for a few minutes until reconstituted.

Source: *Shredded Steak*, 2023

Timeless Cottage Pie

Enjoy this hearty cottage pie, packed with creamy mashed potatoes topped with cheese. Easy to make and perfect for any meal, it's comfort food you'll want again and again!

Ingredients:

- 1 cup freeze-dried diced onion
- 3 cups freeze-dried instant potatoes or mashed potatoes
- 1 cup freeze-dried corn or other desired vegetables
- 2 1/2 cups freeze-dried hamburger
- shredded freeze-dried cheddar cheese
- 2 cups freeze-dried tomato powder
- salt and pepper to taste
- fresh thyme (optional)

Directions:

1. Begin by soaking the cheese in a bowl of cold water to restore its texture. After it has softened, drain the water completely and pat the cheese dry with a paper towel to remove any moisture.
2. Warm the oven to 350 °F (180 °C).
3. Mix the onion, ground beef, tomato powder, and corn or any other vegetables you like. Then add enough hot water to get the consistency you want and heat over medium heat.
4. Season with salt and pepper.
5. Prepare the instant potatoes according to the supplier's directions, or make the mashed potatoes.
6. Place the meat mixture in a casserole dish and sprinkle a little fresh thyme over the meat.
7. Top the meat with the mashed potatoes. You can get creative and carve patterns into the mashed potatoes using a fork.
8. Sprinkle the cheese atop the mashed potatoes.
9. Place in the oven, uncovered, and let your cottage pie bake until the cheese is bubbly and melted. This should take about 30 minutes.
10. Remove from the oven and let the dish rest for about 10 minutes.
11. Serve.

Freeze drying instructions:

1. Spread the cottage pie evenly in trays that are lined with parchment paper or silicone mats.
2. Weigh and note down the weight of the trays of food.

3. Follow the freeze dryer instructions.
4. Once you've finished the freeze drying process, re-weigh the trays. The weight difference shows how much water you need to add to bring it back to its original state.

To reconstitute:

1. Add the recommended amount of hot water.
2. Stir and let it rest for a few minutes until reconstituted.
3. If you like, you can add a little more or less water to get the consistency you want.

Source: *Shepherd's Pie*, 2023

No-Fuss Comfort Pot Roast

Savor the comfort that comes with this quick and simple pot roast. Ideal for busy evenings or cozy weekends, it's sure to be a hit with the whole family.

Ingredients:

- 2 cups beef broth
- 1 yellow onion, chopped into large pieces
- 1 tsp onion powder
- 3 crushed garlic cloves
- 1/2 cup red wine
- 3–4 lb chuck roast
- 1 lb baby potatoes
- 2 tbsp olive oil
- 1 tsp garlic powder
- 4 large sliced carrots
- 3 tbsp Worcestershire sauce
- 1/2 tsp pepper
- 1 tsp salt
- extra salt and pepper to season the roast

Directions:

To roast in the oven

1. Set the oven to 425 °F (220 °C).
2. Heat the olive oil in a large skillet over medium-high heat until it begins to smoke.
3. Season the roast with salt and pepper on both sides.
4. Sear the roast in the skillet for 2–3 minutes per side until a dark brown crust forms.
5. In a large casserole dish, spread the carrots, potatoes, and onion evenly and place the seared roast on top of the vegetables.
6. Combine the beef broth, red wine, Worcestershire sauce, garlic, onion, garlic powder, salt, and pepper in a small bowl.
7. Pour the mixture over the roast and vegetables.
8. Cover the dish with a lid or foil and roast in the oven for 30 minutes.
9. Lower the oven temperature to 300 °F (150 °C) and continue roasting for 4–5 hours until the meat is tender.

In the slow cooker

1. Over medium-high heat, warm the olive oil in a large cast iron skillet until it begins to smoke.
2. Season the roast with salt and pepper on all sides.
3. Sear the roast in the hot skillet for 2–3 minutes per side until a deep brown crust forms.
4. Place the onion, potatoes, and carrots in the bottom of a 5-quart slow cooker.
5. Set the seared roast on top of the vegetables.
6. In a small bowl, mix together the salt and pepper, onion powder, garlic powder, garlic, Worcestershire sauce, beef broth, and red wine.
7. Pour the mixture over the roast and vegetables, then cover and simmer on low heat for 10 hours until the meat is tender.

Freeze drying instructions:

1. Spread the cooled cooked meal out thinly on trays lined with parchment paper or silicone mats.
2. Weigh and note down the weight of the trays of food.
3. Follow the freeze dryer instructions.
4. Once you've finished the freeze drying process, re-weigh and note down the weight of the trays. The weight difference shows how much water you need to add to bring it back to its original state.

To reconstitute:

1. Add the recommended amount of hot water.
2. Stir and let it rest for a few minutes until reconstituted.
3. Adjust the water quantity to reach your desired consistency.

Source: *Fast N Easy Pot Roast*, 2023

Hearty Texas Beef Chili

This Texas chili delivers rich flavors and satisfying heartiness—ideal for quick meals, outdoor adventures, or any time you want genuine slow-simmered comfort.

Ingredients:

For the chili

- 1–2 tbsp avocado or vegetable oil
- 1 diced yellow onion
- 2 cans (4.5 oz each) green chilies
- 1 sliced green pepper
- 1 tbsp cumin
- 5 minced cloves garlic
- 3 lb lean beef chuck, cut into 3-inch cubes
- 1 can (14 oz) crushed fire-roasted tomatoes
- 1 tbsp brown sugar
- 1/4 cup chili powder
- 2 1/2 tsp salt (1 teaspoon per pound of meat; more to taste)

For toppings (optional)

- cornbread or chips
- cheddar cheese
- green onions
- sour cream

Directions:

1. Measure and prepare your ingredients.
2. Heat the oil in a large Dutch oven over high heat.
3. Sear the beef on each side until browned, working in batches if your pan is small.
4. Once browned, remove the beef and place in a slow cooker.
5. Sauté the garlic, green pepper, and onions until the onions are golden in color.
6. Add the salt, spices, and brown sugar and sauté for 3–5 minutes.
7. Add the crushed tomatoes and green chilies and simmer until bubbly; this should take about 3–5 minutes.
8. Add the tomato mixture over the beef in the slow cooker. Make sure that the beef is properly covered in the sauce.
9. Cook on:
    - low heat: 8 hours
    - high heat: 4 hours
10. Once the cooking time is up, shred the beef into large tender chunks and season with salt to taste.
11. Serve with cornbread or chips, cheddar cheese, green onions, and sour cream if desired.

Freeze drying instructions:

1. Spread the Texas beef chili thinly in trays lined with parchment paper or silicone mats.
2. Weigh and note down the weight of the trays of food.
3. Follow the freeze dryer instructions.
4. Once you've finished the freeze drying process, re-weigh the trays. The weight difference shows how much water you need to add to bring it back to its original state.

To reconstitute:

1. Add the recommended amount of hot water.
2. Stir and let it rest for a few minutes until reconstituted.
3. If you like, you can add a little more or less water to get the consistency you want.

Source: *Freeze-Dried Texas Slow Cooker Chili*, 2024

Beef Stroganoff

The hearty aroma alone will convince you to make a double batch. This recipe is versatile, and you can choose if you want the beef to rest on a bed of rice, egg noodles, or low-carb spaghetti squash.

Ingredients:

- 1/2 tsp smoked paprika
- 1 cup sour cream (can be substituted with Greek yogurt or crème fraiche)
- 1 tsp salt (or less to taste)
- 1/2 tsp pepper
- 1/2 finely chopped medium onion
- 1 1/2 cup sliced mushrooms
- 2 cloves garlic, crushed
- 12 oz (340 g) bag egg noodles (cooked), 1 small, cooked spaghetti squash, or 1 1/2 cups cooked rice
- 10 3/4 oz (300 g) canned or homemade cream of mushroom soup
- 1 tbsp butter or olive oil
- 1 tbsp all-purpose flour
- 1 lb (450 g) ground beef
- a few drops of Worcestershire sauce (optional)

Directions:

1. Over medium-high heat, sauté the onions in the butter until the onions are see-through, then add the crushed garlic and continue sautéing for another minute or two to blend the flavors thoroughly.
2. Mix in the ground beef and stir now and again while the beef cooks until brown.
3. Spice the mixture with the paprika, salt, and pepper, then add the mushrooms and flour.
4. Stir in the mushroom soup and let the mixture simmer for about 5–10 minutes.
5. Blend in the sour cream and remove the pan from the heat.
6. Mix in or lay on a bed of egg noodles, spaghetti squash, or rice if you want to eat it right away.

7. To freeze dry, either mix the stroganoff with the pasta or rice, or freeze dry the stroganoff and pasta or rice separately, depending on how you plan to store it. Rehydrate with boiling water poured slowly until the food is barely covered. Wait about 10 minutes, taste test, and pour in more water if needed.

Source: Eaton, 2022

PORK

Tangy Pork Tacos

Enjoy these tasty tacos made with flavorful pulled pork and fresh salsa. Delicious for any meal!

Ingredients:

- 1 can Coca-Cola
- 1/2 cup onion slices
- 1 crushed clove garlic
- 2 cups pulled pork
- 6–8 small corn tortillas
- 1 (15.25 oz) can whole-kernel corn (keep the liquid)
- 1/2 cup cotija cheese
- 1/4 tsp cayenne pepper
- 1 cup instant black beans (rehydrated and chilled in the fridge)

- 2 tbsp lime juice
- 1 cup tomato dices
- 1/2 tsp black pepper
- 1 tsp salt
- cilantro leaves (optional)
- additional salt and pepper as desired

Directions:

1. Mix the Coca-Cola, pulled pork, cayenne, black pepper, garlic, and salt in a covered container. Let the pork marinate for at least 30 minutes.
2. Combine the tomatoes, black beans, corn with juice, lime juice, onions, and cilantro (optional) to make a salsa, then stir it well.
3. Heat the pulled pork in a saucepan over medium heat for 10 minutes.
4. Warm the tortillas on a griddle and then fill them with pork and salsa.
5. Sprinkle with cheese and serve.

Freeze drying instructions:

1. Cook the pulled pork and prepare the salsa, then let both cool completely.
2. Spread the pulled pork and salsa on separate trays lined with parchment paper or silicone mats in thin layers.
3. Weigh each portion for accurate rehydration measurements.
4. Freeze dry following your machine's instructions.
5. Store the freeze-dried pork and salsa in airtight containers or vacuum-sealed bags with oxygen absorbers.
6. Store the tortillas and cheese separately at room temperature.

To reconstitute:

1. Weigh the freeze-dried pulled pork and salsa.
2. Add water equal to 60–70% of their combined weight.
3. Let soak for 5–10 minutes, stirring occasionally.
4. Warm the rehydrated pork mixture in a saucepan over medium heat.
5. Heat the corn tortillas on a griddle or skillet.
6. Assemble the tacos with rehydrated pork, salsa, cheese, and optional cilantro.
7. Serve and enjoy!

Source: Thrive Life, n.d.-a

Smoky BBQ Pulled Pork

Get ready for melt-in-your-mouth pulled pork bursting with smoky BBQ flavor! This easy recipe cooks tender pork to perfection—perfect for sandwiches, sliders, or your favorite BBQ feast.

Ingredients:

- 3 cups BBQ sauce (plus more for serving)
- 2 tbsp liquid smoke
- 3 lb boneless pork sirloin roast, shoulder or butt
- 2 cups low-sodium chicken broth or water
- salt and pepper as desired

Directions:

1. Slice the pork into 4-inch chunks for consistent, rapid cooking.
2. Season all the pork evenly with salt and pepper.

Slow cooker instructions

1. Add the broth or water and liquid smoke to the slow cooker.
2. Place the pork inside, cover, and cook until tender:
    - low: 8–10 hours
    - high: 5–6 hours

Pressure cooker instructions

1. Reduce the broth or water to 1 cup.
2. Pour the water, liquid smoke, and pork into the pressure cooker..
3. Seal the lid.
4. Cook for 55–60 minutes on high pressure, then turn off the pressure cooker.
5. Allow the pressure to drop naturally for 10 minutes, then release any leftover pressure immediately.

Both methods

1. Remove the pork from the cooker and drain most of the liquid, leaving about 1/4 cup.
2. Pull the pork apart with forks.
3. Return the pork to the cooker, add the BBQ sauce, and heat through or keep warm.
4. Serve.

Freeze drying instructions:

1. Place the cooked mix evenly on trays lined with parchment paper or silicone mats.
2. Weigh and note down the weight of the trays of food.
3. Follow the freeze dryer instructions.
4. Once you've finished the freeze drying process, re-weigh the trays. The weight difference shows how much water you need to add to bring it back to its original state.

To reconstitute:

1. Add the recommended amount of hot water.
2. Stir and let it rest for a few minutes until reconstituted.
3. Modify the water amount for the perfect texture.

Source: *BBQ Pulled Pork Recipe, 2023*

Rustic Root Beer Beans

Combining pork and beans with sweet root beer, crispy bacon, and onions, this easy dish is perfect for barbecues and potlucks. Impress your guests with this flavorful, crowd-pleasing side!

Ingredients:

- 3 slices bacon chopped into small bits
- 1/2 cup regular root beer
- 1/4 cup hickory-smoked barbecue sauce
- 1 diced onion
- 1/8 tsp hot sauce
- 2 cans (16 oz each) pork and beans
- 1/2 tsp dry mustard

Directions:

1. Set the oven to 400 °F (200 °C) to ensure it reaches the optimal temperature for cooking.
2. Over medium heat, fry the bacon bits until crisp in a skillet.
3. When crisp, remove the bacon and drain the excess oil on a paper towel. Reserve 2 tablespoons of bacon fat, then sauté the onion in it.
4. Stir together the onion, bacon, and seasonings, and place the mixture in a 1-quart baking dish.
5. Bake, uncovered, in a preheated oven for 55 minutes or until the sauce has thickened to the desired consistency.

Freeze drying instructions:

1. Pour the cooked mix evenly on trays lined with parchment paper or silicone mats.
2. Weigh and note down the weight of the trays of food.
3. Follow the freeze dryer instructions.
4. Once you've finished the freeze drying process, re-weigh the trays. The weight difference shows how much water you need to add to bring it back to its original state.

To reconstitute:

1. Add the recommended amount of hot water.
2. Stir and let it rest for a few minutes until reconstituted.
3. Adjust the water amount to reach the perfect consistency.

Source: *Root Beer Baked Beans*, 2024

Nutritious Homestyle Chili

Everyone loves a warm bowl of chili! This healthy, affordable recipe uses simple ingredients and feeds a crowd. Enjoy it fresh, or freeze dry it for your next adventure!

Ingredients:

- 1 diced large onion
- 6–8 chopped medium Roma tomatoes
- 2 lb ground pork
- 8 tsp chili powder
- 8 cups chicken broth
- 1 tsp smoked paprika
- 2 cups uncooked pinto beans
- 2 cups uncooked red kidney beans
- 6 minced cloves garlic
- 1 tsp Italian seasoning
- 1 tsp cumin
- 3 tsp salt
- 1/2 tsp black pepper

Directions:

1. Soak the pinto and red kidney beans in water overnight, then rinse and drain them.
2. In a large pot, cook the beans in water until tender. Drain and put to one side.
3. Brown the pork in a large Dutch oven over medium heat, then drain the fat.
4. Add the garlic and onion to the pork and cook for approximately 5–7 minutes until the onion is partly translucent.
5. Add and simmer the tomatoes for 5 minutes.
6. Add the salt, pepper, Italian seasoning, paprika, cumin, and chili powder, and mix well.
7. Add the cooked beans and chicken broth to the pot, then stir until fully combined.
8. Adjust the seasoning to taste.
9. Serve hot, garnished with your toppings of choice, such as cilantro, jalapeños, sour cream, or cheese.

Freeze drying instructions:

1. Evenly spread the cooled homestyle chili onto trays lined with parchment paper or silicone mats.
2. Weigh and note down the weight of the trays of food.
3. Follow the freeze dryer instructions.
4. Once you've finished the freeze drying process, re-weigh the trays. The weight difference shows how much water you need to add to bring it back to its original state.

To reconstitute:

1. Add the recommended amount of hot water.
2. Stir and let it rest for a few minutes until reconstituted.

Source: *Simple Chili*, 2025

MIXED MEATS

Steak and Chicken Cheese Melt

Enjoy the perfect blend of tender steak and chicken, sautéed peppers and onions, and melted provolone cheese in this delicious and satisfying sandwich. Easy to make, and a melt you'll want more of!

Ingredients:

- 1 tbsp olive oil
- 1 sliced yellow onion
- 12 oz boneless, skinless chicken breast, thinly sliced
- 10 oz ribeye, thinly sliced
- 1 cup shredded provolone cheese
- 1 tbsp Italian seasoning
- 1 sliced green bell pepper
- 1 sliced red bell pepper
- 2 tsp Worcestershire sauce
- salt and pepper to taste
- sub sandwich rolls (for serving)

Directions:

1. In a large pan, over medium-high heat, heat the olive oil.
2. Add and then sauté the onions and bell pepper until tender. This should take about 5–10 minutes. When soft, place in a bowl and put aside.
3. Cook the chicken and steak until fully browned. Reduce the heat, add the onions and pepper, then season with salt, Italian seasoning, and Worcestershire sauce. Remove from the heat.
4. Put the filling in sub sandwich rolls.
5. Top the filling with cheese.
6. Under the broiler, toast the sandwiches until the cheese melts.

Freeze drying instructions:

1. Place the cooled steak and chicken on trays lined with parchment paper or silicone mats.
2. Weigh and note down the weight of the trays of food.
3. Follow the freeze dryer instructions.

4. Once you've finished the freeze drying process, re-weigh and note down the weight of the trays. The weight difference shows how much water you need to add to bring it back to its original state.

To reconstitute:

1. Add the recommended amount of hot water to the filling.
2. Uncovered, let it rest and keep warm until reconstituted.

Source: *Philly Cheesesteaks*, 2023

PASTA AND RICE DISHES

PASTA DISHES

Cheesy Oven-Baked Jumbo Shells

Delight in these cheesy stuffed shells, filled with a creamy blend of cheeses and baked to perfection in flavorful marinara sauce. An easy Italian classic, perfect for any meal!

Ingredients:

- 1 jar (24 oz) pasta sauce, divided
- 2 tbsp parsley
- 12 oz jumbo shells, cooked perfectly (firm to the bite)
- 1/2 cup grated Parmesan cheese
- 1 beaten egg
- 3 cups cottage or ricotta cheese
- 2 cups shredded mozzarella cheese, divided
- 1/4 tsp Italian seasoning
- salt and pepper to taste

Directions:

1. Set the oven to 375 °F (190 °C).
2. Pour half of the pasta sauce into a 9- by 13-inch baking dish. For a thinner sauce, stir in 1/2 cup of water.
3. In a large bowl, mix together the Italian seasoning, parsley, egg, Parmesan cheese, cottage/ricotta cheese, and 1 cup of mozzarella cheese.
4. Take the cheese filling and fill the pasta shells.
5. Put the filled pasta shells on top of the pasta sauce in the baking dish.
6. Cover the filled pasta shells with the leftover pasta sauce and cover the dish. Bake in the oven for 25–30 minutes.
7. Remove from the oven, uncover, and add the leftover mozzarella cheese over the top.
8. Return to the oven so the cheese on top can melt.

9. Remove from the oven and let the dish rest for 10 minutes before serving.
10. Season with salt and pepper to taste when serving.

Special note:

- To reconstitute more quickly, cut the shells in half before freeze drying.

Freeze drying instructions:

1. Place the cooled pasta shells with some sauce on trays lined with parchment paper or silicone mats.
2. Weigh and note down the weight of the trays of food.
3. Follow the freeze dryer instructions to process.
4. Once you've finished the freeze drying process, re-weigh the trays. The weight difference shows how much water you need to add to bring it back to its original state.

To reconstitute:

1. Place the shells in an oven-safe container and cover with hot water.
2. Cover the container with foil.
3. Bake at 350 °F for 15 minutes.
4. Ensure the shells are fully firm; if not, cover and continue baking.
5. Add more water if needed.
6. After fully rehydrating, take out of the oven and serve.

Source: *Cheese Stuffed Shells*, 2023

Rich Carbonara Pasta

Savor the flavors of this dish, which blends yummy ingredients for a deliciously simple meal that's perfect anytime you want a quick, authentic taste of Italy.

Ingredients:

- 24 cups water
- 1 lb spaghetti, bucatini, or rigatoni
- 4 oz salt-cured pork jowl or bacon
- 2 large eggs
- 4 large egg yolks
- 2 tbsp extra-virgin olive oil
- 2 oz Parmesan cheese
- 3 tbsp salt, plus extra
- ground black pepper

Directions:

1. Over a high heat, heat the water in a large pot.
2. Add salt once the water boils, and cover the pot to speed up boiling.

3. While you wait for the water to boil, cut the pork into 1/4-inch strips.
4. Grate the cheese and put one-quarter aside to use later.
5. In a medium bowl, whisk the yolks and whole eggs until fully blended.
6. Stir the leftover grated cheese into the whisked eggs, add the pepper, and put aside.
7. Warm the oil over medium in a heavy pot, then add the pork or bacon.
8. Stirring occasionally, allow the pork to cook for about 7–10 minutes until crisp around the edges.
9. Remove the pot from the heat and put the pork in a small bowl.
10. Pour the fat into a heatproof measuring cup.
11. Put back 3 tablespoons of fat into the pot. Discard any leftover fat.
12. In the large pot with now boiling water, add the pasta and cook for 2 minutes shy of the package instructions. Stir occasionally.
13. Scoop out 1 3/4 cups pasta liquid just before the pasta is finished cooking.
14. Drain the pasta and add it to the pot.
15. Pour 1 cup of the reserved pasta water into the pot and bring to a boil over medium heat.
16. Stirring constantly, cook the pasta for about 2 minutes until it's al dente and the water is reduced by half.
17. Remove from the heat.
18. Into the egg mixture, whisk 1/4 cup of the reserved pasta water. Then, stirring constantly, slowly steam it in the pot until the egg is thickened and the cheese has melted to form a glossy sauce.
19. Season with salt to taste.
20. Using the remaining 1/2 cup pasta cooking liquid, adding only a spoonful at a time, thin the sauce. Your aim is to have a heavy cream consistency.
21. Add the pork.
22. Divide the pasta into bowls.
23. Top with the remaining cheese and pepper.

Freeze drying instructions:

1. Place the cooled cooked pasta in trays lined with parchment paper or silicone mats.
2. Weigh and note down the weight of the trays of food.
3. Follow the freeze dryer instructions.
4. Once you've finished the freeze drying

process, re-weigh the trays. The weight difference shows how much water you need to add to bring it back to its original state.

To reconstitute:

1. Add the recommended amount of hot water.
2. Stir and let it rest for a few minutes until reconstituted.
3. Slightly modify the water amount for the perfect consistency.

Source: *Pasta Carbonara*, 2024

Creamy Macaroni and Cheese

Stay ahead of hunger with this freeze-dried mac and cheese—creamy, cheesy comfort that's ready whenever you are. Easy to pack, quick to prepare, and loved by little ones, it's the ultimate on-the-go meal.

Ingredients:

For the macaroni and sauce

- 3/4 cup heavy cream
- 1 lb dried elbow macaroni
- 6 tbsp all-purpose flour
- 1/2 cup unsalted butter, plus additional for greasing the baking dish
- 6 cups coarsely grated extra sharp cheddar cheese
- 1 1/2 tbsp mustard powder
- 4 cups whole milk
- 1/2 cup grated Parmesan
- 1 tsp kosher salt, plus more to taste
- 1/2 tsp ground white pepper

For the topping

- 2 tbsp extra-virgin olive oil
- 2 large chopped garlic cloves
- 1/2 cup Parmesan cheese
- 2 tbsp unsalted butter
- 2 cups breadcrumbs
- 1/4 tsp plus 1/8 tsp kosher salt

Directions:

For the macaroni and sauce

1. Warm the oven to 400 °F (200 °C).
2. Boil salted water in a large pot over medium-high heat, then cook the macaroni until al dente.
3. Drain the par-cooked macaroni and put aside. Do not rinse the macaroni.
4. With unsalted butter, grease a 13- by 9-inch baking dish.
5. Over medium-low heat, in a large pot, melt 1/2 cup unsalted butter.
6. Sprinkle the flour into the melted butter and whisk to form a roux.
7. Stir constantly and cook for about 4 minutes until the roux is a light golden color.
8. Whisking continuously, slowly add 3/4 cup heavy cream and 4 cups whole milk.
9. Add the mustard powder, salt, and white pepper.
10. In three batches, whisking continuously until each addition has melted, add the cheddar cheese and Parmesan cheese.
11. Remove from the heat.
12. Add the drained macaroni to the cheese sauce in the pot, then stir thoroughly to evenly coat.
13. Place the macaroni mixture into the prepped baking dish.

For the topping

1. Melt the unsalted butter in a large skillet over medium heat.
2. Pour in the extra-virgin olive oil and stir until the butter foam fades.
3. Add the finely chopped garlic cloves and 2 cups breadcrumbs and cook for 4–6 minutes until the breadcrumbs are golden in color.
4. Put the breadcrumbs into a medium-sized bowl and stir in the Parmesan cheese.
5. Season with salt and set aside.

To assemble

1. Sprinkle the macaroni mixture with the breadcrumbs topping.
2. Bake for 20–22 minutes until bubbling and golden.
3. Remove from the oven.
4. Let the creamy macaroni and cheese dish cool down for about 15 minutes before serving.

Freeze drying instructions:

1. Place the cooled macaroni and cheese evenly on trays lined with parchment paper or silicone mats.
2. Weigh and note down the weight of the trays of food.
3. Follow the freeze dryer instructions.
4. Once you've finished the freeze drying process, re-weigh the trays. The weight difference shows how much water you need to add to bring it back to its original state.

To reconstitute:

1. Add the recommended amount of hot water.
2. Stir and let it rest for a few minutes until reconstituted.
3. Slightly modify the water amount to reach the perfect consistency.

Source: *Freeze-Dried Creamy Macaroni and Cheese*, 2024

Easy Three-Ingredient Egg Noodles

Fresh, simple, and versatile, these homemade egg noodles are easy to make with just three ingredients. Perfect for soups, stir-fries, or your favorite pasta dishes, they bring a comforting touch to any meal!

Ingredients:

- 4 whole eggs
- 1 tsp salt
- 2 cups all-purpose flour

Directions:

1. Combine the salt and flour in a bowl, make a well, crack in the eggs, and whisk, gradually folding in the flour.
2. Start kneading the mixture with your hands as it comes together. Should you feel that the dough is too dry, add some water until you get a doughy consistency.
3. Knead the dough until it's elastic and smooth. If your dough is too sticky, add some more flour, or more water if it's still too dry.
4. Roll the dough into a thin sheet, about 1/8 inch thick.
5. Carefully dust the rolled dough with flour and roll the sheet into a cylinder.
6. Cut the cylinder into strips using a sharp knife.
7. Unroll the strips, gently shaking to separate if needed.
8. Add the fresh noodles to liquid and cook for about 3–5 minutes.

Freeze drying instructions:

1. Place the noodles evenly on trays lined with parchment paper or silicone mats. The trays should be no more than 3/4 full.
2. Weigh and note down the weight of the trays of food.
3. Follow the freeze dryer instructions.
4. Once you've finished the freeze drying process, re-weigh the trays. The weight difference shows how much water you need to add to bring it back to its original state.

To reconstitute:

1. Add the recommended amount of hot water.
2. Stir and let it rest for a few minutes until reconstituted.

Source: *Egg Noodles*, 2025

Simple Buttery Parmesan Fettuccine Alfredo

This rich, velvety fettuccine Alfredo is perfect for satisfying cravings or feeding a crowd, and will quickly become a beloved family dish.

Ingredients:

- 16 oz fettuccine
- 1 1/2 cups heavy cream
- 1 clove crushed garlic
- 6 tbsp butter
- 1 cup grated Parmesan cheese
- salt and pepper to taste
- parsley (optional)

Directions:

1. Bring water to a boil in a large pot.
2. Add the fettuccine and salt to the boiling water; cook per the package instructions, then drain.
3. Heat the butter in a large skillet over medium until melted, add the garlic and sauté for 1-2 minutes, then whisk in the heavy cream until smooth.
4. Stirring occasionally, allow to cook until thickened.
5. Stir in the cheese until fully melted.
6. Add the cooked pasta.
7. Stir to combine all the ingredients well.
8. Serve immediately, optionally topped with parsley and salt and pepper to taste.

Freeze drying instructions:

1. Place the pasta evenly on trays lined with parchment paper or silicone mats.
2. Weigh and note down the weight of the trays of food.
3. Follow the freeze dryer instructions.

4. Once you've finished the freeze drying process, re-weigh the trays. The weight difference shows how much water you need to add to bring it back to its original state.

To reconstitute:

1. Add the recommended amount of hot water.
2. Stir and let it rest for a few minutes until reconstituted.

Source: *Fettuccine Alfredo*, 2025

Cheesy Broccoli Pasta

This recipe is great with either freeze-dried or fresh ingredients and freeze dries well for easy storage. Perfect for busy nights or outdoor adventures—just rehydrate and enjoy!

Ingredients:

- 4 tbsp butter
- 1 tbsp dried basil
- 4 large chopped garlic cloves
- 1 lb bow-tie pasta
- 3 tbsp olive oil
- 1 can (10.5 oz) creamy chicken soup
- 2 cans (14 oz each) chicken broth
- 2 heads broccoli, chopped at the crown
- salt and pepper, to taste
- fresh parsley, to garnish (optional)
- grated Parmesan cheese (optional)

Directions:

1. In a pan with olive oil over medium-high heat, sizzle but do not brown the garlic.
2. Add the butter and then the basil.
3. When the butter has melted, add the broccoli.
4. Gently stir to coat the broccoli.
5. Pour in the chicken broth and soup, cover, and cook over medium heat till the mixture comes to a boil.
6. At the same time, according to the package instructions, cook the pasta.
7. Once the pasta is cooked, drain, then add the pasta to the broccoli mixture.
8. Season with salt and pepper.
9. Sprinkle with Parmesan cheese.
10. Serve hot, garnished with parsley (optional).

Freeze drying instructions:

1. Place the pasta evenly on trays lined with parchment paper or silicone mats.
2. Weigh and note down the weight of the trays of food.
3. Follow the freeze dryer instructions.

4. Once you've finished the freeze drying process, re-weigh and note down the weight of the trays. The weight difference shows how much water you need to add to bring it back to its original state.

To reconstitute:

1. Add the recommended amount of hot water.
2. Stir and let it rest for a few minutes until reconstituted.
3. You can slightly adjust the amount of water to achieve the desired consistency.

Source: *Pasta Broccoli*, 2024

Delicious Cheesy Veggie Lasagna

If your pantry is overflowing with zucchini or you've scored a great deal on squash, this veggie lasagna is the perfect solution. Freeze dried for easy storage, it lets you enjoy a tasty homemade meal wherever you are—just add water and dig in!

Ingredients:

- 1/2 cup white wine
- 2 tbsp olive oil
- 4 whole squash (yellow or zucchini), diced
- 1 whole medium onion
- 1 can (28 oz) whole tomatoes
- 4 cloves garlic
- 24 oz white mushrooms, chopped
- 1 red bell pepper, diced
- 1/2 tsp red pepper flakes
- 1/4 cup fresh parsley
- 2 eggs
- 10 oz lasagna noodles
- 1 lb thinly sliced mozzarella cheese
- 30 oz ricotta cheese
- 1/2 cups grated Parmesan
- extra Parmesan cheese, for sprinkling
- freshly ground black pepper
- 1/2 tsp plus 1/4 tsp kosher salt (more to taste)

✕ fresh parsley, to garnish (optional)

Directions:

1. Preheat the oven to 350 °F (190 °C).
2. Cook the lasagna noodles as per the package instructions.
3. Once cooked, drain and spread the noodles evenly on a sheet of aluminum foil.
4. Warm the olive oil in a large skillet over medium heat.
5. Add the garlic and onions. Allow them to cook for 1 minute.
6. Add the red bell pepper and sauté for another minute or so.
7. Add the mushrooms and squash and cook for a few minutes more.
8. Sprinkle in the red pepper flakes, season with salt and pepper, then add the white wine and mix.
9. Add the tomatoes, using your hands to crush/squeeze them.
10. Stir well to combine all the ingredients, and let the mixture simmer for about 20 minutes.
11. Add the chopped parsley, then combine the salt, pepper, Parmesan cheese, eggs, and ricotta in a bowl.
12. Next, start to assemble the lasagna. In a lasagna pan, spread some of the tomato/vegetable sauce.
13. Lay four cooked noodles in the pan. They can overlap.
14. Layer 1/3 of the ricotta mixture on top of the noodles.
15. Place some mozzarella slices on top of the ricotta mixture.
16. Over the mozzarella, spoon a little less than 1/3 of the tomato/vegetable sauce.
17. Repeat the layering two more times, finishing with a generous amount of tomato and vegetable sauce, topped with a sprinkle of Parmesan.
18. Cover the lasagna with foil and bake in the preheated oven for 20 minutes. Then, remove the foil.
19. Then, for another 5–10 minutes, let the lasagna bake uncovered.
20. Take out of the oven.
21. Let the dish rest for about 10 minutes.
22. Cut into squares.
23. Serve with a fresh parsley garnish (optional).

Freeze drying instructions:

1. Evenly layer the lasagna on trays lined with parchment or silicone mats.
2. Weigh and note down the weight of the trays of food.
3. Follow the freeze dryer instructions.
4. Once you've finished the freeze drying process, re-weigh the trays. The weight difference shows how much water you need to add to bring it back to its original state.

To reconstitute:

1. Add the recommended amount of hot water.
2. Stir and let it rest for a few minutes until reconstituted.
3. Adjust the water slightly to reach the ideal thickness.

Source: *Veggie Lasagna*, 2024

RICE DISHES

Fiesta Rice

This flavorful rice is an easy side dish that goes with almost any meal. Guaranteed, it will taste just like your favorite Mexican restaurant version.

Ingredients:

- 4 tbsp canola oil
- 3 cloves crushed garlic
- 1 large diced onion
- 2 cups rice
- 1 1/2 tsp paprika
- 3 large Roma tomatoes blended to make a puree
- 2 cups chicken or vegetable broth
- 1/4 tsp cumin
- salt and pepper, to taste
- 1 cup peas, diced carrots, etc. (optional)

Directions:

1. Over medium heat, in a saucepan with oil, sauté the rice until it turns light golden brown.
2. Add the onion and sauté until browned.
3. Stirring constantly, add the garlic, paprika, cumin, salt, and pepper.
4. Mix the blended tomatoes with enough chicken broth to make 4 cups and add the mix to the rice.

5. Add your vegetables of choice to the rice (optional).
6. Cover the pot and heat until the liquid reaches a rolling boil.
7. Boil for 15 minutes, then turn the heat down and let the rice simmer until most the water has evaporated. Do not stir the rice as it might turn mushy.
8. Check the rice after 25–30 minutes. When the rice is soft, it's cooked. Serve with chicken as a main dish, or even with your favorite entrée.

Freeze drying instructions:

1. Allow the fiesta rice to cool completely, then spread it evenly on freeze dryer trays lined with parchment or silicone mats.
2. Weigh the trays with the rice to determine the starting weight.
3. Follow your freeze dryer instructions to run a freeze dry cycle.
4. After drying, weigh the trays again. The weight difference shows how much water the rice will need to rehydrate.
5. Store the freeze-dried rice in airtight Mylar bags with oxygen absorbers to preserve the freshness.
6. Label and write the required rehydration water amount on each bag for easy use later.

To reconstitute:

1. Add the recommended amount of hot water.
2. Gently stir and let it rest for a few minutes until reconstituted.
3. Separate the grains with a fork, and serve.

Source: *Freeze Dried Mexican Rice*, 2024

SALADS

Colorful Bean Chili Salad

A colorful bean salad packed with flavor and crunch—perfect for a healthy meal or side. This salad will have your guests dishing out second helpings.

Ingredients:

- 4 cans (each 14 oz) beans (e.g., cannellini, red kidney, mixed)
- 22 oz tinned edamame
- 1 bunch chopped parsley
- 12 oz cucumber, deseeded and diced into 1/3-inch cubes
- 4–6 finely chopped chilies
- 1 large red bell pepper, cut in 1/3-inch dice
- 18 oz tomatoes, cut in 1/3-inch dice
- 1/2 bunch chopped mint
- 9 oz red onion, cut in 1/3-inch dice
- hot chilies, finely sliced (to taste)
- 2 cans (each 14 oz) sweet corn or 1.5 cups freeze-dried corn

Directions:

1. Dice the cucumber, bell pepper, tomatoes, and onion.
2. Drain the edamame, beans, and sweet corn.
3. Chop the chilies, parsley, and mint.
4. Mix all the ingredients together.

Freeze drying instructions:

1. Spread the salad thinly on trays.
2. Freeze dry according to the manufacturer's instructions and then seal in an airtight container.

To reconstitute:

1. Put your freeze-dried salad in a bowl and add enough water to cover.
2. Let sit for a few minute to reconstitute.
3. Drain the excess water and serve.

Source: *Dehydrated Cold-Soak Bean Salad*, n.d.

Chicken and Mayo Salad

Chicken and mayo is a favorite for many people. If you're one of those people, this quick and easy chicken salad made with creamy mayo and flavorful chives will be perfect for a light snack or meal.

Ingredients:

- 2-3 mayonnaise packets
- 1 tbsp chives or scallions
- 1 cup chopped chicken
- salt and pepper to flavor

Directions:

1. Mix the mayonnaise packets with the chopped chives or scallions in a bowl.
2. Add the finely chopped chicken to the bowl and then sprinkle in a pinch of salt and pepper.
3. Mix everything well until fully combined and serve as is or with crackers or tortillas if desired.

Freeze drying instructions:

1. Spread the prepared chicken salad evenly on freeze dryer trays lined with parchment paper or silicone mats.
2. Freeze dry according to your machine's instructions.
3. Store in vacuum-sealed bags or airtight containers.

To reconstitute:

1. Combine the freeze-dried chicken salad with water or mayonnaise, stir, and let it rehydrate for a few minutes.
2. Adjust the moisture to your liking and serve.

Source: *Cold Soak Chicken Salad*, 2025

Summer Pasta Salad

This flavorful pasta salad and dressing is perfect for a quick, healthy meal or side dish.

Ingredients:

Dressing ingredients

- 1 tbsp Italian seasoning
- 6 minced cloves garlic
- 6 tbsp lemon juice
- 5 tbsp nutritional yeast
- 3 tsp spicy mustard or honey
- 6 tbsp red wine vinegar
- 1/2 tsp salt

Salad ingredients

- 1 (15 oz) can black-eyed peas
- 2 chopped red onions
- 1 small broccoli head, chopped
- 1 (2.25 oz) can sliced black olives
- 1 chopped red pepper
- 1 lb cooked pasta noodles
- 1/2 lb halved cherry tomatoes
- 1 chopped cucumber

Directions:

1. Mix all the dressing ingredients well in a small bowl.
2. Toss the salad ingredients together, then drizzle with the dressing.
3. Stir carefully to combine the dressing and salad ingredients well.
4. Chill in the refrigerator and serve.

Freeze dry instructions:

1. Chill the pasta salad fully.
2. Spread the pasta salad evenly on freeze dryer trays lined with parchment paper or silicone mats.
3. Freeze dry as per your machine's guide.
4. Seal in airtight containers with oxygen absorbers.

To reconstitute:

1. Place the freeze-dried salad in a bowl and add enough water to cover it.
2. Stir gently and let it soak for a few minutes.
3. Chill before serving for a cooler, crisper taste.

Source: Renee and Tim, 2024

Celery and Chicken Tossed Salad

Savor this wholesome chicken salad bursting with crisp vegetables, juicy grapes, and crunchy cashews. This simple, flavorful meal is ideal for a quick lunch or a light evening supper.

Ingredients:

- 1/4 cup chopped green onions
- 1/2 cup celery
- 2 cups diced chicken
- 1/2 cup mayonnaise
- 1/2 cup quartered or halved grapes
- garlic powder, to taste
- 1/2 cup cashews (optional)
- salt and pepper, to taste

Directions:

1. Put the green onions, celery, chicken, and grapes in a large bowl.
2. Add water to reconstitute, let sit until fully absorbed, then pour off any surplus liquid.
3. Combine the remaining ingredients and stir well.
4. Place in the refrigerator to chill.
5. Serve.

Freeze drying instructions:

1. Spread the chicken and celery salad evenly on trays lined with parchment paper or silicone mats.
2. Make a note of the weight of the trays of food.
3. Freeze dry according to the machine's instructions.
4. When the process is complete, note down the weight of the trays. The weight difference indicates the amount of water needed for reconstitution.

To reconstitute:

1. Add the recommended amount of cold water.
2. Stir and let it rest for a few minutes until reconstituted.

Source: *Chicken Salad*, 2023

LIGHTWEIGHT CAMPING AND HIKING MEALS

Freeze-dried meals are ideal for the outdoors since they are lightweight and very easy to prepare. Just add boiling water!

Chili for the Trail

Warm up your adventures with this hearty, flavorful backpacker chili—easy to make and perfect for fueling your outdoor journeys!

Ingredients:

- 1 tbsp olive oil
- 2 tbsp granulated sugar
- 1 1/2 cups beef broth
- 1 can (15 oz) petite diced tomatoes
- 1 diced yellow onion
- 1 lb 90% lean ground beef
- 2 tbsp tomato paste
- 1 can (8 oz) tomato sauce
- 1 tbsp garlic powder
- 1 can (16 oz) red kidney beans, drained and rinsed
- 2 1/2 tbsp chili powder
- 2 tbsp ground cumin
- 1/2 tsp ground black pepper
- 1 1/2 tsp salt
- 1/4 tsp cayenne pepper (optional)
- parsley, to garnish (optional)

Directions:

1. Over medium-high heat for 2 minutes, heat the olive oil in a large pot.
2. Add the onion and, stirring occasionally, cook for 5 minutes.
3. Add the ground beef and cook until browned—about 6–7 minutes.
4. Add the cayenne pepper (optional), chili powder, cumin, garlic powder, pepper, salt, sugar, and tomato paste. Mix until everything is combined.

5. Still stirring, add the drained beans, diced tomatoes with their juice, broth, and tomato sauce.
6. Bring to a boil, then reduce to a gentle simmer. Cook uncovered, stirring frequently, for 20–25 minutes.
7. Take the pot off the stove and allow the chili to sit undisturbed for 5–10 minutes.
8. Serve, garnished with parsley (optional).

Freeze drying instructions:

1. Spread the chili thinly in trays lined with parchment paper or silicone mats.
2. Weigh and note down the weight of the trays of food.
3. Follow the freeze dryer instructions.
4. Once you've finished the freeze drying process, re-weigh the trays. The weight difference shows how much water you need to add to bring it back to its original state.

To reconstitute:

1. Add the recommended amount of hot water.
2. Stir and let it rest for a few minutes until reconstituted.
3. Adjust the water to your desired consistency.

Source: *Backpacker Chili*, 2023

Couscous and Brothy Mushroom Soup

The beef broth and mushrooms lend a hearty, full flavor and the couscous adds a delightful texture to this comfort food, which will crown a special day in the wild outdoors.

Ingredients:

- onion and garlic powder, to taste
- salt and pepper, to taste
- 1 cup couscous
- 2 cups boiling water
- 1 cup beef broth
- 1/2 cup chopped mushrooms
4. 1 tbsp butter or full-fat margarine (optional)

Directions:

1. Put the couscous into a mixing bowl or pot.

2. Pour the water over the couscous and stir. For a more creamy taste, stir in a tablespoon of butter.
3. Mix in the broth and mushrooms and add your seasonings to taste.
4. Cover the mixing bowl and let the mixture rest for about 5 minutes.
5. Scrape the mixture onto a lined tray and freeze dry. Package and store until your next outing.
6. To rehydrate the couscous and mushroom soup, add hot or boiling water, stir, and wait a couple of minutes before consuming.

Source: Cook Fanatic Team, 2025

Portable Low-Fat Lasagna

Imagine watching the sun set over a calm lake while sitting in front of a cozy campfire, with coffee brewing over the flames and warm lasagna waiting for dinner. If this appeals to you, you'll also be thrilled to be reminded that freeze-dried lasagna weighs almost nothing and will fit comfortably in your backpack. As an added bonus, this lasagna is low-fat and heart-healthy.

Ingredients:

For the sauce

- 10 oz (300 ml) low-fat milk
- 4 oz (100 g) grated low-fat cheese
- 2 tbsp cornstarch

For the filling

- 7 oz (200 g) lean ground meat (traditionally beef, but mutton is okay)
- 6 lasagna sheets
- 4 oz (100 g) white button mushrooms, washed and cut into quarters
- 1 finely chopped green bell pepper
- 1 finely chopped red bell pepper
- 2 peeled and crushed garlic cloves
- 6 fresh basil leaves, torn
- 1 small chopped onion
- 1 medium trimmed and sliced zucchini
- 14 oz (400 g) fresh or canned chopped tomatoes
- salt and pepper to taste

Directions:

For the sauce

1. In a small saucepan, make a paste from 3 tbsp of milk and the cornstarch.
2. Slowly pour and stir the rest of the milk into the paste and warm over medium heat.
3. Whisk until the sauce has a smooth consistency, then mix in the grated cheese. Leave a little cheese to top the lasagna later.

For the filling

1. While preparing the food, set your oven to preheat at 350 °F (180 °C).
2. Cook the ground beef over medium heat. Keep stirring to avoid clumps.

3. When the ground beef has browned, mix in the zucchini, mushrooms, onion, garlic, and bell peppers. Let the mixture cook for about 5 minutes.
4. Stir in the tomatoes and basil, then season with salt and pepper to taste.
5. Leave the filling to simmer for about 20 minutes with the lid on.

For the lasagna

1. In a lasagna dish, scrape in a third of the filling and lay two sheets of lasagna on top. Above that, lay another layer of filling followed by two lasagna sheets, and then the remaining filling and the last two sheets.
2. Spoon the sauce over the lasagna and sprinkle the remaining cheese on top.
3. Put in the preheated oven for about 25 minutes until the top is golden and the cheese is bubbling.
4. Let it cool, then cut it into slices that are slightly thinner than the height of your freeze drying tray. Lay the slices flat on a lined tray and freeze dry.
5. To rehydrate, slowly add boiling water and wait until the lasagna has absorbed all the water.

Source: British Heart Foundation, n.d.

FRUITS, VEGETABLES, AND VEGGIE DISHES

FRUITS

Freeze-Dried Fruit

Enjoy the natural sweetness and freshness of this freeze-dried fruit recipe—easy to prepare, nutritious, and perfect for snacks or adding to your favorite dishes anytime!

Ingredients:

- fruits of your choice—consider fruits like:
  - raspberries (space generously)
  - oranges (halved and very thinly sliced; space generously)
  - applesauce (arrange on trays in dollops or spread all over in an even layer)
  - passionfruit (sliced or diced)
  - blueberries (halved; arrange skin-side down; space generously)
  - watermelon (remove the rind)
  - nectarines (sliced, with or without skin)
  - bananas (sliced; pretreat with citric acid to avoid discoloration)
  - cantaloupe (diced)
  - pears (sliced or diced)
  - cherries (halve and pit; place cut-side down with ample spacing)
  - kiwi (sliced)
  - pineapple (sliced or diced)
  - lemons (halved and very thinly sliced; space generously)
  - strawberries (sliced)
  - coconut
  - avocado (lightly brush with lemon juice or dip avocado slices in a lemon juice bath—1 cup water and 1 tbsp lemon juice—to avoid discoloration)
  - apricots (sliced, with or without skin)
  - blackberries (space generously)
  - peaches (sliced or diced)
  - grapes (halve or quarter; arrange skin-side down; space generously)

- limes (halved and very thinly sliced; space generously)
- apples (thinly sliced; sprinkle cinnamon over slices before freezing for cinnamon apples)
- mango (sliced or diced)

Please note:

- Cherries take longer to freeze dry because of their high sugar content. To check doneness, bring them to room temperature—you'll know that they're ready when they're completely crunchy, not chewy.

Directions:

1. Prepare the fruit.

Freeze drying instructions:

1. Arrange the fruit on a parchment- or silicone-lined tray and freeze dry according to your machine's guidelines.

Source: *Freeze-Dried Fruit,* 2023

VEGETABLES

Freeze-Dried Vegetables

Freeze-dried vegetables are packed with flavor, nutrition, and convenience. Perfect for busy days or anytime you want a healthy, delicious dish in minutes!

Ingredients:

- vegetables of your choice—consider veggies like:
    - onions (raw or toasted; chopped or sliced)
    - zucchini (sliced, shredded, or spiralized)
    - mushrooms (chopped or sliced)
    - green onions (chopped)

- tomatoes (diced or sliced tomatoes can be ground into a powder after freeze drying for tomato sauce)
- cucumbers (sliced)
- olives
- peppers (jalapeño, bell, etc.; raw or toasted)
- peas (shelled)
- green beans (if freeze drying raw, blanch first, cut into small pieces)
- okra (sliced)
- kale
- spinach
- celery (chopped)
- asparagus (chopped)
- carrots (sliced, diced, or cut into spears)
- potatoes (diced no larger than 1/2 inch thick; for best results, blanch first)
- sweet potatoes (diced no larger than 1/2 inch thick)
- corn (raw or cooked)
- pumpkin (diced no larger than 1/2 inch thick, or pureed)
- squash (diced no larger than 1/2 inch thick)
- eggplant (sliced)
- beet (sliced or diced; peeled and cooked first)

Directions:

1. Prepare the veggies of your choice.

Freeze drying instructions:

1. Arrange the vegetables on parchment paper or silicone mats and freeze dry according to the machine's guidelines.

Source: *Freeze Dried Vegetables*, 2023

VEGGIE DISHES

Ginger Veggie and Tofu Stir Fry

Get ready to sizzle with this stir-fry—a flavorful, quick, and healthy dish that brings fresh veggies, fragrant ginger, and protein-packed tofu together in perfect harmony!

Ingredients:

- 1 tbsp sesame oil
- 3/4 cup water
- 1/4 carrot (cut into half circles)
- 3 cabbage leaves (cut into 3/4-inch squares)
- 1 tsp grated ginger
- 3.5 oz sprouts
- 1 tbsp salt with rice malt (shio-koji)
- 5 tbsp freeze-dried tofu
- salt and pepper, to taste

Directions:

1. Heat the sesame oil in a large pan over medium heat, then add the grated ginger and cook for 1 minute until aromatic.
2. Add the carrot, cabbage, and sprouts to the pan.
3. Stir-fry the vegetables for about 5 minutes until they start to soften, then add the tofu to the pan.
4. Pour in the water and add the salt with rice malt (shio-koji).
5. Stir everything together and cook for another 5 minutes until the tofu is rehydrated and the vegetables are tender.
6. Add salt and pepper to flavor.
7. Serve hot.

Freeze drying instructions for tofu:

1. Cut the tofu into small cubes.
2. Blanch the tofu cubes in boiling water for 1–2 minutes, then drain and pat dry.
3. Arrange the tofu cubes on freeze dryer trays in a single layer, making sure they don't touch.
4. Freeze dry according to your freeze dryer's instructions until fully dried and crispy.
5. Store in a sealed container away from heat and moisture.

To reconstitute tofu:

1. Add the desired amount of freeze-dried tofu to a bowl.
2. Pour warm water (or broth for extra flavor) over the tofu.
3. Let it soak for 5–10 minutes until it softens and rehydrates.
4. Drain excess water before adding the rehydrated tofu to recipes like stir-fries.

Source: Yagi, 2019

Crunchy Seasoned Peas

Seasoned peas make a flavorful and healthy snack. Easily freeze dried and seasoned to your taste, they're perfect for a quick and tasty treat.

Ingredients:

- seasoning of choice like:
    - all-purpose seasoning
    - salt and pepper
    - garlic salt
    - steak seasoning
- fresh or frozen peas

Freeze dry instructions:

1. If you've chosen to use fresh peas, shell them first.
2. Arrange the peas on trays lined with parchment or silicone mats.
3. Sprinkle your seasoning of choice over the peas.
4. Following your freeze dryer's instructions, freeze dry.

To reconstitute:

1. Measure and place the freeze-dried seasoned peas into a container or bowl.
2. Boil or heat water to about 1.5–2 times the volume of the freeze-dried peas.
3. Pour the hot water over the freeze-dried peas, ensuring they're fully submerged.
4. Cover the bowl or container to retain the heat.
5. Let the peas soak for about 10–15 minutes, or until they've fully rehydrated and softened.
6. Stir occasionally during soaking to help even rehydration.
7. Drain any excess water.
8. Use the reconstituted peas in your recipe or serve as desired.

Source: *Crunchy Peas*, 2023

Seasoned Veggie Chips

Try out this healthy, tasty snack made with your favorite veggies. Made from thinly sliced veggies flavored with your favorite seasonings, they're perfect for freeze drying.

Ingredients:

- seasonings like:
  - seasoning blend
  - all-purpose seasoning
  - seasoned salt
- veggies cut into thin rounds like:
  - beets
  - kale
  - squash
  - sweet potato
  - zucchini
- olive oil

Freeze drying instructions:

1. Arrange the vegetables on parchment- or silicone-lined trays, then follow the freeze dryer's instructions.
2. Spritz the freeze-dried vegetables with olive oil.
3. Sprinkle the seasoning on top and coat them by gently tossing.

To reconstitute:

1. Place the desired amount of freeze-dried seasoned veggie chips in a bowl or container.
2. Pour warm water over the chips—enough to fully cover them.
3. Let the chips soak for about 5–10 minutes to rehydrate.
4. Gently stir or press the chips occasionally to help soften them evenly.
5. Once rehydrated to your preferred texture, drain any excess water.
6. Use the reconstituted veggie chips immediately in your dish or as a snack.

Source: *Vegetable Chips*, 2023

Tangy Salt and Vinegar Zucchini Chips

Turn fresh zucchini into crispy, tangy chips you can enjoy all year! Marinated in olive oil, vinegar, and sea salt, these freeze-dried zucchini chips make a tasty, healthy snack or crunchy meal topper.

Ingredients:

- 2 tbsp olive or avocado oil
- 2 tsp salt
- 2 tbsp apple cider or white balsamic vinegar
- 2 medium thinly sliced zucchini with stems removed
- seasoning to taste (optional)

Directions:

1. Using a mixing bowl, make a marinade using the oil, vinegar, and salt.
2. Pour the marinade over the slices of raw zucchini and mix well.

Freeze drying instructions:

1. Arrange the marinated zucchini slices on lined freeze dryer trays and season them (optional).
2. Freeze dry according to the machine's instructions.

To reconstitute:

1. Place the desired amount of freeze-dried salt and vinegar zucchini chips in a bowl or container.
2. Pour cold or room temperature water over the chips—enough to fully cover them.
3. Let the chips soak for about 5–10 minutes to rehydrate, preserving the salt and vinegar flavor.
4. Gently stir or press the chips occasionally to ensure even rehydration.
5. Once they reach your preferred softness, drain any excess water.
6. Use the reconstituted zucchini chips right away in your dish or as a tangy snack.

Source: *Salt and Vinegar Zucchini Chips*, 2024

Creamy Garlic Mashed Potatoes

This creamy roasted garlic mashed potatoes recipe is delicious. It's perfect for freeze drying and quick rehydration whenever you want a comforting, cheesy side dish.

Ingredients:

- 4 tbsp butter
- 1/4–1/2 cup milk
- 2/3 cup shredded Parmesan cheese
- 7–9 peeled and cubed potatoes
- 1 head roasted garlic
- salt and pepper to season, as desired
- chopped chives for garnish (optional)

Directions:

1. Boil the potatoes in salted water over medium-high heat until tender and easily pierced, then drain and transfer to a bowl.
2. Add the salt and pepper, butter, cheese, and garlic to the bowl.
3. Combine all the ingredients and mash until the butter fully dissolves, using a masher or mixer.
4. Add the milk slowly until you have the desired consistency.
5. Garnish with chives, and serve hot.

Freeze drying instructions:

1. Spread the mashed potatoes evenly on parchment-lined or silicone-lined trays.
2. Weigh and make a note of the weight of the trays of food.
3. Process according to the freeze dryer's instructions.
4. Weigh the trays immediately after freeze drying. The difference in weight will be the recommended amount of water you'll need to use to reconstitute the dish.

To reconstitute:

1. Add the recommended amount of hot water.
2. Stir and let it rest for a few minutes until reconstituted.
3. You can add a little more or less water depending on your desired consistency.

Source: *Roasted Garlic Mashed Potatoes*, 2023

Veggie Crispies

It's super easy to make crispy vegetable chips if you use freeze-dried ingredients.

Ingredients:

- 1 cup freeze-dried green beans
- 1 cup freeze-dried carrots
- 2 tbsp olive oil
- 1 cup freeze-dried zucchini
- seasonings to taste

Directions:

1. Set your oven to 325 °F (160 °C) to preheat
2. Mix your preferred seasonings and the olive oil with the freeze-dried veggies in a bowl.
3. Lightly oil your baking tray or spray with a nonstick baking product and spread the prepared vegetables on the tray.
4. Pop in the oven until the veggies are crispy, which takes around 10–15 minutes.
5. Take your veggie crispies out of the oven and let them cool before eating.

Source: Wolfe, 2023

Sweet Potato Crunchy Chips

In the previous recipe, we made crunchy veggie chips from freeze-dried ingredients. This recipe shows you how to make crunchy chips from sweet potato and freeze dry them to last about 5 years (using oil) or 25 years (if you use an oxygen absorber and don't use oil).

Ingredients:

- 2 lb (900 g) sweet potato
- seasoning of your choice (such as 1 tbsp salt, 2 tsp onion powder, or 2 tsp smoked paprika for savory chips, or 1/3 cup brown sugar and 1 tbsp cinnamon for sweet chips)
- 1 tbsp olive oil or any other neutral oil you prefer

Directions:

1. Set your oven to 400 °F (200 °C) to preheat.
2. Peel the sweet potatoes, then slice them evenly to about 1/8 inch (3 mm) thickness.
3. Put the sweet potato slices in a bowl and cover them with cold water for a 30-minute soak.
4. Drain the slices in a colander and rinse them off with cold water. Leave the wet slices on a clean kitchen towel to dry.
5. When the sweet potato chips are dry, put them into a large mixing bowl. Toss the chips with the oil to coat the slices.
6. Add the seasoning and toss until all the chips are covered.
7. Place the chips in a single layer on baking trays lined with parchment.
8. Put the trays in the oven for 10 minutes, then rotate the trays, putting them back in the oven for another 10 minutes. Remove them from the oven after the full 20 minutes even if they aren't crispy, and leave them to cool.
9. While the chips are cooling, start up your freeze dryer. You'll have to wait a certain time (depending on the model and manufacturer) for the chamber to cool.
10. Load the freeze dryer trays with the chips in a single layer and load into the appliance. Close the drain valve and continue the cycle (18–36 hours).
11. When the chips are dry, package and store them.

Source: Becky, 2024a

DESSERTS AND SWEET TREATS

DESSERTS, PUDDINGS, AND SWEET TREATS

Chill and Shake Soft Serve Ice-Cream

Enjoy a creamy and delicious soft serve vanilla ice cream made quickly and easily with freeze-dried ice cream powder. This no-fuss recipe lets you create a cool, smooth treat right at home with just a few simple steps.

Ingredients:

- freeze-dried ice-cream powder

Directions:

1. Place the freeze-dried ice cream powder in a bowl and add the recommended reconstitution amount of water to it, then mix well.
2. Now grab a cooler, and put the jar in it under some ice.
3. Let it rest for about an hour.
4. Enjoy.

Source: *Soft Serve Vanilla Ice Cream Recipe*, 2023

Granny Smith's Secret Apple Pie

Packed with tangy Granny Smith apples, this homemade apple pie is a timeless classic made easy. With a delicious double crust and just the right touch of sweetness, it's perfect for sharing any time of year!

Ingredients:

- 6 cups Granny Smith apples
- 3 tbsp flour
- 1 9-inch double-crust thawed pie crust
- 1 tbsp butter
- 1/2 cup brown sugar
- 3 tbsp flour
- 2 tsp freeze-dried apple powder
- 3 tbsp plus 1 tsp water
- 1/2 cup white sugar plus extra for sprinkling

Directions:

1. Warm the oven to 425 °F (220 °C).
2. Peel and core the Granny Smith apples; set aside.
3. Melt the butter over medium heat, then whisk in the flour until smooth.
4. Add the freeze-dried apple powder, sugars, and water, then bring to a boil.
5. Allow the mixture to simmer uncovered for 3–5 minutes, then take it off the heat.
6. Press one pie crust into a 9-inch pie dish.
7. Roll out the remaining dough to overlap the crust by 1/2 inch; cut into eight 1-inch strips.
8. Evenly place the apple slices in the crust.
9. Lay four strips across the apples; fold and weave with the remaining strips to form lattice.
10. Trim and crimp the edges.
11. Slowly pour the liquid over the lattice and apples.
12. Brush the liquid over the lattice top; sprinkle with sugar (optional).
13. Bake for 15 minutes.
14. Lower the oven to 350 °F (180 °C) and bake until the apples are soft—about 35 minutes.
15. Serve warm or chilled.

Source: *Homemade Apple Pie*, 2025

Smooth and Creamy Cocoa Pudding

Satisfy your sweet tooth with this creamy, dreamy homemade pudding! Rich, silky, and oh-so-satisfying, this classic dessert is the perfect way to treat yourself anytime.

Ingredients:

- 2 tsp vanilla extract
- 3 tbsp cornstarch
- 3 egg yolks
- 1/2 cup cocoa powder
- 3 cups whole milk
- 1 1/2 cups granulated sugar

Directions:

1. Add the cocoa, cornstarch, and granulated sugar to a medium-sized saucepan.
2. Whisk the ingredients in the saucepan until they're well mixed.
3. Slowly add the milk and the egg yolks, stirring constantly until the mixture is smooth.

4. Stir continuously over medium-high heat until the mixture boils and thickens to your preference, then remove from the heat.
5. Stir in the vanilla extract.
6. Let the pudding cool and place it in your desired serving dishes.
7. Place the serving dishes in the refrigerator to completely cool down.
- Serve.

Freeze drying instructions:

1. Place trays lined with parchment paper or silicone mats on a clean, dry surface.
2. Pour the pudding into molds and pre-freeze before freeze drying for poppable bites, or spread thinly in trays to freeze dry into power form. Alternatively, you can drop spoonfuls of pudding onto trays to make cookie-like shapes.
3. Weigh and note down the weight of the trays of food.
4. Follow the freeze dryer instructions.
5. Once you've finished the freeze drying process, re-weigh the trays. The weight difference shows how much water you need to add to bring it back to its original state.

To reconstitute:

1. Add the recommended amount of water.
2. Stir and let it rest for a few minutes until reconstituted.
3. For optimal taste, refrigerate before serving.

Source: *Homemade Chocolate Pudding*, 2025

Cinnamon Pumpkin Roll Treat

This pumpkin roll is a deliciously soft spiced cake wrapped around a creamy, dreamy filling—perfect for cozy gatherings and festive celebrations. Let's roll up some pumpkin-flavored magic!

Ingredients:

For the cake

- 3/4 cup all-purpose flour
- 1 tsp vanilla extract
- 1 tsp ground cinnamon
- 2/3 cup freeze-dried pumpkin
- 3 large eggs
- 1 tsp baking soda
- 1 tsp pumpkin pie spice
- 1 cup granulated sugar
- 1/4 tsp salt

For the filling

- 1 tsp vanilla extract
- 8 oz cream cheese, softened
- 1 cup powdered sugar, plus extra for dusting (optional)
- 2 tbsp butter, softened

Directions:

1. Warm the oven to 350 °F (180 °C).
2. Line a 15- by 10-inch jelly roll pan with parchment, extending the paper beyond the long edges for easy lifting.
3. Whisk the baking soda, cinnamon, salt, flour, and pumpkin spice in a large bowl.
4. In another bowl, blend the sugar, pumpkin, vanilla, and eggs until smooth.
5. Mix the dry ingredients into the wet until no dry streaks remain.
6. Spread the batter evenly in pan and bake for 12–15 minutes, checking doneness with a toothpick. The batter will be ready when, after pricking the batter with a toothpick, the toothpick comes out clean.
7. Lift the hot cake using the parchment paper and carefully roll it with the paper from one short end. Cool completely on a wire rack.

8. Beat the butter, cream cheese, vanilla, and powdered sugar until smooth and airy.
9. Unroll the cake, spread the filling evenly, then roll up gently without the parchment paper.
10. Wrap in plastic wrap and chill in the fridge for at least 1 hour.
11. Optionally, dust with powdered sugar before slicing and serving.

Freeze drying instructions:

1. Prepare the pumpkin roll according to the recipe, including baking, filling, rolling, and refrigerating it.
2. After chilling, slice the pumpkin roll into individual serving portions.
3. Arrange the slices in a single layer on freeze dryer trays lined with parchment paper or silicone mats, without touching or overlapping.
4. Place the trays in the freeze dryer and begin the cycle.
5. Once the freeze drying is complete, remove the slices and store them in airtight vacuum-sealed bags or containers to maintain freshness and prevent moisture absorption.
6. Keep the freeze-dried pumpkin roll slices in a cool, dry spot, shielded from sunlight.

To reconstitute:

1. To rehydrate a freeze-dried pumpkin roll slice, remove it from the airtight packaging and place it on a plate or paper towel.
2. Lightly mist the slice with water using a spray bottle, or sprinkle a few drops of water evenly over the slice to moisten it.
3. Cover the slice loosely with plastic wrap or place it in a sealed container.
4. Let it sit at room temperature for about 10–20 minutes to absorb the moisture and soften.
5. Optionally, warm the rehydrated slice gently in a microwave for 10–15 seconds to enhance the texture and flavor.
6. Plate and, if desired, lightly sprinkle with powdered sugar.

Source: *Pumpkin Roll*, 2023

Freeze-Dried Berry or Fruit Cheesecake

This cheesecake recipe is suitable for your favorite berry or fruit and will delight even the most picky of taste buds.

Using freeze-dried berries with their intensified flavor will give your cheesecake a colorful, natural, and irresistible taste. This recipe has a secret ingredient (spices) that complements the aroma of the filling. The spices won't overwhelm the berries or fruit but will enhance the fruity flavors.

The cream cheese you use can affect the consistency. Philadelphia cream cheese works best.

Ingredients:

Spices

The spices you use will depend on your choice of fruit:

- 1/4 tsp Chinese five-spice powder for strawberry
- 1/4 tsp almond extract for cherry
- 1/8 tsp cardamom for mango
- 1/8 tsp ground cloves for banana
- 1/8 tsp ground cinnamon and 1/8 tsp ground cloves for cranberry

For the filling

- 3/4 cup sugar
- 1 3/4 cup heavy cream
- 16 oz (455 g) cream cheese (full fat and unflavored)
- 3 cups freeze-dried fruit or berries of your choice
- 3 tbsp fresh lemon juice (or orange juice if you're using cranberry)

For the crust

- 5 tbsp unsalted melted then cooled butter
- 2 cups graham crackers, Oreo wafers, or the biscuit of your choice
- pinch of kosher or table salt to taste

Directions:

1. Put the cookies in a strong bag and give it a couple of bashes with a rolling pin, or crumb them in a food processor.
2. Mix the crumbled cookies with the cooled melted butter. You can add a pinch of salt to the cookie–butter mix if that is to your taste.
3. Press the moist cookie mix into the bottom and sides of a shallow pie dish as evenly as you can. Put the pan in your fridge while making the cheesecake filling.
4. Use a mortar and pestle or food processor to make a powdered freeze-dried fruit or berry and sugar mix.
5. Stir the sugar mix with the cream cheese, a touch of spice matching the fruit or berry of your choice, and the lemon juice.
6. Use a wooden spoon or stand mixer with a paddle to blend the ingredients until the mixture is completely smooth.
7. Whisk the heavy cream into the sweet, creamy mixture until everything is thick and firm enough to hold a stiff peak.
8. Scrape the firm filling onto your crust in the pie pan in an even layer.
9. The cheesecake has to go into the fridge for about six hours to thicken. If you can resist eating the cheesecake right away, you can keep it in the fridge for a week.
10. Serve in slices as is or with fresh fruit slices or berries on top as an extra temptation.

Source: Parks, 2023

Chocolate Bark

Mixing fresh fruit into molten chocolate ruins the texture because there is simply too much moisture. Freeze-dried fruit blends perfectly and keeps the chocolate smooth and creamy.

Ingredients:

- 2 tbsp chopped nuts (optional)
- 1 cup freeze-dried berries of your choice
- 8 oz (28 g) white, milk, or dark chocolate chips

Directions:

1. Lay parchment paper on a baking tray.
2. Use a double boiler or your microwave to melt the chocolate chips.
3. Scrape the chocolate onto the paper and even it out.
4. Sprinkle the berries and nuts over the chocolate while it is still hot.
5. Refrigerate for 30 minutes to harden the chocolate bark.
6. To serve, break the bark into pieces of the desired size.

Source: Wolfe, 2023

FROSTINGS AND SWEET INGREDIENTS

Raspberry-Kissed Buttercream Frosting

Sweet and perfectly creamy, this raspberry-infused buttercream frosting is a vibrant twist on a classic favorite. Made with real freeze-dried raspberries, it's easy to whip up and adds a burst of berry flavor!

Ingredients:

- 3/4 cup freeze-dried raspberries
- 1 tsp pure vanilla extract
- 1/2 cup unsalted butter, softened
- 1/2 cup vegetable shortening
- 3 1/2 cups sifted powdered sugar
- pinch of salt

Directions:

1. Using a food processor, grind 3/4 cup freeze-dried raspberries into a fine powder.
2. On a high-medium speed, using a mixer, whip the vegetable shortening and butter until creamy. This should take about 1–2 minutes.
3. Add the crushed freeze-dried raspberries and vanilla extract, then blend on medium until smooth and combined.
4. Gradually incorporate the powdered sugar, adding 1 cup at a time while blending on a low setting.
5. Add the salt and, on low speed, mix for about 1–2 minutes until smooth and fully combined.
6. Spread onto 12 large cupcakes or a 9- by 13-inch cake.
7. Garnish with freeze-dried or fresh mint and raspberries.

Freeze drying instructions:

1. Prepare the buttercream frosting according to the recipe.
2. Spread the prepared frosting in a thin, even layer on freeze dryer trays lined with parchment paper or silicone mats.
3. Load the trays into the freeze dryer and initiate the drying process.
4. Once fully freeze dried, break the dried frosting into smaller pieces or grind into powder if desired.
5. Store the freeze-dried frosting pieces or powder in airtight vacuum-sealed bags or containers to prevent moisture absorption.
6. Store in a cool, dry, and shaded place.

To reconstitute:

1. To rehydrate freeze-dried buttercream frosting, place the desired amount of freeze-dried pieces or powder in a mixing bowl.
2. Gradually add room temperature unsalted butter or heavy cream to the powder while mixing on low speed.
3. Mix until the frosting reaches a smooth and creamy consistency, similar to fresh buttercream. Add additional liquid or butter as needed to adjust the texture.
4. Use immediately to frost cupcakes, cakes, or other desserts.
5. Refrigerate any leftovers and bring to room temperature before using.

Source: *Freeze Dried Raspberry Buttercream Frosting*, 2024

Homemade No-Cook Sweetened Condensed Milk

Make your own creamy sweetened condensed milk at home with a few ingredients. The result can be used in recipes that need 1 can of sweetened condensed milk. Perfect for baking, desserts, and all your favorite recipes—quick, easy, and delicious!

Ingredients:

- 3 tbsp butter
- 2/3 cup sugar
- 1 cup milk
- 1/3 cup boiling water

Directions:

1. Combine all the ingredients in a large bowl and blend until smooth using an electric mixer.

Freeze drying instructions:

1. Pour the sweetened condensed milk into trays lined with parchment paper or silicone mated.
2. Weigh the condensed milk trays, then follow the freeze dryer instructions to process.

To reconstitute:

1. Add the recommended amount of hot water.
2. Stir and let it rest for a few minutes until reconstituted.

Source: *Sweetened Condensed Milk*, 2023

CANDY, SNACKS, AND HEALTH BARS

CANDY

Butterscotch Treats

Indulge in these rich, buttery homemade caramel candies that melt in your mouth! With just a few ingredients and easy steps, you'll have sweet, chewy treats in no time.

Ingredients:

- 1 1/4 cups light corn syrup
- 2 cups heavy cream
- 2 1/4 cups sugar
- 6 tbsp unsalted butter, diced
- 1/2 tsp vanilla extract
- vegetable oil, for baking sheet
- 1/2 tsp coarse salt

Directions:

1. Grease a 9- by 13-inch pan, line with parchment extending 2 inches on the long sides, and lightly oil the paper.
2. In a large saucepan over high heat, bring the corn syrup, sugar, cream, and butter to a boil, stirring until the sugar dissolves.
3. Lower the heat to medium-high and cook for 15 minutes, checking with a sugar thermometer. Remove from the heat when the caramel reaches 248 °F (120 °C); stir in the vanilla and salt.
4. Pour onto the baking sheet and let sit uncovered at room temperature for 8–24 hours.
5. Transfer to a cutting board and slice into 3/4- by 1/4-inch pieces. Wrap each piece in cellophane or waxed paper for storage.

Freeze drying instructions:

1. Arrange the caramel pieces in a single layer on freeze dryer trays lined with parchment paper or silicone mats, making sure they don't touch or overlap.
2. Place the trays carefully into the freeze dryer.
3. Use the standard candy or sweet cycle on your freeze dryer.
4. After the cycle finishes, check that the caramels are fully dried, crisp, and no longer sticky or soft.
5. Keep in airtight or vacuum-sealed containers to block moisture.
6. tore in a cool, dry place for a longer shelf life.

To reconstitute:

1. Place the desired freeze-dried caramel pieces in a bowl.
2. Add just enough warm water or cream to cover the caramels lightly.
3. Soak for 10–15 minutes until soft, then drain the liquid.
4. Enjoy.

Source: Stewart, 2019

Fluffy Pillow Marshmallows

These homemade marshmallows are a cloud-like treat you can enjoy anytime! With just a few ingredients, you'll have melt-in-your-mouth marshmallows perfect for snacking, hot chocolate, or roasting by the fire.

Ingredients:

- 1 scraped vanilla bean pod
- 25 oz white caster sugar
- oil
- 13 leaves gelatin
- 3/4 cup cold water
- 1 1/4 cup water
- 3 large egg whites
- 1 1/2 tbsp liquid glucose

For dusting

- 4 tbsp cornstarch
- 4 oz powdered sugar

Directions:

1. Beat the egg whites in a large heatproof bowl with an electric mixer until soft peaks form; set aside.
2. Soak the gelatin in 3/4 cup cold water until softened.
3. In a large saucepan, combine 1 1/4 cups water, the liquid glucose, and the caster sugar.
4. Bring to a boil over medium-high heat and cook until the syrup reaches 266 °F (130 °C); remove from the heat.
5. Stir the softened gelatin into the hot syrup until dissolved, then transfer to a heatproof jug.
6. Whip the egg whites again until stiff peaks form.
7. Slowly pour the warm syrup into the egg whites while continuously mixing.
8. Beat until the mixture is smooth and glossy, then add the vanilla seeds.
9. Continue mixing for 8–10 minutes until thickened.
10. Line a large rectangular dish with plastic wrap and lightly oil it.
11. Combine the cornstarch and powdered sugar, then sift one-third of the mix into the dish to coat.
12. Pour the marshmallow batter into the dish, smooth the surface, and let it set for 2 hours.
13. Lay baking parchment on your workspace and sprinkle 1/3 of the cornstarch/sugar mixture evenly over it.
14. Turn the set marshmallow out onto the parchment and remove the plastic wrap.
15. Dust the marshmallow's top and a sharp knife with the cornstarch/sugar.
16. Cut into your desired shapes, dusting the cut edges and knife with more cornstarch/sugar to prevent sticking.
17. Coat all sides of the marshmallows with cornstarch/sugar.
18. Serve or refrigerate in a sealed container for up to 48 hours, placing parchment paper between each layer.

Freeze drying instructions:

1. Arrange the marshmallows in a single layer on freeze dryer trays lined with parchment paper or silicone mats, ensuring they don't touch.
2. Place the trays in the freeze dryer and run the freeze dry cycle.
3. Once freeze dried, store the marshmallows in airtight, moisture-proof containers or vacuum-sealed bags.

To reconstitute:

1. To rehydrate freeze-dried marshmallows, place the desired pieces in a bowl.
2. Lightly mist or sprinkle a small amount of water over the marshmallows.

3. Cover and leave at room temperature for 10–20 minutes to soften.
4. Enjoy.

Source: Nice, n.d.

Chewy Jelly Gummies

Get ready to make your own deliciously chewy, fruity gummy candies right at home! With simple ingredients and easy steps, these homemade gummies are a fun treat you can customize just the way you like.

Ingredients:

- 1/3 cup granulated sugar
- 3 tbsp plus 1 tsp unflavored gelatin dissolved in 1/3 cup water or juice
- extra 2/3 cup juice
- nonstick spray
- few drops flavoring or food coloring (optional)
- 1/8–1/4 tsp citrus zest (optional)

Directions:

1. Spray flat containers or silicone molds with nonstick spray and wipe off the excess. Set aside.
2. In a small bowl, dissolve the gelatin in 1/3 cup water or fruit juice.
3. Let the gelatin mix sit for 5 minutes.
4. In a saucepan, combine 1/3 cup sugar and 2/3 cup fruit juice. Constantly stir the mixture over medium heat until it reaches a boil and the sugar dissolves.
5. Stir the gelatin into the boiling mixture until fully dissolved and simmer for 5 minutes.
6. Remove from the heat, skim off any foam, and add the flavoring or food coloring and citrus zest if you so choose.
7. Pour into molds, then let rest at room temperature for 5 minutes.
8. Refrigerate for at least 1 hour until fully set, then remove.
9. For flat molds, run a knife around the edges, remove the gummy sheet, and cut into shapes.
10. Keep the gummies sealed at room temperature for no more than 7 days.

Freeze drying instructions:

1. Place the fully set gummy candies in a single layer on freeze dryer trays lined with parchment paper or silicone mats, ensuring they don't touch or overlap.
2. Arrange the trays carefully in the freeze dryer machine.
3. Set the freeze dryer to its standard fruit or candy freeze dry cycle.
4. Start the freeze drying process.
5. Once the cycle is complete, check that the gummies are thoroughly dry, crisp, and no longer sticky or soft.
6. Transfer the freeze-dried gummies to an airtight container or vacuum bag immediately to keep them dry.
7. Keep the freeze-dried gummies in a cool, dry place for an extended shelf life.

To reconstitute:

1. Place the desired amount of freeze-dried gummies in a bowl.
2. Add just enough water or fruit juice to cover the gummies lightly.
3. Let the gummies soak for about 10–15 minutes until they regain a soft, chewy texture.
4. Drain the excess liquid.
5. Enjoy!

Source: Ostrander, 2022

SNACKS

Classic Blueberry-Vanilla Muffins

Filled with juicy berries and a hint of vanilla, these muffins are the perfect treat. Easy to make and delicious to enjoy fresh or freeze dry for later!

Ingredients:

- 2 cups all-purpose flour
- 2 eggs
- 3/4 cup blueberries or aronia berries
- 1 tsp vanilla extract
- 1 1/2 tsp baking powder
- 3/4 cup milk
- 3/4 cup sugar

- 1/2 cup butter
- 1/2 tsp salt

Directions:

1. Set the oven to 375 °F (190 °C).
2. Beat the butter and sugar in a bowl. Add the vanilla, eggs, and milk; mix well. Set aside.
3. In another bowl, mix the dry ingredients (except the berries).
4. Gently mix the wet and dry ingredients.
5. Fold in the blueberries or aronia berries and let the batter sit for a few minutes.
6. Lightly oil the muffin tin, fill each cup 3/4 full, and bake for 25–30 minutes until a toothpick inserted in the center comes out clean.
7. Let the muffins rest for 5 minutes.
8. Serve hot or cold.

Freeze drying instructions:

1. Cool the muffins completely. Slice into halves or quarters.
2. Lay the muffin pieces in a single layer on freeze dryer trays.
3. Freeze dry per your machine's instructions.
4. Store the freeze-dried muffins in airtight containers or vacuum-sealed bags with oxygen absorbers. Correctly stored, they can be kept for 10–25 years.

To reconstitute:

1. Weigh the freeze-dried muffin pieces.
2. Add water equal to 60–70% of the muffins' weight.
3. Let soak until softened. Add more water if needed.

Source: Harvest Right, 2020

Creamy Citrus and Vanilla Cookies

These cookies taste like your favorite popsicle with a citrus burst and vanilla. Soft, chewy, and perfect for any snack or gathering!

Ingredients:

- 2 tbsp freeze-dried oranges (ground into powder) or orange zest
- 1/4 cup white sugar
- 3 oz orange Jell-O
- 1/4 cup flour
- 1 box white cake mix
- 6 tbsp butter, softened
- 1 cup powdered sugar
- 1 cup white chocolate chips
- 2 large eggs

Directions:

1. Preheat the oven to 375 °F (190 °C).
2. Cream the butter until light and fluffy.
3. Add the Jell-O and white cake mix, and mix well.
4. Beat in the eggs, then the freeze-dried oranges or zest.
5. Incorporate the flour until fully combined.
6. Fold the chocolate chips in lightly, then cover and place in the fridge to chill for about 30 minutes.
7. Next, combine the white sugar and powdered sugar in a small bowl.
8. Form the dough into 1/2-inch balls.
9. Roll each ball in the sugar mixture and put them on a greased or lined cookie sheet.
10. Place the cookie sheet into the preheated oven and bake for 10–12 minutes.

Source: *Orange Creamsicle Cookies*, 2024

Mini Yogurt Treats

These bite-size yogurt snacks are a healthy, refreshing treat anytime!

Ingredients:

- yogurt (Greek yogurt is not recommended)

Directions:

1. Arrange the yogurt in teaspoon-sized dollops on trays lined with parchment paper or silicone mats using a piping bag or spoon.
2. Follow the freeze dryer's guidelines to process.

To reconstitute:

1. Place the desired amount of freeze-dried yogurt bites in a bowl.
2. Add a small amount of warm water to lightly cover them.
3. Let them soak for a few minutes until they soften and regain a creamy texture.
4. Enjoy your refreshing yogurt bites as is or topped with fruit of your choice!

Source: *Yogurt Bites*, 2023

Crunchy Power Snack

This tasty trail mix combines crunchy nuts, sweet chocolate, and flavorful freeze-dried fruits for a perfect on-the-go snack. Quick to make and great to store!

Ingredients:

- 1/4 cup plain coconut flakes
- 1/4 cup chocolate chips or candies
- 1 cup freeze-dried fruit like:
    - blueberries
    - mango
    - pineapple
- 1/2 cup pepitas
- 1 cup roasted almonds
- 1 cup cashews

Directions:

1. Combine the ingredients in a bowl and then seal them in an airtight container or bag.

Source: *Trail Mix*, 2023

HEALTH BARS

Blueberry Power Bars

Blueberry bars are a wholesome and convenient snack! Made with juicy blueberries, oats, and naturally sweet applesauce, they're perfect for a quick, nourishing treat.

Ingredients:

- 3/4 cup raw oats
- 3 cups blueberries
- 1 cup applesauce

Directions:

1. Line freeze dryer trays with parchment paper or silicone mats, then position the tray dividers securely on top.
2. Put the blueberries in a blender, and blend till they're a puree.
3. Add the oats and applesauce to the blueberries and blend again.
4. Pour the blended mixture into your lined freeze dryer trays.
5. Place the lids on the freeze dryer trays, then freeze them in a standard freezer.
6. When frozen, place the trays in the freeze dryer.
7. Select frozen mode and process.
8. Once processed, bag and store.

To reconstitute:

1. Take the desired amount of freeze-dried blueberry bars.
2. Add warm water gradually to the bars, starting with about half the volume of the bars you want to rehydrate.
3. Let the bars soak for several minutes until they soften and regain a chewy texture.
4. Add more water if needed to reach your preferred consistency.
5. Enjoy your blueberry bars!

Source: *Blueberry Bars*, 2025

Fruity Crunch Bars

Crunchy and packed with fruit flavor, these cereal bars are the perfect easy snack to fuel your day. Made with your favorite cereal, fruit, and a splash of milk or creamer, they're quick to whip up and great anytime!

Ingredients:

- fruit
- cold cereal
- yogurt, cream, or coffee creamer
- milk

Directions:

1. Place tray dividers onto parchment paper or silicone mats inside freeze dryer trays.
2. Fill the prepared trays with cereal and your choice of fruit.
3. Pour milk, yogurt, or cream over the fruit and cereal until fully submerged. This liquid acts as the binding agent for all of the ingredients. For an ideal texture, I recommend a mix of 90% milk and 10% sugar-free creamer.
4. Secure the trays with freeze dryer lids and place them in the regular freezer to pre-freeze.
5. Once frozen solid, load the trays into the freeze dryer and process in frozen mode.
6. Package and store the dried snacks or enjoy them immediately.

Source: *Freeze-Dried Cereal Bars*, 2024

Spiced Pumpkin Oat Bars

Enjoy the comforting flavors of pumpkin pie bars—a delicious twist on a classic dessert. A nutty oat and pecan crust pairs perfectly with a creamy spiced pumpkin filling made from pumpkin puree and warm autumn spices.

Ingredients:

For the crust

- 1/4 melted coconut oil, plus extra for greasing
- 1/2 tsp ground cinnamon
- 1/4 cup maple syrup
- 1 tsp vanilla extract
- 1/4 tsp ground ginger
- 1 cup pecans
- 1 1/2 cup rolled oats
- 1/2 tsp sea salt

For the filling

- 1 tsp vanilla extract
- 1/4 cup full-fat coconut milk
- 1/2 cup maple syrup
- 15 oz pumpkin puree
- 1/2 tsp ground nutmeg
- 1 tsp ground ginger
- 1/8 tsp ground cardamom
- 1 pinch ground cloves
- 1 tsp ground cinnamon
- 2 eggs
- 1/4 tsp salt

Directions:

1. Preheat the oven to 350 °F (180 °C).
2. Grease an 8- by 8-inch baking pan with coconut oil and line it with parchment paper.

Prepare the crust

1. Place the rolled oats and pecans in a food processor and blend on high until they're finely ground into a flour-like texture.
2. After blending, pour the oatmeal and pecan mixture into a large bowl, then add the cinnamon, ginger, and sea salt. Mix well to combine.
3. Combine the coconut oil, maple syrup, and vanilla with oats until thickened.
4. Pour the mixture into the baking dish and press it down firmly and evenly with your hands, making sure to cover all the corners.
5. Pierce the crust repeatedly with a fork.
6. Bake for 10–12 minutes until the edges are golden brown.
7. When the crust is done baking, take it out of the oven and let it sit for around 5 minutes to cool slightly.

Prepare the filling

1. In a large bowl, mix together all the filling ingredients, whisking until fully combined. Then set it aside.

Complete the pumpkin bars

1. Once the crust has cooled, evenly pour the filling over it and bake for 45–50 minutes until set.

2. When done, take the dish out of the oven and let it cool completely.
3. Once cooled, cut into 9 squares.

To freeze dry:

1. Prepare and bake the pumpkin pie bars as per the recipe and allow them to cool completely.
2. Cut the bars into individual squares.
3. Arrange the squares in a single layer on freeze dryer trays lined with parchment paper or silicone mats, ensuring they don't touch or overlap.
4. Place the trays in the freeze dryer and run the freeze-drying cycle according to your machine's instructions until the bars are fully dried and crisp.
5. Remove the freeze-dried bars and store them in airtight containers or vacuum-sealed bags to keep moisture out.

To reconstitute:

1. Take the desired number of freeze-dried pumpkin pie bars.
2. Add warm water slowly to the bars, starting with around half the volume of the bars.
3. Allow the bars to soak for several minutes until they soften and regain a moist texture.
4. Add more water if needed to achieve your preferred consistency.
5. Enjoy!

Source: *Pumpkin Pie Bars*, 2023

SUPER QUICK FREEZE-DRIED YUMMIES

The following recipes are so quick that the prep time is just a minute or two. The addition of a freeze-dried ingredient gives a master chef's touch to foods you already have.

Veggie Party Dip

A vegetable-based dip is perfect for parties where some of the guests are vegan or vegetarian. Carnivores will also love the taste! Use sour cream or plain Greek yogurt as a base, then add seasonings such as salt, pepper, paprika, and onion powder with ground freeze-dried vegetables. Stir until all the ingredients are well mixed. Put into a shallow container and serve as is.

Savory Summer Popsicles

Aren't popsicles supposed to be sweet? Yes—unless you are a creative freeze dryer! Mix tomato juice with rehydrated veggies and season according to your taste. Put them in the freezer and enjoy for a surprisingly delicious and refreshing treat.

Fruit Leather

Fruit leather's concentrated taste makes freeze-dried fruit the ideal ingredient. Rehydrate the freeze-dried fruit of your choice, puree it, and use the back of a spoon to spread it evenly on parchment paper in a baking tray. Leave to dry, then break off pieces to eat as is.

Trail Mix

Add a handful of freeze-dried banana, pineapple, or berries to your trail mix, or make your own trail mix from scratch with peanuts, rolled oats, chocolate chips, coconut, and freeze-dried fruits in the combination of your taste. Surprise your loved ones with this treat in their lunchboxes, or take a bagful along on a hike for an energizing, filling snack on the go.

French Toast Voilà!

French toast is a trusted old favorite in many a kitchen. Simply dip bread in whisked and seasoned raw egg and fry in a pan on both sides. Some people prefer to eat it with a little cinnamon sugar on top, some with tomato sauce. As a freeze-dried fruit expert, you have more choices—sprinkle ground freeze-dried berries, apricots, or peaches on your French toast with perhaps a little maple syrup.

Next-Level Yogurt Snack

What takes this yogurt snack to the next level is its healthy ingredients and incredible taste. Mix Greek yogurt with honey or maple syrup and vanilla (or coconut oil for a creamier texture) according to taste and stir in a handful of your favorite freeze-dried fruits or berries. Spoon bite-sized amounts onto a lined freeze dryer tray and freeze dry. Eat the snack as is or pour a little molten chocolate over the pieces for extra sweetness.

Sweet and Red Bites

This snack is made from sweetened cranberries and can be eaten freeze dried without rehydration. Take 4 lb frozen or fresh cranberries and chop them manually or with a food processor on the pulse setting. Mix the berries with 4 cups orange juice or apple cider and 1 1/2 cups sugar. After thoroughly mixing everything together, wait about 30 minutes for all the sugar to dissolve. Pour the mixture onto your lined tray and freeze dry. Break the product into smaller pieces and package with an oxygen absorber.

If you prefer this snack rehydrated, pour water slowly over the freeze-dried cranberries. The secret is to rehydrate without adding too much water, because if you have so much added water that it pools at the bottom of your container, the taste will be lost. It will just taste bland and boring instead of being the sweet and tart combination you want.

Oatmeal Refuelers

This protein-rich snack beats the afternoon slump in a tasty, filling way that won't spoil your dinnertime appetite. Slice apples, pears, or peaches evenly to about 1 inch (2.5 cm) thickness. Add the slices to cooked oatmeal and mix thoroughly. Spoon bite-sized scoops onto a lined freeze dryer tray. Freeze dry, package, and enjoy as is when you need a tummy refill or an energy refuel.

Peckish for a Pickle

To enjoy the taste of pickle juice without an overwhelmingly strong flavor, soak sliced cucumber in a bowl of pickle juice for a day or two. Put in a colander to drain, pat dry with a clean kitchen towel, and freeze dry. These pickle-flavored cucumbers can be eaten as is.

BEVERAGES

Floral and Fruit Fusion Water

Stay refreshed with this easy freeze-dried infused water! Packed with natural fruit and floral flavors, it's a tasty way to enjoy water.

Ingredients:

Pick your preferred fruits and botanicals to freeze dry; some favorites might include:

- cucumber
- hibiscus
- lavender
- lemons
- mint
- orange
- pineapple
- raspberries
- rose
- strawberries

Freeze drying instructions:

1. Evenly layer the botanicals or fruit onto trays lined with parchment paper or silicone mats.
2. Follow your freeze dryer's specific guidelines to complete the drying process.

To reconstitute:

1. Select your favorite freeze-dried fruits and botanicals and add them to a pitcher or water dispenser.
2. Fill the pitcher or water dispenser with water and ice to keep it cool.
3. Let the botanicals or fruit reconstitute and their flavors blend into and infuse the water.

4. Enjoy your refreshing, naturally flavored drink!

Source: *Freeze-Dried Infused Water*, 2023

Peach Pineapple Refresher

This bright and tasty blend of juicy peaches and sweet pineapple is a perfectly refreshing drink any time of day! Your taste buds will thank you for this delicious beverage.

Ingredients:

- 6 cups water
- 1/2 cup pineapple pieces
- 3 cups sliced peaches
- 1/2 carton frozen apple juice concentrate

Directions:

1. Using a blender, combine the ingredients until completely smooth.
2. Strain the blend through a fine sieve into a large bowl to remove pulp.
3. Pour into glasses.
4. Enjoy.

Freeze dry instructions:

1. Pour the juice into freeze dryer trays.
2. Freeze dry until dry flakes form.
3. Store in airtight containers.

To reconstitute:

1. Combine 1 part freeze-dried juice powder with 3–4 parts water.
2. Stir until dissolved; adjust the water to taste.
3. Serve chilled.

Source: Thrive Life, n.d.-d

On-the-Go Lemonade Blend

Quench your thirst with this refreshing freeze-dried lemonade! This easy-to-make mix captures all the tangy, sweet goodness of fresh lemonade and is perfect for on-the-go sipping or brightening up any drink.

Ingredients:

- 2 large lemons, pith stripped
- 2 tbsp plus 1 tsp granulated sugar
- 5 cups cold water

Directions:

1. Wash the lemons well.
2. Extract the white pith from the lemons. You can do this by cutting the lemon in half, then using a spoon or knife to carefully scrape out the white pith from inside without damaging the rind.
3. Slice the lemons, keeping the rind intact. You can do this by slicing the lemon crosswise or lengthwise with a sharp knife, cutting through the flesh but leaving the rind intact.
4. Blend until smooth.
5. Add the cold water and granulated sugar.
6. Transfer the mixture onto silicone-lined freeze drying trays.
7. Freeze dry according to the machine's instructions.
8. Grind into a fine powder and then store.

How to use:

1. Mix 1 cup of water with 1/3 cup of powder until dissolved.
2. Refrigerate before serving.

Source: *Freeze-Dried Lemonade*, 2024

Berry Bliss Lemonade

Bright, sweet, and tangy, strawberry lemonade is the perfect refreshing drink. Made with freeze-dried strawberries for a burst of flavor, it's a delicious twist on a classic favorite!

Ingredients:

- 3 tbsp granulated sweetener
- 3 cups homemade or store-bought lemonade
- 3 cups freeze-dried strawberries

Directions:

1. Grind the strawberries into a fine powder.
2. Add 3 tablespoons of granulated sweetener to the strawberries and place in a blender.
3. Pour 1 cup of lemonade into the blender and pulsate.
4. Add the remaining lemonade and stir well.
5. Chill in the fridge before serving.

Source: *Strawberry Lemonade*, 2024

Festive Berry Bliss Punch

Celebrate the season with this delicious punch! Bursting with berries and citrus flavors, this drink promises to be a sparkling, refreshing crowd-pleaser perfect for any occasion.

Ingredients:

- 1/2 cup orange juice
- 4 cups ice
- 1 cup freeze-dried strawberries
- 1/4 cup lemon juice
- 1/2 cup freeze-dried cranberries
- 1/2 cup freeze-dried raspberries
- 3 cups ginger ale, Sprite, or sparkling water
- 4 cups cran-strawberry juice
- 1/2 cup freeze dried pineapple (optional)

Directions:

1. In a large container of your choice, add all the juices and stir.
2. Stir in the freeze-dried fruit, making sure that all the fruit is covered with liquid.
3. Add the ginger ale, Sprite, or sparkling water.
4. Place the container in the fridge for about an hour so the fruit can soften.
5. When the fruit softens, transfer the punch to a bowl and add ice.
6. Serve.

Source: *Fruity Holiday Punch*, 2024

Immunity Boosting Emergen-C

Stay healthy with this easy Immunity Boosting Emergen-C! Made from freeze-dried citrus and ginger, just mix the powder with water for a tasty, refreshing drink that helps support your immune system.

Ingredients:

- 2 tbsp freeze-dried orange
- 1/2-inch piece sliced, freeze-dried ginger
- 2 cups freeze-dried tangerine segments
- 1 tsp freeze-dried lemon
- 1/2 cup maple syrup powder

Directions:

1. Grind all the ingredients, except the tangerine segments and maple syrup powder, into a fine powder in a coffee grinder or a food processor.
2. Add the tangerine segments and maple syrup powder and grind into a fine powder again.
3. Place the fine powder in an airtight container.

To reconstitute:

1. Add 1 or 2 tablespoons of the powder into 8 oz of water and stir.

Source: *DIY Emergen-C*, 2023

Nature's Green Boost Smoothie

Start your day with this easy, healthy smoothie. Blend fruits and vegetables with ice for a quick, revitalizing drink.

Ingredients:

- 8–10 ice cubes
- 1 cup milk or water
- 1 freeze-dried kiwi
- 1/2 chopped freeze-dried pear
- 1/2 small cucumber, peeled and diced
- 1 roughly chopped freeze-dried green apple
- 1 chopped freeze-dried celery stalk
- 1/2 freeze-dried medium avocado
- 3/4 cup freeze-dried baby spinach

Directions:

1. Combine all the ingredients in a high-speed blender and process on maximum for 45–60 seconds until silky smooth.
2. Enjoy and be refreshed.

Special note:

- Give it a quick taste and tweak it to your liking—add extra fruit or a splash of pineapple or apple juice for that perfect sweet kick!

Source: *Green Goddess Smoothie*, 2024

Nutmeg-Kissed Creamy Eggnog

Who can resist the smooth, velvety charm of eggnog? With freeze-dried homemade eggnog, you can savor that luscious, creamy delight anytime and anywhere you want.

Ingredients:

- 6 large egg yolks
- 1/2 tsp ground nutmeg
- 1/2 cup granulated sugar

- 2 cups milk
- 1 cup heavy whipping cream
- 1/4 tsp vanilla extract
- salt to taste
- ground cinnamon (optional)
- aniseed (optional)

Directions:

1. In a medium bowl, beat the egg yolks and sugar until the mixture becomes creamy and light.
2. Over medium-high heat in a saucepan, stirring frequently, combine the nutmeg, salt, milk, and whipping cream until the mixture just starts to simmer.
3. Spoonful by spoonful, slowly add the hot milk to the egg mixture, whisking quickly after each addition.
4. Return the mixture to the saucepan and heat it on the stove. Add the ground cinnamon and aniseed if you've chosen to use these ingredients.
5. Whisk briskly for 1–2 minutes until the mixture thickens slightly and reaches 160 °F. Remove from the heat and stir in the vanilla as it cools and thickens further.
6. Pour the mixture through a fine sieve to remove lumps, then transfer to a container.
7. Cover the container and chill in the refrigerator until cold.

Freeze drying instructions:

1. Pour the eggnog onto trays lined with parchment paper or silicone mats.
2. Weigh and note down the weight of the trays of food.
3. Follow the freeze dryer instructions.
4. Once you've finished the freeze drying process, re-weigh the trays. The weight difference shows how much water you need to add to bring it back to its original state.

To reconstitute:

1. Add the recommended amount of water.
2. Stir and let it rest for a few minutes until reconstituted.

Source: *Creamy Homemade Eggnog*, 2024

Sweet Strawberry Milk Blend

Savor the fresh, sweet flavor of homemade strawberry milk made with real freeze-dried strawberries. This simple, natural mix is perfect for kids and adults.

Ingredients:

- 2 tbsp sugar
- 2/3 cup freeze-dried milk
- 3/4 cup freeze-dried strawberries
- pinch salt

Directions:

1. Combine the ingredients.
2. Rehydrate with 2 cups of milk when you're ready, or double the recipe to have a convenient mix ready to go. It's also tasty with cookies or cupcakes, or on ice cream!

Source: *Strawberry Milk Mix*, 2024

Icy Strawberry Coconut Milk Delight

Enjoy this cool, creamy strawberry milk drink made with smooth coconut milk and bursting with the natural sweetness of strawberries. It's a refreshing treat that's perfect when you want a fruity, icy beverage.

Ingredients:

- 1 oz coconut milk
- 1 cup ice cubes
- 1 oz strawberry fruit puree
- 1/4 cup freeze-dried strawberries

Directions:

1. Mix the strawberry puree with 2/3 cup ice, then add the coconut milk and stir in the strawberries.
2. Fill the rest of the cup with a few more freeze-dried strawberries if you like, and the rest of the ice.

Special note:

- The longer the freeze-dried strawberries soak in the drink, the more tender they'll become.

Source: *Pink Drink Copycat*, 2023

PETS AND HOME

DOG FOOD

Tail-Wagging Turkey and Veggie Mix

Every dog lover wants to make sure their beloved fur babies are also eating healthy food. This recipe will have your pet both happy and healthy.

Ingredients:

- 2 cups brown rice
- 8 oz mixed frozen broccoli, carrots, and cauliflower
- 1 tsp dried rosemary
- 1 lb ground turkey
- 6 cups water

Directions:

1. Put the rice, water, and rosemary in a large pot.
2. Break the turkey into small pieces and add it to the mix.
3. Combine thoroughly to ensure the turkey is evenly distributed throughout.
4. Bring the mixture to a boil over high heat, then simmer gently for 20 minutes over low heat.
5. Add the frozen vegetables, cook for 5 minutes, then remove from the heat to cool.
6. Refrigerate until you need to use it.

Freeze drying instructions:

1. Put your four-legged kid's meals evenly on trays lined with parchment paper or silicone mats.
2. Weigh and note down the weight of the trays of food.
3. Follow the freeze dryer instructions.
4. Once you've finished the freeze drying process, re-weigh the trays. The weight difference shows how much water you need to add to bring it back to its original state.

To reconstitute:

1. Add the recommended amount of hot water.
2. Stir and let it rest for a few minutes until reconstituted.

Special note:

- Larger dog breeds can be fed 2 cups in the morning and in the afternoon.

Source: *Freeze-Dried Dog Food*, 2023

CAT FOOD

Kitty's Purrfectly Tender Chicken Delight

Treat your furry friend to a homemade delight with this irresistible chicken cat food recipe! Packed with tender chicken and wholesome ingredients, it's a purr-fect way to show your kitty some love.

Ingredients:

- 1 tsp olive oil
- 3 oz baked dark chicken meat
- 1/4 cup boiled potato
- 1/4 cup boiled white rice

Directions:

1. Mix the ingredients together, and meow! The dish is ready to be served.
2. Seal leftovers in airtight containers and store in the fridge.

Freeze drying instructions:

1. Put the ready-to-be-enjoyed cat food evenly on trays lined with parchment paper or silicone mats.
2. Weigh and note down the weight of the trays of food.
3. Follow the freeze dryer instructions.
4. Once you've finished the freeze drying process, re-weigh the trays. The weight difference shows how much water you need to add to bring it back to its original state.

To reconstitute:

1. Add the recommended amount of hot water.
2. Stir and let it rest for a few minutes until reconstituted.

Source: *Cat Food*, 2023

PET TREATS

Pet treats made from freeze-dried ingredients are cost-effective, versatile, and nutritious. Many store-bought pet treats are unhealthy, may cause allergies, and are brimming with additives and artificial preservatives. Making the treats at home gives you control over the ingredients so you can give your furry companions the yummy treats they deserve.

Meat and Sweet Potato Bites

Cut two chicken breasts (or turkey, ham, beef, fish, or mutton) into small blocks and thinly slice a sweet potato or pumpkin (peeled or unpeeled; either will do). Lay them out on a lined tray and freeze dry. Package and store, or hand them out right away to your cat or dog.

Peanut Butter Sweet Banana Treat

To make this treat, which is loved by most four-legged housemates, simply spread some unsalted peanut butter over sliced banana and freeze dry. Hand out the treats every time your furry buddy looks at you with pleading eyes.

Liver Slivers

This super-nutritious snack is ridiculously easy to make. Slice beef livers to about 1 inch (2.5 cm) thickness or cut chicken livers in half, then freeze dry. Hand out only as occasional treats since liver is very nutrient-dense.

HOME ESSENTIALS

Natural Heartwarming Simmer Pot

Infuse your home with the cozy, inviting scents of this Natural Heartwarming Simmer Pot, made with ingredients that fill the air with comforting aromas perfect for any season.

Ingredients:

- 3–4 freeze-dried orange slices
- 4 cups water
- 3–4 freeze-dried apple slices
- 2–3 crushed freeze-dried rosemary sprigs for even blending
- 2–3 cinnamon sticks
- 1/4 cup freeze-dried cranberries
- essential oils of choice (optional)

Directions:

1. Put 4 cups water in a pot to help rehydrate the ingredients.
2. Over low to medium heat, bring the pot to a gentle simmer. As the pot simmers, enjoy the scents that fill your home. If the water level becomes low, add more water.

Special note:

- This simmer pot lasts for days; just add water and reheat to renew the scent.

Source: *Freeze-Dried Holiday Simmer Pot*, 2023

ABOUT THE AUTHOR

Charles Johansson is a seasoned expert in food production and preservation with years of hands-on experience in freeze drying techniques. Combining his deep knowledge of the science behind food preservation with a passion for discovering delicious, practical recipes, Charles aims to empower home cooks to confidently preserve their food and reduce waste.

As a trusted advisor who understands the impact of global trends on food safety and quality, he blends technical expertise with real-world insight. Charles also enjoys sailing the world and sharing his journey of faith and adventure. His mission is to help others discover the art and joy of freeze drying, making it accessible and enjoyable for every home cook.

"Watch ye therefore, and pray always, that ye may be accounted worthy to escape all these things that shall come to pass, and to stand before the Son of man." Luke 21:36 KJV

REFERENCES

Andress, E., & Harrison, J. (n.d.). *Preparing an emergency food supply, short term food storage.* College of Family and Consumer Sciences, University of Georgia. https://www.fcs.uga.edu/extension/preparing-an-emergency-food-supply-short-term-food-storage

Backpacker chili. (2023, July 20). Prep4Life. https://p4lfood.com/blogs/recipes/backpacker-chili

BBQ pulled pork recipe. (2023, July 24). Prep4Life. https://p4lfood.com/blogs/recipes/bbq-pulled-pork-recipe

Becky. (2024a, June 4). *Freeze dried sweet potato chips.* The Seasonal Homestead. https://www.theseasonalhomestead.com/freeze-dried-sweet-potato-chips/

Becky. (2024b, November 2). *Freeze dried cranberries recipe.* The Seasonal Homestead. https://www.theseasonalhomestead.com/freeze-dried-cranberries/

Becky. (2024c, December 18). *How to use a freeze dryer & tips.* The Seasonal Homestead. https://www.theseasonalhomestead.com/how-to-use-a-freeze-dryer-tips/

Best green bean casserole. (2023, December 22). Prep4Life. https://p4lfood.com/blogs/recipes/best-green-bean-casserole

Blueberry bars. (2025, February 3). Prep4Life. https://p4lfood.com/blogs/recipes/blueberry-bars

bobtaylor12. (2023, July 20). *The pros and cons of repairing vs. replacing appliances.* Service Works. https://blog.service.works/service-business/appliance-repair/the-pros-and-cons-of-repairing-vs-replacing-appliances/

British Heart Foundation. (n.d.). *Low-fat lasagne recipe.* https://www.bhf.org.uk/informationsupport/support/healthy-living/healthy-eating/recipe-finder/low-fat-lasagne-recipe

Bucket brine smoked turkey. (2023, November 8). Prep4Life. https://p4lfood.com/blogs/recipes/bucket-brine-smoked-turkey

Butternut squash casserole. (2024, September 26). Prep4Life. https://p4lfood.com/blogs/recipes/butternut-squash-casserole

Butternut squash soup. (2024, September 5). Prep4Life. https://p4lfood.com/blogs/recipes/butternut-squash-soup

Buttery herb stuffing. (2024, October 30). Prep4Life. https://p4lfood.com/blogs/recipes/buttery-herb-stuffing

Campbell, R. (2024, August 30). *Freeze-drying could boost food sustainability and security*. Engineering News. https://www.engineeringnews.co.za/article/freeze-drying-could-boost-food-sustainability-and-security-2024-08-14-1

Cat food. (2023, February 23). Prep4Life. https://p4lfood.com/blogs/recipes/cat-food

Cheddar broccoli soup with The CUBE. (2024, November 6). Prep4Life. https://p4lfood.com/blogs/recipes/cheddar-broccoli-soup-with-the-cube

Cheese stuffed shells. (2023, February 23). Prep4Life. https://p4lfood.com/blogs/recipes/cheese-stuffed-shells

Cheeseburger casserole recipe. (2023, August 26). Prep4Life. https://p4lfood.com/blogs/recipes/cheeseburger-casserole-recipe

Cheesy potato soup. (2023, February 23). Prep4Life. https://p4lfood.com/blogs/recipes/cheesy-potato-soup

Chicken and vegetable stew. (n.d.). Whatsfordinner. https://whatsfordinner.co.za/r/chicken-and-vegetable-stew.html/212483

Chicken and zucchini casserole. (2023, August 14). Prep4Life. https://p4lfood.com/blogs/recipes/chicken-and-zucchini-casserole

Chicken bacon ranch casserole. (2023, December). Prep4Life. https://p4lfood.com/blogs/recipes/chicken-bacon-ranch-casserole

Chicken salad. (2023, February 23). Prep4Life. https://p4lfood.com/blogs/recipes/chicken-salad

Cold soak chicken salad: Just-add-water backpacking recipe. (n.d.). Road Trip Addict. https://roadtripaddict.com/backpacking-recipes/cold-soak-chicken-salad/

Comparing freeze-dried vs. traditional food storage methods. (2024, January 24). Flex Foods. https://www.flexfoodsltd.com/blog/comparing_freeze_dried_vs_traditional_food_storage_methods.php

Cook Fanatic Team. (2025, March 9). *10+ freeze drying recipes for deliciously preserved treats*. Cook Fanatic. https://cookfanatic.com/freeze-drying-recipes/

Crack chicken chili. (2024, September 26). Prep4Life. https://p4lfood.com/blogs/recipes/crack-chicken-chili

Crack chicken soup. (2023, December 28). Prep4Life. https://p4lfood.com/blogs/recipes/crack-chicken-soup

Creamy homemade eggnog. (2024, December 9). Prep4Life. https://p4lfood.com/blogs/recipes/creamy-homemade-eggnog

Crock pot green enchilada chicken soup. (2023, November 3). Prep4Life. https://p4lfood.com/blogs/recipes/crock-pot-green-enchilada-chicken-soup

Crock pot lemon chicken. (2023, November 3). Prep4Life. https://p4lfood.com/blogs/recipes/crock-pot-lemon-chicken

Crunchy peas. (2023, February 23). Prep4Life. https://p4lfood.com/blogs/recipes/crunchy-peas

CryoDry. (2024, February 12). *How to know when freeze drying is complete*. https://cryodry.biz/2024/02/how-to-know-when-freeze-drying-is-complete/

Customer support (n.d.). Harvest Right. https://harvestright.com/support/

D'Argy, J. (2023a, January 18). *10 lesser-known benefits of freeze dried food*. Candy Jan Co. https://candyjan.com/blogs/news/10-benefits-of-freeze-dried-food-you-didn-t-know-about

D'Argy, J. (2023b, November 29). *Can all food be freeze dried? Considerations*. Candy Jan Co. https://candyjan.com/blogs/news/can-all-food-be-freeze-dried-things-to-consider

David. (2023, April 8). *Beyond food: Discover what you can freeze-dry*. The Freeze Dried Business. https://freezedriedbusiness.com/beyond-food-discover-what-you-can-freeze-dry/

Dehydrated cold-soak bean salad. (n.d.). Slower Hiking. https://slowerhiking.com/recipes/dehydrated-cold-soak-bean-salad

Diane. (2023, December 20). *The complete guide to oxygen absorbers*. Homemade Food Junkie. https://www.homemadefoodjunkie.com/the-complete-guide-to-oxygen-absorbers/

Diane. (2024, January 31). *How to freeze dry beef: A simple guide*. Homemade Food Junkie. https://www.homemadefoodjunkie.com/how-to-freeze-dry-beef-a-simple-guide/

Differences between home freeze dryers and commercial freeze dryers. (n.d.). Vikumer. https://vikumer.com/differences-between-home-freeze-dryers-and-commercial-freeze-dryers/

DIY emergen-C. (2023, February 23). Prep4Life. https://p4lfood.com/blogs/recipes/diy-emergen-c

Document recovery. (n.d.). European Freeze Dry. https://www.europeanfreezedry.com/document-recovery/

An easy guide to setting up your freeze dryer. (2024, January 29). Stay Fresh Freeze Dryer. https://stayfreshfreezedry.com/blogs/freeze-dryer-101/your-easy-guide-to-setting-up-your-freeze-dryer

Eaton, T. (2022, November 16). *What to do with leftover beef stroganoff: Freeze dry*. Awesome Cooking Ideas. https://awesomecookingideas.com/leftover-beef-stroganoff/

Egg noodles. (2025, February 12). Prep4Life. https://p4lfood.com/blogs/recipes/egg-noodles

Eggplant casserole. (2023, December 1). Prep4Life. https://p4lfood.com/blogs/recipes/eggplant-casserole

Fast n easy pot roast. (2023, December 28). Prep4Life. https://p4lfood.com/blogs/recipes/fast-n-easy-pot-roast

Fettuccine Alfredo. (2025, January 7). Prep4Life. https://p4lfood.com/blogs/recipes/fettuciini-alfredo-with-chicken

Foods you should not freeze dry. (2023, October 10). Green Thumb Depot. https://greenthumbdepot.com/blogs/guides/foods-you-should-not-freeze-dry

Freeze dried baby food. (2023, February 23). Prep4Life. https://p4lfood.com/blogs/recipes/baby-food

Freeze-dried cereal bars. (2024, December 17). Prep4Life. https://p4lfood.com/blogs/recipes/freeze-dried-cereal-bars

Freeze-dried creamy macaroni and cheese. (2024, February 16). Prep4Life. https://p4lfood.com/blogs/recipes/freeze-dried-creamy-macaroni-and-cheese

Freeze-dried dog food. (2023, February 23). Prep4Life. https://p4lfood.com/blogs/recipes/freeze-dried-dog-food

Freeze-dried fruit. (2023, February 23). Prep4Life. https://p4lfood.com/blogs/recipes/freeze-dried-fruit

Freeze-dried holiday simmer pot. (2023, November 24). Prep4Life. https://p4lfood.com/blogs/recipes/freeze-dried-holiday-simmer-pot

Freeze-dried infused water. (2023, July 19). Prep4Life. https://p4lfood.com/blogs/recipes/freeze-dried-infused-water

Freeze-dried lemonade. (2024, July 24). Prep4Life. https://p4lfood.com/blogs/recipes/homemade-lemonade

Freeze dried meat. (2023, November 20). Homesteading Family. https://homesteadingfamily.com/freeze-dried-meat/

Freeze dried Mexican rice. (2024, November 25). Prep4Life. https://p4lfood.com/blogs/recipes/mexican-rice

Freeze dried packaging: The complete FAQ guide in 2025. (n.d.). Allpack. https://www.allpackchina.com/freeze-dried-packaging/

Freeze-dried paprika recipe. (2024, September 18). Prep4Life. https://p4lfood.com/blogs/recipes/freeze-dried-paprika-recipe

Freeze dried pumpkin puree. (2023, November 30). Prep4Life. https://p4lfood.com/blogs/recipes/freeze-dried-pumpkin-puree

Freeze dried raspberry buttercream frosting. (2024, August 8). Prep4Life. https://p4lfood.com/blogs/recipes/freeze-dried-raspberry-buttercream-frosting

Freeze-dried Texas slow cooker chili. (2024, February 16). Prep4Life. https://p4lfood.com/blogs/recipes/freeze-dried-texas-slow-cooker-chili

Freeze dried tzatziki seasoning mix. (2024, March 4). Prep4Life. https://p4lfood.com/blogs/recipes/freeze-dried-tzatziki-seasoning-mix

Freeze dried vegetables. (2023, February 23). Prep4Life. https://p4lfood.com/blogs/recipes/freeze-dried-vegetables

Freeze dried yogurt bites. (2024, November 6). Freeze Drying Mama. https://freezedryingmama.com/freeze-dried-yogurt-bites/

Freeze dryer's problem: Common solutions. (2025, January 8). AELAB. https://aelabgroup.com/freeze-dryer-problems-and-solutions/

Freeze-drying as a preservation method. (n.d.). Barnalab Liofilizados. https://www.barnalab.com/en/how-we-freeze-dry/

Freeze drying fact vs fiction. (n.d.). Millrock Technology. https://www.millrocktech.com/freeze-drying-fact-vs-fiction/

Freeze drying steps. (n.d.). Vikumer. https://vikumer.com/freeze-drying-steps/

Freeze drying terminology. (n.d.). Millrock Technology. https://www.millrocktech.com/lyosight/lyobrary/freeze-drying-terminology/

Fruity holiday punch. (2024, December 19). Prep4Life. https://p4lfood.com/blogs/recipes/fruity-holiday-punch

Galusha, H. (2020, September 10). *Troubleshooting your freeze dryer & vacuum pump*. New Life Scientific. https://newlifescientific.com/blogs/new-life-scientific-blog/troubleshooting-your-freeze-dryer-vacuum-pump

Greek chickpea soup with lemon. (2024, September 26). Prep4Life. https://p4lfood.com/blogs/recipes/greek-chickpea-soup-with-lemon

Green goddess smoothie. (2024, January 24). Prep4Life. https://p4lfood.com/blogs/recipes/green-goddess-smoothie

Grow your own healing garden with these 10 medicinal herbs. (n.d.). Sow Right Seeds. https://sowrightseeds.com/blogs/planters-library/create-a-healing-medicinal-herb-garden

Guest. (2018, June 23). *Harvest Right freeze dryer - Cost analysis*. Common Sense Home. https://commonsensehome.com/harvest-right-freeze-dryer/

Guide to beginner - automated cycle. (2024, March 22). Stay Fresh Freeze Dryer. https://stayfreshfreezedry.com/blogs/freeze-dryer-101/guide-to-beginner-automated-cycle

Habek, K. (2023, March 29). *Why is buying items in bulk cheaper?* Reel. https://www.reelpaper.com/blogs/reel-talk/why-is-buying-items-in-bulk-cheaper

Ham & potato soup. (2023, February 23). Prep4Life. https://p4lfood.com/blogs/recipes/ham-potato-soup

Hamburger seasoning recipe. (2023, June 15). Prep4Life. https://p4lfood.com/blogs/recipes/hamburger-seasoning-recipe

Hansen, J. (n.d.). *The benefits of garden-to-table produce versus supermarket varieties*. GardenTech. https://www.gardentech.com/blog/gardening-and-healthy-living/garden-to-table-goodness-and-nutrition

Harvest Right. (2017a, March 17). *Celebrate National Meatball Day the healthy way*. https://harvestright.com/blog/2017/celebrate-national-meatball-day-the-healthy-way/

Harvest Right. (2017b, November 15). *Freeze-dried turkey noodle soup*. https://harvestright.com/blog/2017/freeze-dried-turkey-noodle-soup/

Harvest Right. (2018, February 22). *Freeze drying homemade soup*. https://harvestright.com/blog/2018/freeze-drying-homemade-soup/

Harvest Right. (2020, July 10). *National blueberry muffin day*. https://harvestright.com/blog/2020/national-blueberry-muffin-day/

Harvest Right Help Squad. (2025, February 3). *Using all of the trays in your freeze dryer is important for multiple reasons: 1. Even drying: Distributing your product* [Image attached. Facebook. https://www.facebook.com/permalink.php/?story_fbid=122199468638167608&id=61555028267412

Henney, J. E., Taylor, C. L., & Boon, C.S. (Eds). (2010). *Strategies to reduce sodium intake in the United States*. National Academies Press.

Home freeze dryer's owner's manual: The essential guide for every home freeze dryer owner. (n.d.). Harvest Right. https://images.thdstatic.com/catalog/pdfImages/72/72419fc2-473b-4d0b-9dee-05c16420fc29.pdf

Homemade apple pie. (2025, January 28). Prep4Life. https://p4lfood.com/blogs/recipes/homemade-apple-pie

Homemade applesauce. (2025, March 18). Prep4Life. https://p4lfood.com/blogs/recipes/homemade-applesauce

Homemade chocolate pudding. (2025, March 18). Prep4Life. https://p4lfood.com/blogs/recipes/homemade-chocolate-pudding

Homemade freeze-dried dog treats: Easy recipes. (2024, November 24). Petme. https://petme.social/homemade-freeze-dried-dog-treats/

How to freeze dry candy: Easy step-by-step guide. (2024, October 28). Homesteading Family. https://homesteadingfamily.com/how-to-freeze-dry-candy/

How to freeze dry food from home without a machine. (2019, April 13). Valley Food Storage. https://valleyfoodstorage.com/blogs/inside-vfs/freeze-drying-food-from-home-without-a-machine

How to grow a frozen food business. (2024, June 15). HostPapa. https://www.hostpapa.com/ideas/business/how-to-grow-a-frozen-food-business/

How to store freeze dried food. (2024, November 13). Homesteading Family. https://homesteadingfamily.com/how-to-store-freeze-dried-food/

Howard, R. (2016, November 7). *Freeze dried after school snacks*. Harvest Right. https://harvestright.com/blog/2016/freeze-dried-after-school-snacks/

Johnston, A. (n.d.). *How to blanch vegetables before preserving*. University of Minnesota Extension. https://extension.umn.edu/preserving-and-preparing/vegetable-blanching-directions-and-times-home-freezer-storage

Jones, L. (n.d.). *How to properly manage food stock rotation and date labelling*. Pilla. https://yourpilla.com/blog/stock-rotation

Kathleen. (2025, March 16). *Beef stew: Freeze-dried backpacking meal recipe*. The Hungry Hiker. https://the-hungry-hiker.com/2025/03/16/beef-stew-freeze-dried-backpacking-meal-recipe/

Kibblewhite, B. (2016, November 30). *Bulk density and product loading on trays*. Cuddon Freeze Dry. https://info.cuddonfreezedry.com/blog/bulk-density-and-product-loading-on-trays

King, E. (2024, December 13). *Parchment paper vs. silicone mats: What every home baker needs to know*. Serious Eats. https://www.seriouseats.com/parchment-paper-vs-silicone-baking-mats-8761072

Klein, J. (2021, December 7). How smoked meat can be kept for a long time. American Made Grills. https://americanmadegrills.com/blogs/grilling-tips/how-smoked-meat-can-be-kept-for-a-long-time

LaBorde, L., Herneison, A., & Zapp, M. (2023, April 13). *Let's preserve: Drying fruits and vegetables (dehydration)*. Penn State Extension. https://extension.psu.edu/lets-preserve-drying-fruits-and-vegetables-dehydration

Liivat, K. (2024a, September 12). *How to prevent freezer burn in your kitchen (7 tips)*. FoodDocs. https://www.fooddocs.com/post/freezer-burn

Liivat, K. (2024b, October 3). *How to freeze dry food: All your freeze dried food questions answered*. FoodDocs. https://www.fooddocs.com/post/how-to-freeze-dry-food

Marinara sauce recipe. (2024, February 29). Prep4Life. https://p4lfood.com/blogs/recipes/marinara-sauce-recipe

MasterClass. (2022, April 4). *How long does dehydrated food last? 4 storage tips*. https://www.masterclass.com/articles/how-long-does-dehydrated-food-last

McCarty, K. (2024, April 25). *Tips for freeze drying at home*. University of Maine Cooperative Extension. https://extension.umaine.edu/food-health/2024/04/25/tips-for-freeze-drying-at-home/

NASA. (2020). *Freeze-dried foods nourish adventurers and the imagination*. NASA Spinoff. https://spinoff.nasa.gov/Spinoff2020/cg_2.html

Nice, M. (n.d.). *Marshmallows*. BBC Good Food. https://bbcgoodfood.com/recipes/marshmallows

Onion soup mix. (2023, February 23). Prep4Life. https://p4lfood.com/blogs/recipes/onion-soup-mix

Oota Box. (n.d.). *Uncover the pros and cons of homemade vs. store-bought food - which is best for you?* https://ootabox.com/uncover-the-pros-and-cons-of-homemade-vs-store-bought-food-which-is-best-for-you/

Orange creamsicle cookies. (2024, August 17). Prep4Life. https://p4lfood.com/blogs/recipes/orange-creamsicle-cookies

Ostrander, M. (2022, September 9). *Super simple homemade 4-ingredient gummy candy*. Mostly Bakes. https://mostlybakes.com/super-simple-homemade-4-ingredient-gummy-candy/

Parks, S. (2023, November 7). *No-bake cheesecake with freeze-dried fruit recipe*. Serious Eats. https://www.seriouseats.com/no-bake-cheesecake-with-freeze-dried-fruit

Pasta broccoli. (2024, July 24). Prep4Life. https://p4lfood.com/blogs/recipes/pasta-broccoli

Pasta carbonara. (2024, March 4). Prep4Life. https://p4lfood.com/blogs/recipes/pasta-carbonara

Perthel, J. (2023, September 22). *Emergency food rotation: How to ensure freshness in your stockpile*. Proactive Foods. https://proactivefoods.co.za/blogs/news/emergency-food-rotation-how-to-ensure-freshness-in-your-stockpile

Perthel, M. (2023, April 19). *The pros and cons of freeze drying in comparison to other types of food preservation*. Forever Fresh Foods. https://foreverfresh.co.za/blogs/news/the-pros-and-cons-of-freeze-drying-in-comparison-to-other-types-of-food-preservation

Philly cheesesteaks. (2023, February 23). Prep4Life. https://p4lfood.com/blogs/recipes/philly-cheesesteaks

Pilet, J. (2025, February 24). *Food safety news*. Food Safety News. https://www.foodsafetynews.com/2025/02/at-home-freeze-drying-a-growing-trend-with-food-safety-concerns/

Pink drink copycat. (2023, February 23). Prep4Life. https://p4lfood.com/blogs/recipes/pink-drink-copycat

Pizza casserole. (2023, August 17). Prep4Life. https://p4lfood.com/blogs/recipes/pizza-casserole

Pumpkin pie bars. (2023, November 9). Prep4Life. https://p4lfood.com/blogs/recipes/pumpkin-pie-bars

Pumpkin roll. (2023, November 30). Prep4Life. https://p4lfood.com/blogs/recipes/pumpkin-roll

Queensland Government. (2021, June 9). *Cross contamination*. (2021, June 9). https://www.qld.gov.au/health/staying-healthy/food-pantry/food-safety-for-consumers/food-safety-and-your-health/cross-contamination

Ranch dressing mix. (2024, October 8). Prep4Life. https://p4lfood.com/blogs/recipes/ranch-dressing-mix

Randal, D. (n.d.). *How long does freeze-dried food last? A guide to shelf life*. Trimleaf. https://www.trimleaf.com/blogs/articles/how-long-does-freeze-dried-food-last-a-guide-to-shelf-life

Rankin, J. (2024, July 3). *How to freeze dry flowers for resin projects*. Jewelry Made by Me. https://jewelrymadebyme.com/blogs/news/how-to-freeze-dry-flowers-for-resin-projects

Recipe analyzer. (n.d.). HappyForks. https://happyforks.com/analyzer/result

Rehydrating freeze dried foods. (2024, February 10). Homesteading Family. https://homesteadingfamily.com/rehydrating-freeze-dried-foods/

Renee and Tim. (2024, June 29). *Easy pasta salad that's freeze dried and cold-soakable for backpacking*. Thruhikers: Renee and Tim. https://thruhikers.co/freeze-dried-pasta-salad/

Rhonda. (2020, September 18). *How to freeze dry herbs for medicinal purposes*. https://freezedryingmama.com/how-to-freeze-dry-herbs/

Rich, S. R., & Gumpert, D. E. (1985, May). *How to write a winning business plan*. Harvard Business Review. https://hbr.org/1985/05/how-to-write-a-winning-business-plan

Roasted garlic. (2023, February 23). Prep4Life. https://p4lfood.com/blogs/recipes/roasted-garlic

Roasted garlic mashed potatoes. (2023, February 23). Prep4Life. https://p4lfood.com/blogs/recipes/roasted-garlic-mashed-potatoes

Roberti, R. (2024, May 24). *Can you legally start a freeze-dried food business from home in Florida?* LinkedIn. https://www.linkedin.com/pulse/can-you-legally-start-freeze-dried-food-business-from-damian-roberti-tu9ne/

The role of pre-treatment in freeze-dried herbs processing. (2023, June 15). Flex Foods. https://www.flexfoodsltd.com/blog/The-role-of-pre-treatment-in-freeze-dried-herbs-processing.php

Root beer baked beans. (2024, April 25). Prep4Life. https://p4lfood.com/blogs/recipes/root-beer-baked-beans-prep4life-cube-freeze-dryer

Salt and vinegar zucchini chips. (2024, September 4). Prep4Life. https://p4lfood.com/blogs/recipes/salt-and-vinegar-zucchini-chips

Shaozhi, Z., Yu, P., Dongpo, L., Youming, Z., Guangming, C., & Heng, L. (2016). A thermophysical study on the freeze drying of wooden archaeological artifacts. *Journal of Cultural Heritage*, *17*, 95–101. https://doi.org/10.1016/j.culher.2015.07.003

Shelf life of freeze dried and dehydrated food. (n.d.). Food Assets. https://foodassets.com/info/bulk-food-shelf-life.html

Shepherd's pie. (2023, February 23). Prep4Life. https://p4lfood.com/blogs/recipes/shepherd-s-pie

Shredded steak. (2023, February 23). Prep4Life. https://p4lfood.com/blogs/recipes/shredded-beef

Simple chili. (2025, February 19). Prep4Life. https://p4lfood.com/blogs/recipes/simple-chili

Skillet chicken fajitas recipe. (2023, September 1). Prep4Life. https://p4lfood.com/blogs/recipes/skillet-chicken-fajitas-recipe

Smoky quinoa and black bean stew. (2023, November 3). Prep4Life. https://p4lfood.com/blogs/recipes/smoky-quinoa-and-black-bean-stew

Soft serve vanilla ice cream recipe. (2023, July 4). Prep4Life. https://p4lfood.com/blogs/recipes/soft-serve-vanilla-ice-cream-recipe

Spinach casserole recipe. (2023, September 15). Prep4Life. https://p4lfood.com/blogs/recipes/spinach-casserole-recipe

Stewart, M. (2019, January 19). *Classic caramel candies*. Martha Stewart. https://marthastewart.com/948380/classic-caramel-candies

Storing freeze-dried foods in mason jars: A guide. (n.d.). Gubba Homestead. https://gubbahomestead.com/food-preservation/storing-freeze-dried-foods-in-mason-jars-a-guide/

Strawberry lemonade. (2024, July 24). Prep4Life. https://p4lfood.com/blogs/recipes/strawberry-lemonade

Strawberry milk mix. (2024, September 4). Prep4Life. https://p4lfood.com/blogs/recipes/strawberry-milk-mix

Sweet potato casserole with marshmallows. (2023, December 22). Prep4Life. https://p4lfood.com/blogs/recipes/sweet-potato-casserole-with-marshmallows

Sweetened condensed milk. (2023, August 4). Prep4Life. https://p4lfood.com/blogs/recipes/sweetened-condensed-milk

Taco soup. (2023, February 23). Prep4Life. https://p4lfood.com/blogs/recipes/taco-soup

Theory to practice: CryoDry® freeze drying best practice and techniques. (2023). CryoDry. https://unitedscientific.co.za/images/Products/CryoDry/CD8/CryoDry_Freeze_Drying_Best_Practice_and_Techniques_V1.pdf

Thomas, C. (2022, February 26). *Freeze-dried or frozen chicken pot pie*. Homesteading Family. https://homesteadingfamily.com/freeze-dried-or-frozen-chicken-pot-pie/

Thrive Life. (n.d.-a). *Coca Cola pork street tacos*. https://thrivelife.com/recipe/coca-cola-pork-street-tacos

Thrive Life. (n.d.-b). *Creamy tomato sauce with parmesan*. https://thrivelife.com/recipe/creamy-tomato-sauce-with-parmesan

Thrive Life. (n.d.-c). *Hashbrown breakfast casserole*. https://thrivelife.com/recipe/hashbrown-breakfast-casserole

Thrive Life. (n.d.-d). *Pineapple and peach juice*. https://thrivelife.com/recipe/pineapple-and-peach-juice

Top freeze dryer brands for home and commercial use. (n.d.). SED Pharma. https://sedpharma.com/news-events/freeze-dryer-brands/

Trail mix. (2023, February 23). Prep4Life. https://p4lfood.com/blogs/recipes/trail-mix

Troubleshooting your vacuum pump error message. (2024, August 23). Freeze Drying Mama. https://freezedryingmama.com/vacuum-pump-troubleshooting-steps/

Try our recipe nutrition calculator. (n.d.). Verywell Fit. https://www.verywellfit.com/recipe-nutrition-analyzer-4157076

U.S. Department of Agriculture. (2013, June 15). *The big thaw — safe defrosting methods*. https://www.fsis.usda.gov/food-safety/safe-food-handling-and-preparation/food-safety-basics/big-thaw-safe-defrosting-methods

U.S. Department of Health & Human Services. (n.d.). *4 steps to food safety*. FoodSafety.gov. https://www.foodsafety.gov/keep-food-safe/4-steps-to-food-safety

Van Drunen Farms. (n.d.). *Advantages of freeze-drying: Preserving the value of whole foods*. https://www.vandrunenfarms.com/blog/advantages-freeze-drying/

Vegetable broth. (2024, March 4). Prep4Life. https://p4lfood.com/blogs/recipes/vegetable-broth

Vegetable chips. (2023, February 23). Prep4Life. https://p4lfood.com/blogs/recipes/vegetable-chips

Veggie lasagna. (2024, April 12). Prep4Life. https://p4lfood.com/blogs/recipes/veggie-lasagna

West Coast Chief Repair. (2022, May 10). *The pros & cons of buying used appliances*. https://chiefappliance.com/the-pros-and-cons-of-buying-used-appliances/

What foods cannot be freeze dried. (2023, July 24). Homesteading Family. https://homesteadingfamily.com/what-foods-cannot-be-freeze-dried/

White bean chicken chili. (2025, February 25). Prep4Life. https://p4lfood.com/blogs/recipes/white-bean-chicken-chili

Wolfe, A. (2023, October 14). *16 genius uses for freeze-dried ingredients*. Be Prepared - Emergency Essentials. https://www.beprepared.com/blogs/articles/16-genius-uses-for-freeze-dried-ingredients

Yagi, K. (2019, September 28). *Koya-tofu(freeze-dried tofu) and vegetable stir fry*. Cookpad. https://cookpad.com/eng/recipes/10715675

Yogurt bites. (2023, February 23). Prep4Life. https://p4lfood.com/blogs/recipes/yogurt-bites

Zaman, F. (2024a, May 6). *Freeze drying weed | Complete guide*. Green Thumb Depot. https://greenthumbdepot.com/blogs/guides/freeze-drying-weed

Zaman, F. (2024b, May 13). *Harvest Right freeze drying time chart*. Green Thumb Depot. https://greenthumbdepot.com/blogs/guides/harvest-right-freeze-drying-time-chart

IMAGE REFERENCES

Alexas_Fotos. (2016, January 4). *Gummy bear, giant gummy bear, gummi bear image* [Image]. Pixabay. https://pixabay.com/photos/gummy-bear-giant-gummy-bear-1114951/

AlexP. (2022, July 23). *Full shot of various nuts* [Image]. Pexels. https://pexels.com/photo/full-shot-of-various-nuts-12955793/

American Heritage Chocolate. (2023, January 12). *Two bowls of chocolate pudding with raspberries on the side* [Image]. Unsplash. https://unsplash.com/photos/two-bowls-of-chocolate-pudding-with-raspberries-on-the-side-YxjIO0LmDO0

Anderson, S. (2020, January 12). *Bowl of vegetable soup* [Image]. Unsplash. https://unsplash.com/photos/bowl-of-vegetable-soup-x4l4U-pHF9s

andrejbujna. (2018, September 16). *Mushrooms, dried mushrooms, oak trees* [Image]. Pixabay. https://pixabay.com/photos/mushrooms-dried-mushrooms-oak-trees-3680251/

armendes. (2018, May 16). *Fruit dehydrated, apple, fruit* [Image]. Pixabay. https://pixabay.com/photos/fruit-dehydrated-apple-fruit-3405839/

ASnowKnows. (2019, April 16). *Baking, fondant, confectionery* [Image]. Pixabay. https://pixabay.com/photos/baking-fondant-confectionery-4130764/

Auraz, A. (2020, May 19). *3 carrots on brown wooden table* [Image]. Unsplash. https://unsplash.com/photos/3-carrots-on-brown-wooden-table-R198mTymEFQ

Azouagh, I. R. (2021, November 20). *A pink drink with ice cubes in it* [Image]. Unsplash. https://unsplash.com/photos/a-pink-drink-with-ice-cubes-in-it-_gQYLSXkhb4

Bailey, J. (2018, February 6). *Three baked muffin with strawberry filling on top* [Image]. Pexels. https://pexels.com/photo/three-baked-muffin-with-strawberry-filling-on-top-853004/

Bailey, J. K. (2021, August 11). *White ceramic bowl with white cream* [Image]. Unsplash. https://unsplash.com/photos/white-ceramic-bowl-with-white-cream-eBjjnr5pwE0

Bayar, M. (2022, January 5). *Resin wall art with flower design* [Image]. Pexels. https://www.pexels.com/photo/resin-wall-art-with-flower-design-10753701/

Beefy bean taco soup. (2025 June 26). [AI-generated image].

Belousova, A. (2021, November 22). *Colorful jelly candies* [Image]. Pexels. https://www.pexels.com/photo/colorful-jelly-candies-10325488/

Beneli, F. (2021, October 13). *Fried zucchini slices with cottage cheese* [Image]. Pexels. https://pexels.com/photo/fried-zucchini-slices-with-cottage-cheese-9883451/

Berry smoothie. (2025). [AI-generated image].

Bożek, M. (2018, July 23). *Person showing blueberry lot* [Image]. Unsplash. https://unsplash.com/photos/person-showing-blueberry-lot-nKVMyxLS3ik

Bronzini, E. (2020, December 6). *Close-up photo of dried sage* [Image]. Pexels. https://www.pexels.com/photo/close-up-photo-of-dried-sage-6103379/

Brown, R. (2020, August 18). *First aid and surival kits* [Image]. Pexels. https://www.pexels.com/photo/first-aid-and-surival-kits-5125690/

Carneiro, A., Jr. (2025, March 12). *Delicious lasagna with fresh salad on a plate* [Image]. Pexels. https://www.pexels.com/photo/delicious-lasagna-with-fresh-salad-on-a-plate-31119072/

Casserole dish filled with fiesta rice. (2025, June 26). [AI-generated image].

Chandak, V. (2021, April 23). *White ceramic bowl with baked food* [Image]. Pexels. https://www.pexels.com/photo/white-ceramic-bowl-with-baked-food-7625714/

Cheddar-topped green bean bake in a modern baking dish. (2025, June 26). [AI-generated image].

Cheesy broccoli pasta. (2025, June 26). [AI-generated image].

Cheesy chicken and pepper frajitas. (2025, June 26). [AI-generated image].

Cheesy eggplant casserole in a perfectly shaped rustic casserole. (2025, June 26). [AI-generated image].

Cheesy stuffed shells in a modern bowl with perfectly shaped and neatly arranged shells. (2025, June 26). [AI-generated image].

Cheesy velveeta potato soup served in a modern white bowl, garnished with fresh herbs. (2025, June 26). [AI-generated image].

Chicken and celery salad with all ingredients well mixed, showing the creamy texture with visible pieces of shredded chicken, diced celery, quartered grapes, chopped green onions, and cashews. (2025, June 26). [AI-generated image].

Chicken and white bean chili served in a rustic Dutch oven. (2025, June 26). [AI-generated image].

Chiemsee2024. (2016, February 18). *Puppy, golden retriever, nature* [Image]. Pixabay. https://pixabay.com/photos/puppy-golden-retriever-dog-young-1207816/

Chili for the trail. (2025, June 26). [AI-generated image].

ClickerHappy. (2015, May 16). *Illustration of hose* [Image]. Pexels. https://www.pexels.com/photo/black-and-white-hose-refill-valves-4194/

Cooked sausage and hash brown casserole in a baking dish. (2025, June 26). [AI-generated image].

Coreen. (2022, February 11). *A white plate topped with pasta covered in sauce* [Image]. Unsplash. https://unsplash.com/photos/a-white-plate-topped-with-pasta-covered-in-sauce-OBxF5lHY3zo

Country-style chicken stew cooking in a large pot. (2025, June 26). [AI-generated image].

CrafterChef. (2023, October 11). *Alfredo, fettuccine, pasta* [Image]. Pixabay. https://pixabay.com/photos/alfredo-fettuccine-pasta-cheese-8305773/

Creamy and rich carbonara. (2025, June 26). [AI-generated image].

Creamy potato and ham soup served in a rustic bowl, garnished with fresh herbs. (2025, June 26). [AI-generated image].

Creamy ranch chicken and bacon casserole in a rustic casserole dish, ready to be served. (2025, June 26). [AI-generated image].

Creamy spinach and cheese casserole, fresh out of the oven and ready to be served. (2025, June 26). [AI-generated image].

Creamy zucchini and chicken casserole in a modern, perfectly shaped casserole dish, ready to be served. (2025, June 26). [AI-generated image].

Cup of Couple. (2021, April 26). *Kiwi fruit juice on a clear drinking glass*. Pexels. https://pexels.com/photo/kiwi-fruit-juice-on-a-clear-drinking-glass-7656397/

Dehydration, orange, fruit [Image]. (2019, December 16). Pixabay. https://pixabay.com/photos/dehydration-orange-fruit-dried-4699184/

Delicious cheesy veggie lasagna. (2025, June 26). [AI-generated image].

ds_30. (2020, February 17). *Broth, vegetable, nature* [Image]. Pixabay. https://pixabay.com/photos/broth-vegetable-grass-dinner-meal-4855760/

felix_w. (2020, April 9). *Dog, puppy, catch* [Image]. Pixabay. https://pixabay.com/photos/dog-puppy-catch-treat-5021242/

Free, S. (2024a, December 19). *Delicious pumpkin Swiss roll with cream filling*. Pexels. https://pexels.com/photo/delicious-pumpkin-swiss-roll-with-cream-filling-29849799/

Free, S. (2024b, December 19). *Warm holiday eggnog with star anise and cinnamon*. Pexels. https://pexels.com/photo/warm-holiday-eggnog-with-star-anise-and-cinnamon-29849802/

Fresh, tangy dressing in a modern glass dish with fresh herbs. (2025, June 26). [AI-generated image].

Garcia, V. (2020, December 29). *Anonymous man cooking on camping stove after hiking in forest* [Image]. Pexels. https://www.pexels.com/photo/anonymous-man-cooking-on-camping-stove-after-hiking-in-forest-6324408/

Golden turmeric turkey noodle soup. (2025, June 26). [AI-generated image].

Green and Great. (2022, August 4). *A bowl of food* [Image]. Unsplash. https://unsplash.com/photos/a-bowl-of-food-auTqcVC96X4

Gromov, D. (2022, July 20). *Close-up shot of a tasty casserole* [Image]. Pexels. https://pexels.com/photo/close-up-shot-of-a-tasty-casserole-12916865/

Haillard, S. (2022, March 24). *A pan filled with sliced apples on top of a stove* [Image]. Unsplash. https://unsplash.com/photos/a-pan-filled-with-sliced-apples-on-top-of-a-stove-w1wM3CMumqA

Hearty enchilada chicken soup served in a rustic bowl, accompanied by crispy tortilla chips. (2025, June 26). [AI-generated image].

hello aesthe. (2023, August 19). *Lemons in pot* [Image]. Pexels. https://pexels.com/photo/lemons-in-pot-18038733/

Henderson, G. (2019, February 18). *Oatmeal on white bowl beside yellow banana* [Image]. Unsplash. https://unsplash.com/photos/oatmeal-on-white-bowl-beside-yellow-banana-djY0xDWCEUM

HeVoLi. (2019, June 6). *Fruit, strawberries, vitamins* [Image]. Pixabay. https://pixabay.com/photos/fruit-strawberries-vitamins-healthy-4255924/

Holmes, K. (2020, November 17). *Crop woman frying meat on pan* [Image]. Pexels. https://pexels.com/photo/crop-woman-frying-meat-on-pan-5908057/

Ibrahimzade, F. (2020, November 9). *Cooked food on black ceramic bowl* [Image]. *Unsplash*. https://unsplash.com/photos/cooked-food-on-black-ceramic-bowl-KpOl9jV2aJM

Ibrahimzade, F. (2021, July 13). *Green ceramic bowl with soup* [Image]. Unsplash. https://unsplash.com/photos/green-ceramic-bowl-with-soup-PY0L46NEl5s

jereskok. (2017, August 18). *Beef fillet, roast beef, steak* [Image]. Pixabay. https://pixabay.com/photos/beef-fillet-roast-beef-steak-2654315/

JetalProduções. (2023, November 15). *Food, Christmas, chicken* [Image]. Pixabay. https://pixabay.com/illustrations/food-christmas-chicken-natal-foods-8379847/

jusminmari. (2019, November 7). *Cold milk, pink, sweet* [Image]. Pixabay. https://pixabay.com/photos/cold-milk-pink-sweet-cool-sugar-4608842/

kaboompics. (2015, May 31). *Table setting, celebration, feast* [Image]. Pixabay. https://pixabay.com/photos/table-setting-celebration-feast-791148/

Kaboompics.com. (2020a, July 27). *Hands cutting cauliflower* [Image]. Pexels. https://www.pexels.com/photo/hands-cutting-cauliflower-4963672/

Kaboompics.com. (2020b, September 22). *Woman hand mixing pumpkin pure* [Image]. Pexels. https://pexels.com/photo/woman-hand-mixing-pumpkin-pure-5421510/

Kamp, A. (2019, March 5). *Round pie on tray* [Image]. Unsplash. https://unsplash.com/photos/round-pie-on-tray-fGiLO1V8zH4

Kapoor, P. (2021, June 22). *Person holding red plastic cup with red liquid* [Image]. Unsplash. https://unsplash.com/photos/person-holding-red-plastic-cup-with-red-liquid-Cyy2btrRYIE

khezez. (2024, December 25). *Delicious beef stroganoff meal with vegetables* [Image]. Pexels. https://www.pexels.com/photo/delicious-beef-stroganoff-meal-with-vegetables-29935503/

kifotofotografia. (2023, July 27). *Drumstick, chicken, food* [Image]. Pixabay. https://pixabay.com/illustrations/drumstick-chicken-food-dip-sauce-8151626/

KRivrs. (2023, July 26). *Italian, pasta, nature* [Image]. Pixabay. https://pixabay.com/photos/italian-pasta-salad-garden-healthy-8147681/

LauKritz. (2021, October 17). *Pressure gauge, pressure indicator* [Image]. Pixabay. https://pixabay.com/photos/pressure-gauge-pressure-indicator-6715671/

Le, Y. (2025). *Garlic mashed potato* [Image]. Unsplash. https://unsplash.com/s/photos/garlic-mashed-potato

Lernestorod. (2017, July 24). *Fruit punch, drink, mojito image* [Image]. Pixabay. https://pixabay.com/photos/fruit-punch-drink-mojito-cherry-2535967/

May, C. (2020, November 21). *Glass of cold iced water with rose petals* [Image]. Pexels. https://pexels.com/photo/glass-of-cold-iced-water-with-rose-petals-5946990/

MichWich. (2023, May 29). *Soup, vegetable soup, minestrone* [Image]. Pixabay. https://pixabay.com/photos/soup-vegetable-soup-minestrone-8021569/

Mini yogurt treats. (2025, June 26). [AI-generated image].

Monstera Production. (2020, January 27). *Tasty dishes and wine on table served for Thanksgiving dinner* [Image]. Pexels. https://pexels.com/photo/tasty-dishes-and-wine-on-table-served-for-thanksgiving-dinner-5876742/

MorganLaFé. (2020, May 21). *Apple pie, tea, dessert* [Image]. Pixabay. https://pixabay.com/photos/apple-pie-tea-dessert-pastry-pie-5195808/

Mozzarella and sausage pizza casserole in a casserole dish. (2025, June 26). [AI-generated image].

No-fuss comfort pot roast. (2025, June 26). [AI-generated image].

Olalde, J. (2021, May 12). *Grilled meat on black and orange kettle grill* [Image]. Unsplash. https://unsplash.com/photos/grilled-meat-on-black-and-orange-kettle-grill-YDLHa1DEfhU

Panchenko, K. (2022, February 9). *A bowl filled with chickpeas sitting on top of a table* [Image]. Unsplash. https://unsplash.com/photos/a-bowl-filled-with-chickpeas-sitting-on-top-of-a-table-5352eOUYay4

Partheeban, G. (2019, December 15). *Food pack lot* [Image]. Unsplash. https://unsplash.com/photos/food-pack-lot-bAzFhYZ0PbU

Paulitasolange. (2020, December 5). *Cookies, chocolate chips, vanilla* [Image]. Pixabay. https://pixabay.com/photos/cookies-chocolate-chips-vanilla-5804140/

Peas, vegetables, food [Image]. (2022, December 17). Pixabay. https://Pixabay.com/photos/peas-vegetables-food-healthy-7658492/

Pixabay. (2016, November 5). *Red and blueberry cake on brown wooden surface* [Image]. Pexels. https://www.pexels.com/photo/red-and-blueberry-cake-on-brown-wooden-surface-221068/

planet_fox. (2022a, February 14). *Burger, pork, pulled pork* [Image]. Pixabay. https://pixabay.com/photos/burger-pork-pulled-pork-pig-food-7009893/

planet_fox. (2022b, February 14). *Pork, pulled pork, pig* [Image]. Pixabay. https://pixabay.com/photos/pork-pulled-pork-pig-flesh-7009879/

polatdover. (2020, September 21). *Meat, beef, vegetables* [Image]. Pixabay. https://pixabay.com/photos/meat-beef-vegetables-spices-food-5587780/

Ralph. (2021, May 17). *Close-up shot of a black and white cat eating on the grass* [Image]. Pexels. https://pexels.com/photo/close-up-shot-of-a-black-and-white-cat-eating-on-the-grass-7174121/

Ralphs_Fotos. (2019, September 26). *Pumpkin, fruit, fall* [Image]. Pixabay. https://pixabay.com/photos/pumpkin-fruit-fall-pumpkin-plant-4459053/

RDNE Stock project. (2021, July 28). *A close-up shot of a bowl of chips* [Image]. Pexels. https://www.pexels.com/photo/a-close-up-shot-of-a-bowl-of-chips-8964243/

remcoosculiflowers. (2017, May 9). *Garlic, roasted, oven* [Image]. Pixabay. https://pixabay.com/photos/garlic-roasted-oven-food-foodporn-2293120/

Ri_Ya. (2021, December 5). *Bubbles, lemon, slice of lemon* [Image]. Pixabay. https://pixabay.com/photos/bubbles-lemon-slice-of-lemon-citrus-6841040/

RitaE. (2016, May 16). *Salad, cucumbers, tzatziki* [Image]. Pixabay. https://pixabay.com/photos/salad-cucumbers-tzatziki-tomato-1390743/

RitaE. (2017, March 17). *Potato soup, potato, soup* [Image]. Pixabay. https://pixabay.com/photos/potato-soup-potato-soup-wild-garlic-2152254/

RitaE. (2019, October 9). *Paprika, paprika powder, Capsicum annuum* [Image]. Pixabay. https://pixabay.com/photos/paprika-paprika-powder-4535689/

RitaE. (2022, August 26). *Spare ribs, ribs, grill* [Image]. Pixabay. https://pixabay.com/photos/spare-ribs-ribs-grill-bbq-7410911/

Root beer beans dish in an oven baking dish. (2025, June 26). [AI-generated image].

Rosario, K. (2021, May 18). *Brown wooden spoon on brown wooden spoon* [Image]. Unsplash. https://unsplash.com/photos/brown-wooden-spoon-on-brown-wooden-spoon-2bEl8oxzAxg

Sabrina_Ripke_Fotografie. (2016, October 27). *Pumpkin, vegetables, autumn* [Image]. Pixabay. https://pixabay.com/photos/pumpkin-vegetables-autumn-basket-1768857/

saniusman89. (2020, November 29). *Meat, bowl, marinate* [Image]. Pixabay. https://pixabay.com/photos/meat-bowl-marinate-marination-5573857/

Savory squash and ricotta casserole in a rustic baking dish. (2025, June 26). [AI-generated image].

Shared Food. (n.d.). *Healthy chili* [Image]. Burst.shopify. https://shopify.com/stock-photos/photos/healthy-chili?q=homestyle+chili

Skibka. (2016, September 27). *Moldy, food, broken* [Image]. Pixabay. https://pixabay.com/photos/moldy-food-broken-green-yellow-1693929/

Smoky bacon chicken chili freshly cooked and served in a slow cooker. (2025, June 26). [AI-generated image].

Smoky bean and quinoa stew. (2025, June 26). [AI-generated image].

Sophkins. (2017, March 12). *Blueberry muffins, muffins, cupcakes* [Image]. Pixabay. https://pixabay.com/photos/blueberry-muffins-muffins-cupcakes-2136749/

Steak and chicken cheese melt sandwich sliced in half on a perfectly round white plate. (2025, June 26). [AI-generated image].

stevepb. (2015, July 13). *Plumbing, pipe, wrenches* [Image]. Pixabay. https://pixabay.com/photos/plumbing-pipe-wrenches-plumber-840835/

Sweet potato casserole. (2025, June 26). [AI-generated image].

Taco dish featuring seasoned ground beef with taco and ranch seasoning, mixed beans, corn, diced tomatoes, topped with . (2025, June 26). [AI-generated image].

takedahrs. (2020, May 9). *Freeze-dried bean curd, Japanese meal, Japanese food* [Image]. Pixabay. https://pixabay.com/photos/freeze-dried-bean-curd-japanese-meal-5143853/

TastyLens. (2023, December 1). *Ice cream, vanilla, ice* [Image]. Pixabay. https://pixabay.com/photos/ice-cream-vanilla-ice-dessert-bowl-8419129/

TheUjulala. (2016). *Milkmaid, sweetened condensed milk, sugar milk* [Image]. Pixabay. https://pixabay.com/photos/milkmaid-sweetened-condensed-milk-1237364/

Three ingredient egg noodles. (2025, June 26). [AI-generated image].

Timeless cottage pie fresh out of the oven in a rustic casserole dish. (2025). [AI-generated image].

Tjena. (2017, September 8). *Tomato sauce, tomato puree, Tjena-kitchen* [Image]. Pixabay. https://pixabay.com/photos/tomato-sauce-tomato-puree-2729689/

Turkey meatballs. (2025, June 26). [AI-generated image].

Ultimate cheeseburger mac casserole in a rustic casserole dish, garnished with fresh herbs and accompanied by a serving spoon. (2025, June 26). [AI-generated image].

Vegetable chips. (2025, June 26). [AI-generated image].

Volkovitskaia, O. (2022, May 15). *Kitchen, vegetables, cook* [Image]. Pixabay. https://pixabay.com/photos/kitchen-vegetables-cook-food-7193219/

Weber, T. (2021, May 28). *Pouring water on orange juice* [Image]. Pexels. https://pexels.com/photo/pouring-water-on-orange-juice-8679597/

Weber, T. (2022, May 28). *A yellow liquid on a clear drinking glass* [Image]. Pexels. https://pexels.com/photo/a-yellow-liquid-on-a-clear-drinking-glass-8679372/

WikimediaImages. (2017, April 4). *Caramel, candy, sweet* [Image]. Pixabay. https://pixabay.com/photos/caramel-candy-sweet-sugar-brown-2201902/

Yilmaz, E. (2023, July 6). *Pieces of white chocolate with strawberries and pistachios* [Image]. Pexels. https://www.pexels.com/photo/pieces-of-white-chocolate-with-strawberries-and-pistachios-17498808/

zweifelsfreimitb. (2022, January 13). *Dish, beef stew, flatlay* [Image]. Pixabay. https://pixabay.com/photos/dish-beef-stew-flatlay-beef-meat-6930432/

www.ingramcontent.com/pod-product-compliance
Lightning Source LLC
Chambersburg PA
CBHW060338010526
44117CB00017B/2871